★ ★ ★ ★ ★

Abraham Lincoln's Statesmanship and
the Limits of Liberal Democracy

Abraham Lincoln's Statesmanship and the Limits of Liberal Democracy

Jon D. Schaff

Southern Illinois University Press
Carbondale

Southern Illinois University Press
www.siupress.com

22 21 20 19   4 3 2 1

Jacket illustration: photograph of Abraham Lincoln, cropped and
    tinted; Library of Congress

Library of Congress Cataloging-in-Publication Data
Names: Schaff, Jon D., 1971– author.
Title: Abraham Lincoln's statesmanship and the limits of liberal
    democracy / Jon D. Schaff.
Description: Carbondale : Southern Illinois University Press,
    [2019] | Significant revision of author's thesis (doctoral)—
    Loyola University Chicago, 2002, titled The domestic Lincoln :
    presidential leadership, realignment and public policy. | Includes
    bibliographical references and index.
Identifiers: LCCN 2018044128 | ISBN 9780809337378 (cloth : alk.
    paper) | ISBN 9780809337385 (e-book)
Subjects: LCSH: Lincoln, Abraham, 1809–1865. | Presidents—
    United States—Biography. | Political leadership—
    United States—History. | United States—Politics and
    government—1861–1865. | United States—History—Civil War,
    1861–1865.
Classification: LCC E457 .S33 2019 | DDC 973.7092 [B] —dc23 LC
    record available at https://lccn.loc.gov/2018044128

Printed on recycled paper ♻
This paper meets the requirements of ANSI/NISO Z39.48-1992
    (Permanence of Paper). ∞

Ad majorem Dei gloriam

Contents

Introduction   1

Part I.   Lincoln and the Architecture of Democracy's Soul
1. Lincoln and the Political Virtues of
   Prudence and Moderation   11
2. Lincoln and the Defense of Natural Rights   41
3. Lincoln's Political Economy in the American Tradition   79

Part II.   The Domestic Lincoln: Presidential Power and the Second
American Revolution
4. Lincoln and the Second American Revolution   133
5. Whigs and Lincoln: A Realignment Reconsidered   160
6. The Domestic Lincoln and Congressional Government   180

Conclusion   207

Acknowledgments   215
Notes   217
Bibliography   243
Index   253

★ ★ ★ ★ ★

Abraham Lincoln's Statesmanship and
the Limits of Liberal Democracy

Introduction

In his work *The Everlasting Man*, G. K. Chesterton argues that the best way to gain knowledge of something is to be either very close to it or very far away from it. The worst perspective is that of the person who is just close enough to a thing to gain superficial knowledge but not close enough to know it well nor far enough away to look at it dispassionately. Chesterton says, "There are two ways of getting home; and one of them is to stay there. The other is to walk round the whole world till we come back to the same place."[1]

Such is the nature of the contemporary attitude of Americans toward their democracy. In Chesterton's terms, we are just familiar enough with it to take advantage of its forms and mores but not close enough or far away enough to appreciate its virtues. This is why, for example, when teaching the Declaration of Independence to my introductory American Government students, I start by giving them the basics of ancient political thought. One way to appreciate the qualities of the Declaration is to compare them with something quite different. The typical student has a passing familiarity with the principles of the Declaration, just enough to be able to mouth those principles in the form of thoughtless platitudes but not enough to actually understand them, much less cherish them.

One of the many virtues of Abraham Lincoln is that he seemed able to stand both inside and outside democracy at the same time. He revered the doctrines of the Declaration and the moral cause of democracy while being able to offer friendly critiques of democracy's excesses. The clarity with which Lincoln saw the hope and potential tragedy of a democratic people has seldom been replicated in history. Democracy, thought Lincoln, could recognize and raise the dignity of the individual while also potentially subjecting the individual to the whim of the mob. Lincoln's day saw the possibility of democracy's decay into democratic despotism, all the more tempting because that despotism confused itself with justice. The people, as it has often been said, sometimes confuse their own voice for the voice of God. Lincoln would agree with this passage from Chesterton:

> If there is one fact we really can prove, from the history that we really do know, it is that despotism can be a development, often a late development and very often indeed the end of societies that have been highly democratic. A despotism may almost be defined as a tired democracy. As fatigue falls on a community, the citizens are less inclined for that eternal vigilance which has truly been called the price of liberty; and they prefer to arm only one single sentinel to watch the city while they sleep.[2]

It is in this Chestertonian spirit that the present consideration of the statesmanship and presidency of Abraham Lincoln has been written. In a time when many of the qualities that make liberal democracy worth treasuring are under stress (freedom of speech, intellectual diversity, and due process of the law are some examples), Lincoln's model has much to teach regarding the virtues of basic liberal democratic principles while warning us against the kind of corruption that is a particular risk for a democratic people.

My own interest in Lincoln was sparked many years ago as I noted a dearth of writing on his presidency from the varying perspectives political science can offer. This is especially true of what I came to call the "domestic Lincoln," reflected in those acts by President Lincoln that had little or nothing to do with the Civil War. The appellation "domestic" is somewhat ironic in that a civil war is by its nature a domestic affair, but the term was meant to differentiate what modern political observers would call domestic policy—concerned with economics, budgets, commerce, and the like—from military or foreign policy. When my interest in Lincoln began, there was a scholarly movement emerging within political science called American political development, which applied the methods of history to the study of American political phenomena, typically looking at the evolution of American political institutions over time.

As my own study of politics gained both depth and breadth, I began to see Lincoln in a slightly different light, as I was better able to place him within a tradition of American political thought. Through a deeper examination of the American founding and especially a growing interest in the thought of Alexis de Tocqueville, I started to gain a sense of the fragility of free government and the delicacy of the institutions that have marked American history for nearly two and a half centuries. My appreciation for Lincoln's statesmanship was renewed and deepened. Lincoln's statesmanship was essential to the preservation of this noble experiment in free government and provides an example to which modern citizens of that republic, and those devoted to liberty around the world, can look for inspiration. This book attempts to give a greater appreciation for that statesmanship by demonstrating Lincoln's dedication to and defense of honorable political principles such as prudence, moderation, and natural rights. In addition, Lincoln's economic vision and his conduct as president regarding the nonwar "domestic" measures provide lessons to contemporary readers seeking to find solutions to the stresses put on our political system through such phenomena as the globalization of economics and the rise of a presidency-centered government. While it may be easy to dismiss the relevance of a statesman from the mid-nineteenth century, the aim here is to show that the power of Lincoln's thought is precisely its continued ability to speak across time to our present situation.

Andrew Ferguson, in his characteristically breezy and readable take on Lincoln's America, notes that our view of Lincoln has taken on an element of triteness. "He's been hated and loved, pondered and studied, honored and mourned so intensely for so long," writes Ferguson, "that it doesn't seem to matter why. He's reached the zenith of American celebrity. He's famous for being famous."[3] As with Chesterton's earlier comments, we are close enough to Lincoln to have some knowledge of his greatness but far enough away that this knowledge has become stale. One can know a thing or a person so well that one loses sight of the greatness or uniqueness of that thing or person. Take, for example, the song "Over the Rainbow" from the 1939 film version of *The Wizard of Oz*. It is widely considered one of the finest popular songs ever written, yet most of us have heard it so many times that we have long ceased to admire its quality. It often takes hearing it in an unusual or unique arrangement to renew our appreciation. My hope is that this book is analogous to a unique arrangement of the often-heard song, helping us better honor the man who may be the pivotal figure in America's history, the quality of his poetic words, and the profundity of his actions.

We too often take Lincoln for granted— as if his greatness was always assured, the Union would always be restored, the end of slavery was always inevitable. And I fear that our complacency regarding Lincoln that Ferguson identifies is part and parcel of a complacency regarding democracy. We are so used to it that we think of democracy as the natural state of a people, requiring no effort on the part of the citizenry to maintain it. But given the rise of extremist groups on both the right and left (for example, the so-called alt-right and the Antifa movement), we cannot be indifferent toward statesmanship.

Just as we cannot assume Lincoln's eminence, we cannot assume the continuation of that democracy that Lincoln sought to nobly advance. Glenn Thurow notes, "To the question, Is democracy good?, common opinion answers, Yes, because the people are wise and just. Lincoln, too, in the moment when American democracy was put to its greatest test, thought democracy to be finally good only if the people are wise and just. . . . If the people are not ultimately just, then there is no reason other than expediency why they should decide questions of justice."[4] Just as a garden does not spontaneously bear a healthy yield, neither do people effortlessly become wise and just. People, like a garden, need cultivation. This assumes a cultivator, a gardener—or in political life, a statesman and his or her purposeful action.

The relationship between citizens and statesman is symbiotic because people must be cultivated in the first place in order to recognize the statesman and avoid the demagogue. Those responsible for acculturating the citizenry must help them form the proper habits and dispositions that will allow them to tell the difference between those two kinds of leaders. A healthy democracy, based as it is on the opinions of the people, requires statesmen to assist in interpreting the times. They help shape popular opinions by seeing more clearly than most the definitive trends of the day, understanding and explaining with great articulation the meaning of the historical moment and showing how present circumstances are to be understood. This is often done in light of certain fundamental principles and the enduring commitments of the political community.

The idea of statesmanship can be explained via the concept of time.[5] The tendency of the ancient world and still today in many Eastern philosophies is to view time as a circle, a continual reoccurrence of events. In this view there is no movement or progress; rather, we live within a repetition. One might think of the cycle of seasons as an example. The modern Western view of time tends to be linear, one thing occurring after another. The assumption is that the line slants upward, so to speak, so that time is progressive, meaning that things get better as our knowledge and mastery of the world increase. But what if time partakes of both of these characteristics, both continuity and change? This is a conception of time as a spiral. We are progressing linearly through time and experiencing change while at the time same revisiting or returning to certain fundamentals, enduring ideas, practices, or self-conceptions, reinter-preted in the light of new circumstances. As Russian novelist Eugene Vodolazkin puts it, this notion of time as spiral is useful, as throughout history "events repeat, but on another level, under other conditions." Certain foundational ideas or principles recur across time, but as they are occurring under "other conditions" a statesman is needed to interpret these foundations anew. This task is not reserved only to statesmen, but certainly this is a role that the best statesmen play.[6] In Lincoln's case, he needed to explain natural rights, the rule of law, and the role of the pres-idency to a new generation of Americans whose vision of the founding ideas of the nation was already dimming.

The central argument of this book is that for free people to remain free, they must live within limits. Some of that limitation can be achieved through properly constructed institutions, but ultimately the imposition of limits must come from the people themselves; it must be a self-impo-sition. If free people want something bad enough for long enough, no limitation in law will be sufficient to withstand their demands. While limits imposed by the rule of law are fundamental to a free society, as Lincoln himself argued, in the end the people's will rules. Ultimately democracy trumps constitutionalism. Lincoln believed strongly that a democracy must exist within limits in order to be a just democracy, for the notion of rule without limits is the very definition of tyranny, whether it be one ruler or many. In a democracy the limits must be self-imposed by the people, as a democracy works fundamentally from the opinions of the people.

Lincoln's defense of democratic limits manifested itself in various ways. First, he was devoted to the moderating effect of the law. The ma-jority should rule, but only within the limits of a process that protects the minority from capricious rule. Arbitrariness is the seed of tyranny, perhaps most frightening when pursued in the name of abstract justice. The road to tyranny, like the road to Hell, is paved with good intentions.

Second, Lincoln vigorously defended natural rights. He argued that natural justice exists beyond popular opinion. The task of democratic statesmanship is to conform opinion to this natural justice to the largest extent possible.

Third, Lincoln's view of the powers of government suggest that while Lincoln favored a strong national government that promoted a kind of economic dynamism, he stopped well short of the view held by many today that there should be no principled limits on governmental power.

The fourth manner in which Lincoln demonstrated moderation was in his views concerning political economy. Lincoln the statesman was at least as concerned about the manner in which an economy shaped the character of a people as he was with wealth creation or with what contemporary observers might call economic justice. Lincoln's political economy was not about promoting economic efficiency so as to maximize wealth and consumption but about maintaining the kind of economy that is consistent with a free people. For what does it profit a citizenry to gain material wealth but lose its democratic soul?

Finally, Lincoln's moderation extended to his use of the powers of the presidency in regard to the "domestic" functions discussed above. The Civil War Congresses were active in producing economic legislation involving land, railroads, education, banking, and currency. Lincoln's leadership on these issues belies the typical depiction of the modern activist presidency. Lincoln arose from a tradition skeptical of executive power. Still, while aggressively exercising the war powers of the presidency, he tended to defer to Congress on other matters. This is not simply because he was distracted by war. Despite his reputation as a forceful president, Lincoln's view of presidential power is at odds with our presidency-centered politics that seeks to make the chief executive the very embodiment of the federal government. Lincoln believed that it was impossible to personify the people's will in one individual while remaining faithful to free government. Perhaps one reason why modern Americans seem consistently disappointed in their presidents is that they ask more than those presidents can deliver. As Gene Healy puts it in his critique of the "cult of the presidency," "We want what we cannot have, and as a result, we get what we do not like."[7]

In each of these five aspects of Lincoln's statesmanship—rule of law, natural rights, powers of government, political economy, and presidential power—Lincoln asked Americans to live within limits, to moderate their desire for power, control, and wealth. The case for a moderate, principled democracy is made in the pages that follow. As such, the work is divided in two parts. Part 1 deals largely with Lincoln's political thought. The first chapter defines the terms "prudence" and "moderation" and then proceeds to demonstrate how Lincoln defended and practiced those political virtues. Chapter 2 illustrates Lincoln's defense of natural rights, focusing particularly on Lincoln's six-year battle with Senator Stephen Douglas, a fellow Illinoisan. Chapter 3 delineates Lincoln's view of the appropriate reach of government. This is accomplished by showing the consistency of Lincoln's views with those of Alexander Hamilton and the Whig Party, in which Lincoln cut his political teeth. Within this chapter I consider whether Lincoln can be considered as a forerunner of the Progressive movement. One purpose of the chapter is to contrast Lincoln's defense of strong, effective but limited government with the principled defense of unlimited government made by the Progressives. This chapter concludes with a unique argument, namely that there is much agreement between Lincoln's political economy and the twentieth-century Catholic economic movement known as distributism. For Lincoln, the final good of an economy is not the production of wealth but the manner in which an economy promotes dignified liberty. To this extent, Lincoln's theory of labor, like that of the distributists, calls for a limit on the pursuit of material wealth in the name of a higher ideal.

Part 2 contains three chapters that collectively consider Lincoln's presidency as it relates to domestic policy, particularly whether Lincoln's presidential statesmanship is in harmony with the presidency-centered politics of contemporary America. Chapter 4 is an extended discussion of the thesis put forth by noted historian James McPherson that Lincoln led a "second American Revolution" by supporting the domestic agenda that did much to help usher in the Industrial Revolution. I will investigate McPherson's own sources for this contention to see if they offer support for his thesis. Here I will also set forth how political science goes about investigating this claim through a brief overview of literature on presidential power, public policy, and electoral realignments. Chapter 5 provides a concise history of the American Whig Party and examines the reasons for its collapse and what role Lincoln may have had in forming the Republican Party that replaced the Whigs. I will also consider the extent to which economic policy rather than the controversy over slavery was the cause of this realignment. This chapter addresses the election of 1860 as a mandate for the historically significant economic policies that followed. Finally, the sixth chapter presents a legislative history of five key pieces of legislation arising from the Civil War Congresses: the Homestead Act, the Land-Grant College Act, the Pacific Railroad Act, the National Bank Act, and the Legal Tender Act. Lincoln is often depicted as the aggressive exception to the typically weak nineteenth-century presidents; the chapter examines whether Lincoln acted like a modern president in leading Congress or whether he was more deferential. The goal of part 2 and its emphasis on the "domestic Lincoln" is to show that Lincoln saw the presidency as a limited office. While an assertive war president, he rejected the notion that the president was at the heart of our governing order—that public policy starts with the presidential initiatives that Congress merely endorses. These three chapters operate together to suggest that rather than setting a precedent for a broad view of presidential power in addressing domestic issues, Lincoln's presidency provides a more modest, limited view of executive power.

Introduction

By the book's end it is fondly hoped that the reader will come to a greater appreciation of Lincoln's place in the American political tradition and of the qualities of his statesmanship. At the core of this statesmanship is the preaching of a political gospel of limitations. Essential to the endurance of our political institutions is the dedication of political leaders and people alike to more humble expectations of democratic politics. Abraham Lincoln gave his life so that the promise of democracy and its ideals would not perish from this earth. It is for us, the living, to not assume the perpetuation of American institutions and ideals but to work to make sure they endure for generations to come.

Part I

★ ★ ★ ★ ★

**Lincoln and the
Architecture of Democracy's Soul**

1

★ ★ ★ ★ ★

Lincoln and the Political Virtues
of Prudence and Moderation

One of the common complaints in contemporary American politics is the lack of statesmanship on the part of political leadership. Governed by polls and petty partisanship, our politicians cannot rally the American people to a common purpose. Rarely in contemporary political discourse do elected officials make a good faith appeal to those with whom they disagree, choosing instead to preach to the converted. This is a problem, as our political rhetoric is thus dominated by language destined to highlight differences rather than bring about conciliation. It is not a surprise, then, that polarization and tribalism are on the rise.

Part of our frustration is caused by a lack of understanding of fundamental qualities of the statesman. Two central political ideals that govern the statesman are prudence and moderation, but our contemporary political discourse tends to denigrate or misunderstand these two grand principles. Prudence, when it is considered at all, is often confused with pragmatism or mere opportunism. Meanwhile, a moderate politician is defined as one who holds some positions of one political party and some of the other party. A Republican like Maine senator Susan Collins or a Democrat like West Virginia's Joe Manchin are described as "moderates" because they sometimes vote against their party's typical policy preferences, but this is a confusion of centrism for moderation.

Aristotelian definitions of prudence and moderation, discussed in greater detail below, offer a better guide to the importance of these central political virtues. People cannot understand the activity of a statesman if they cannot accurately describe the definitive characteristics of statesmanship. The career of Abraham Lincoln, perhaps America's greatest statesman, shows how his political philosophy and political activity embody these virtues. It is in part Lincoln's prudence and moderation that make him an object of persistent fascination and continued study. Lincoln's careful use of language allowed him to stake out certain positions while generally avoiding association with controversy. This skill encouraged listeners to read their own prejudices into Lincoln's equivocal words. This equivocation also influences scholars: Lincoln's rhetoric provides evidence for those who wish to see him as a radical or revolutionary but also fodder for those who view him as the cautious conservative.

One example will suffice to introduce the concept. The 1850s saw the rise of the Native American Party, a secret society and political party formed in opposition to both immigration and slavery. Members gained the appellation "Know-Nothings" after they said, when asked if they belonged to the group, that they "knew nothing." The antislavery portion of the Know-Nothing platform surely appealed to Lincoln, but he had little patience with the anti-immigrant stance. The Know-Nothings presented a political conundrum, however. Being antislavery, they could participate in a coalition that would give the nascent Republican Party, and not coincidently Lincoln himself, electoral success. However, their opposition to immigrants threatened to alienate other potential members of that coalition, such as recent Irish and German immigrants. In 1854 Lincoln commented on the Know-Nothings:

> And he would say on the start, that, like many others he *Knew Nothing* in regard to the Know-Nothings, and he had serious doubts whether such an organization existed—if such was the case, he had been slighted, for no intimation thereof had been vouchsafed to him. But he would say in all seriousness, that if such an organization, secret or public, as Judge [Stephen] Douglas had described, really existed, and had for its object interference with the rights of foreigners, the Judge could not deprecate it more severely than himself. If there was an order styled the Know-Nothings, and there was any thing bad in it, he was unqualifiedly against it; and if there was anything good in it, why, he said God speed it! [Laughter and applause.] But he would like to be informed on one point: if such a society existed, and the members were bound by such horrid oaths as Judge Douglas told about, he would really like to know how the Judge found out his secrets? [Renewed laughter.][1]

This is classic Lincoln. He begins by doubting such a group as the Know-Nothings exists. But if it does exist and it is contrary to the rights of foreigners, then he is as opposed as his archrival Stephen Douglas. And then he closes with a joke to diffuse the topic. If one is predisposed to be against Know-Nothingism, there is enough here to recommend Lincoln. If one supports the Know-Nothings, Lincoln's denunciation is mild enough and is coupled with humor to make one believe that Lincoln is not too serious in opposition. Lincoln portrays Know-Nothings as more silly than dangerous. We now know that privately Lincoln was fiercely opposed to the Know-Nothings, but judging them the lesser threat than Douglas or proslavery Southern politicians, he considered it counterproductive to weigh in too heavily on the controversy.[2] As Douglas Wilson puts it, "Rather than trying to convince strangers to alter their preconceptions, he understood that he would be better served by simply giving them reasons to believe that, whatever his faults, he was essentially honest and trustworthy."[3]

Harry Jaffa states,

> But a man who makes enemies and aliens of friends and fellow citizens corrupts the soul of the body politic. To create strife where there was none, or where there need have been none, as a means of one's own fame, is to make honor the reward not of virtue or public benefit but of baseness and mischief-making. If the order of talents of the man who does this is high, so much the more reprehensible is his action.[4]

Lincoln wished, as much as possible, to win enemies over as friends. How else does one succeed politically? He also saw the need for the democratic statesman to temper his rhetoric, to soothe rather than stoke the passions of the people and of himself should the desire for power tempt him to tyranny. At the heart of Lincoln's statesmanship was "a conscious effort to avoid extremes, especially those of moral idealism and moral cynicism in politics."[5] Joseph Fornieri aptly describes Lincoln as a "philosopher statesman" concerned with "timeless truths about human nature and politics." Students of politics would be wise to consult Lincoln as they consider the question of what makes a good statesman.[6]

Before discussing Lincoln's prudence and moderation, let us see how Aristotle defines the terms.

The Tradition of Prudence and Moderation

In the *Nicomachean Ethics*, Aristotle describes prudence, or practical wisdom, thusly: "Now, the capacity of deliberating well about what is good and advantageous for oneself is regarded as typical of a man of practical wisdom." This characterization suggests that practical wisdom is right reasoning about good ends. As Aristotle puts it, those who possess practical wisdom "calculate well with respect to some worthwhile end."[7] While practical wisdom does not help us learn what is good and noble, as that is the work of theoretical wisdom, it helps us bring *into being* what is good and noble. The purpose of practical wisdom "is not to know what is just, noble and good, but to become just, noble, and good."[8] Aristotle's invocation of the great Athenian leader Pericles indicates that practical wisdom is a particular virtue of the statesman: "That is why we think that Pericles and men like him have practical wisdom. They have the capacity of seeing what is good for themselves and for mankind, and these are, we believe, the qualities of men capable of managing households and states."[9] Aristotle argues that "the main concern of politics is to engender a certain character in the citizens and to make them good and disposed to perform noble actions."[10]

Moderation, while chiefly considered by Aristotle as an individual virtue, has political ramifications. It is well known that Aristotle describes moral virtue as the mean between the excess and deficiency of a particular virtue. For example, "Excess as well as deficiency of physical exercise destroys our strength. . . . The man who shuns and fears everything and never stands his ground becomes a coward, whereas a man who knows no fear at all and goes to meet every danger becomes reckless."[11] To be virtuous is to experience the right things in the right amount; this is moderation. "Accordingly, he is courageous who endures and fears the right things, for the right motive, in the right manner, and at the right time, and who displays confidence in a similar way."[12] A person who exemplifies the virtue of courage is one who is afraid of the right things (for example, a household intruder wielding a gun) but not the wrong things (a household intruder that is simply a harmless spider). Likewise with the example of physical exercise. It seems more obvious how one can exercise too little, thus becoming weak and perhaps overweight, but one can also damage one's health by exercising too much and injuring the body.

While we tend to discuss moderation as the middle between two extremes, Aristotle says that the mean or moderate position is actually relative. For instance, healthy eating is not the middle point between anorexia and obesity; it is eating each thing in its proper amount. This requires judgment as to what the "right amount" is. The kind of diet that might be healthy for a typical teenager will not be healthy for someone in middle age. Similarly the "right amount" of exercise for a teenager is different from that of an elderly person. Moderation is not subjective, but it is relative. It takes judgment—prudence—to know what the right amount is.

What are the political implications of these qualities? As stated above, prudence allows us to use the right means to get a good thing. This teaches us that it is not enough to want a good thing. We must have the wisdom to secure that good thing. The virtue of moderation aids in this task. Take this moral example from Aristotle: "Anyone can get angry—that is easy—or can give away money or spend it; but to do all this to the right person, or the right extent, at the right time, for the right reason, and in the right way is no longer something easy that anyone can do. It is for this reason that good conduct is rare, praiseworthy, and noble."[13] The states-man must make sure to have the appropriate response to injustice, and he or she must ensure that the people believe similarly. There *are* some things worth being angry about; we call this righteous indignation. But anger is not an end in itself. Anger must be directed toward removing the injustice. Thus we have to reason rightly as to what methods are to be used to correct an injustice. In any given political situation there are competing goods. The statesman makes sure that the political society has each of these good things in the right amount. Harry Clor, in his excellent work on moderation, states, "The root idea here is that there are always diverse and competing desiderata in political life, and that this reality determines the fundamental task of statesmanship, that of balancing and reconciling."[14] In modern liberal democracies, for instance, we tend to value liberty, rule of law, equality, and consent, to name some basic political goods. The liberal statesman must make sure that each of these political goods gets its due. These goods are sometimes in conflict. For example, sometimes public opinion (that is, consent) favors something that is at odds with the liberty of a minority. Sometimes the rule of law dictates that a guilty person escapes legal punishment. How does the statesman balance these frequently competing goods, such as consent and liberty, the rule of law and the desire for justice? He or she must moderate the various demands coming from the people. Prudence will tell the statesman how precisely to do that.

One can see how prudence and moderation are necessary for sound po-litical leadership by considering Aristotle's discussion of statesmanship in his *Politics*. Aristotle points to two perils that particularly tempt the demo-cratic statesman. The first danger is that of the demagogue. The demagogue, far from leading the people toward the good or noble in a moderate way, plays upon the people's passions. The statesman, in contrast, must defend the rule of law as a check upon political passion. In a democracy it is the people who are the rulers, so it is they who must be checked.

But where the laws are not sovereign, there you find demagogues. The people becomes a monarch, one person composed of many, for the many are sovereign, not as individuals but as an aggregate. . . . Such a people, in its role as a monarch, not being controlled by law, aims at sole power and becomes like a master, giving honour to those who curry its favor. Such a democracy is the counterpart of tyranny among monarchies. Hence its general character too is exactly the same: both play the master over the better sort of person, and the decrees of democracy are the directives of tyranny.[15]

By catering to every passion, the demagogue encourages the people to immoderation. As Aristotle puts it, "They began to do everything with a view to pleasing the people, just as if they were humoring a tyrant."[16] Without the virtue of moderation, the people, in a sense acting as one, cannot govern toward the noble or good. They or their leaders cannot then make use of practical wisdom, which by definition is aimed at the good. A prudent and moderate statesman (as opposed to the demagogue) must wisely manage the desires of the people so they aim at the good rather than at merely fleeting passionate desires. Aristotle states, "Freedom to do exactly as one likes cannot do anything to keep in check that element of badness which exists in each and all of us."[17]

All of us, it must be admitted, carry within us certain unsavory passions. We are alternatively jealous, envious, greedy, angry, indulgent. Surely nearly everyone has seen someone who has a life of relative material ease and felt that twinge of envy aimed at that person who has what we want but cannot have. Multiply this among "the many" and there is the perennial problem of the "have-nots" who envy the "haves." The statesman must encourage the "have-nots" to control their envy while at the same time attempting to reconcile any real injustice. The demagogue, alternatively, might attempt to gain power by stoking and encouraging the many "have-nots" in their resentment toward the "haves" or by encouraging the "haves" in an excessive fear or contempt of the "have-nots."

The second danger of imprudent and immoderate leadership is what we might call ideology. Aristotle writes, "Some people, believing that this virtue is a single one, push it to extremes. . . . So too it is with constitutions: both oligarchy and democracy may be tolerably good . . . but if one carries either of them to excess, the constitution will first become worse and finally not a constitution at all."[18] This immoderation, believing one good thing to be the only good thing, can be described as ideology and its purveyor the ideologue. The ideologue has an idea of what justice is and tries to cram reality into that idea. Fornieri describes the ideologue as one who tends "toward a puritanical equation of law and morality in politics."[19] The danger here is that the people, exaggerating one good to the extent that it stops being good, become impatient with the very balancing that is needed for a just and moderate polity. For example, if one takes a good thing such as liberty and then pursues liberty to the exclusion of societal stability or the rule of law, then liberty in this sense ceases to be a good. In the excessive love of liberty one turns a virtue into a vice. Moderation requires some forms of compromise, of balancing one good thing against another good thing. The balancing of moderation requires prudence to know when to give and when to take. But under sway of the demagogue or the ideologue, the people have neither prudence nor moderation.

The quest for an unsullied politics is at the heart of the fallacy "Voting for the lesser of two evils is still voting for evil." It is not. It is voting to mitigate an evil, which is a good. Anyone who is seeking purity in politics is expecting the impossible and will then cease to advance any good because one is unwilling to even touch anything with the slightest stain. Consider what would happen, for example, if we made our choice of spouse in this manner. All honest people recognize that no one is perfect, and therefore the choice of spouse necessarily entails some form of compromise. Indeed, the faithfulness of a good marriage relates precisely to the notion that we stick by our spouse in spite of his or her shortcomings, and our spouse's attitude toward ourselves is the same. The pursuit of perfection in a husband or wife will leave one alone and embittered. This is true of a quest for purity in politics as well.

The democratic statesman must take care of the opinions of the people to ensure that they have a moderate love of the goods democracy has to offer. This was Lincoln's charge. As Harry Jaffa puts it, "Noble things are difficult, said Aristotle, and the nobler more difficult. Lincoln saw popular government as most noble and most difficult."[20] An investigation of Lincoln's actions throughout his life will demonstrate that he was a prudent and moderate statesman in the Aristotelian tradition.

Lincoln on Prudence and Moderation

Certainly many scholars dissent from the idea that Lincoln exemplified the virtues of prudence and moderation. In his history of the Civil War, Shelby Foote describes Lincoln as a man "who would hold to principles only so long as he had more to gain than lose by them."[21] Harold Holzer, in his book on Lincoln's 1860 speech at Cooper Union in New York City, disagrees with the notion that Lincoln was moderate in his approach.

Indeed, Lincoln was "a vigorous antislavery man in conservative's clothing, invoking historical precedent and denying confrontationism to set the stage for a powerful call for resistance to immoral compromise."[22] Richard Striner's *Father Abraham: Lincoln's Relentless Struggle to End Slavery* is self-consciously written to debunk the notion that Lincoln was politically moderate. Striner dismisses the notion that Lincoln was a "saintly 'moderate'" and the idea that Lincoln's moderation stood in contrast to the "extremism" of the abolitionists.[23] Striner describes Lincoln's plans for postwar reconstruction: "Here is yet another major item in the orthodox legend of Lincoln the 'moderate': his 'lenient' plan for reconstruction. But Lincoln's earliest plan for reconstruction was clearly just a temporary ploy if we consider his position on the issue as it changed in the months before he died."[24]

Holzer and Striner are defenders of Lincoln's record, but Lincoln critics share the appraisal that Lincoln was no moderate. Thomas DiLorenzo is mystified as to how Lincoln could defend natural rights while opposing "social and political equality" of black and white people. For DiLorenzo this is just an example of Lincoln's lack of principles. He also notes that in Lincoln's eulogy of Henry Clay, Lincoln had questioned whether slavery could be eliminated without "producing a greater evil, even to the cause of human liberty itself."[25] DiLorenzo's Lincoln is simply an unprincipled politician seeking personal power. Lerone Bennett, who depicts Lincoln as a defender of white supremacy, chastises him in the strongest language for not being as radical in his opposition to slavery as other Republicans such as Thaddeus Stevens, Charles Sumner, and Salmon P. Chase. In Lincoln's famous speech of 1838 at the Springfield Young Men's Lyceum, Bennett contends, his unwillingness to directly confront the murder of Illinois abolitionist Elijah Lovejoy illustrates his weak antislavery credentials.[26]

In this same Lyceum speech and in one before the Washington Temperance Society in 1842, Lincoln laid out his basic political theory and defended prudence and moderation. These speeches illustrate Lincoln's preternatural appreciation for these political virtues.

Lincoln's appearance before the Lyceum took the title "On the Perpetuation of Our Political Institutions." The title itself indicates that Lincoln understood the role of the statesman in preserving the political order. In the speech he gives his diagnosis of the threat to American political institutions and then his solution to that threat. What is the threat? The menace, Lincoln argues, does not come from without but from within. The United States has been blessed with two large oceans protecting it from violent threats, sheltering it from external invasion. As Lincoln puts it, "As a nation of freemen, we must live through all time, or die by suicide."[27] What particularly concerns Lincoln is a rise in lawlessness: "I mean the increasing disregard for the law which pervades the country." This lawlessness is in the free states and slave states, in the North and in the South.

But it is not an accident that Lincoln's two examples of lawlessness both happen to come from slave states.[28] One took place in Mississippi. A mob there went after and hanged a group of gamblers. Then, caught up in a frenzy, the mob pursued "Negroes" who were plotting an "insurrection." Finally the throng turned against white citizens and total strangers until the violence escalated and no one was safe. "Thus went on this process of hanging, from gamblers to negroes, from negroes to white citizens, and from these to strangers; till, dead men were seen literally dangling from the boughs of trees upon every road side; and in numbers almost sufficient, to rival the native Spanish moss of the country, as a drapery of the forest." Lincoln then turns to a "horror-striking scene" in St. Louis, Missouri: a "mulatto man" by the name of McIntosh was lynched, "seized in the street, dragged to the suburbs of the city, chained to a tree, and actually burned to death."[29]

Is Lincoln upset that these people were killed? In some sense he is not.

> Abstractly considered, the hanging of the gamblers at Vicksburg, was of but little consequence. They constitute a portion of population, that is worse than useless in any community; and their death, if no pernicious example be set by it, is never matter of reasonable regret with any one. . . . Similar too, is the correct reasoning, in regard to the burning of the negro at St. Louis. He had forfeited his life, by the perpetration of an outrageous murder, upon one of the most worthy and respectable citizens of the city; and had not he died as he did, he must have died by the sentence of the law, in a very short time afterwards.[30]

We here learn additional information about McIntosh. He was not an innocent man. He had killed a man—in fact, a police officer. So, "abstractly considered," the deaths of the gamblers and the murderer are not injustices. So what is Lincoln's complaint? What is the problem with the mob? After all, is not the mob the voice of the people?

Lincoln has various objections to mob justice. First, and most obviously, the mob tends to be indiscriminate. "When men take it in their heads to day, to hang gamblers, or burn murderers, they should recollect, that, in the confusion usually attending such transactions, they will be as likely to hang or burn some one, who is neither a gambler nor a murderer

[as] one who is."[31] The mob is undiscerning in that even when it comes to the guilty it may administer punishment beyond the crime. Also, and more seriously, it may sweep up the innocent along with the guilty.

But this is not the worst of it, argues Lincoln. The prevalence of the mob encourages the "lawless in spirit" to become "lawless in practice." This is Lincoln's second critique of mob rule. Political scientist Kenneth Meier has a clever way of elucidating the phenomenon that Lincoln is addressing.[32] Meier, in a study of moral policy, divides the populace into three categories. The first contains individuals Meier labels "nerds." These are people who no matter the situation will always do the right thing. The second category is made up of people Meier calls "perverts." They, no matter the incentives, will always choose to do the wrong or immoral thing. But most of us, says Meier, are simply sinners. We sometimes do wrong things, but we are trying to be good and respond to incentives to do so. This is what moral policy does: it increases the incentives to do the right thing, or, put differently, it increases the disincentives to do the wrong thing. This, I believe, is Lincoln's essential point. For the many who, in Meier's schema, are neither nerds nor perverts, the existence of law is one important factor in restraining our behavior. Lincoln contends that if we perceive that we may break the law without consequence, then we are more likely to do so. Almost all are a little bit "lawless in spirit." So if we observe that we can do wrong and no one will care, we are more likely to do wrong.

Finally, Lincoln argues that the truly good man, whose spirit is to defend the law, becomes frustrated at the law's inability to protect him and his property: "Good men, men who love tranquility . . . seeing their property destroyed; their families insulted, and their lives endangered; their persons injured; and seeing nothing in prospect that forebodes a change for the better; become tired of, and disgusted with, a Government that offers them no protection." The final evil of the "mobocratic spirit" is to destroy the "attachment of the people" to its laws.[33] The truly good person, seeing democracy turn into a mob, loses his or her faith in democracy. That individual will be more likely to turn to the authoritarian leader who can at least promise order.

There is an unstated example that Lincoln's audience could not have helped but consider. Shortly before Lincoln's speech, abolitionist editor Elijah Lovejoy had been murdered in Alton, Illinois, across the Mississippi River from St. Louis. He had been shot and his printing press thrown into the river. It was Lovejoy who had publicized the lynching of McIntosh. Lincoln never mentions Lovejoy by name but makes a reference when he denounces mobs that "throw printing presses into rivers, shoot editors." Only a truly thick person in Lincoln's audience would have missed the allusion. Lerone Bennett is wrong when he criticizes Lincoln for failing to mention Lovejoy.

Given the perceived decline in the respect for the law, what is the cure Lincoln prescribes? Reverence for the law. In one of his most quoted passages, Lincoln states,

> Let every American, every lover of liberty, every well wisher to his posterity, swear by the blood of the Revolution, never to violate in the least particular, the laws of the country; and never to tolerate their violation by others. As the patriots of seventy-six did to the support of the Declaration of Independence, so to the support of the Constitution and Laws, let every American pledge his life, his property, and his sacred honor;—let every man remember that to violate the law, is to trample on the blood of his father, and to tear the character [charter?] of his own, and his children's liberty. Let reverence for the laws, be breathed by every American mother, to the lisping babe, that prattles on her lap— let it be taught in schools, in seminaries, and in colleges;—let it be written in Primmers, spelling books, and in Almanacs;—let it be preached from the pulpit, proclaimed in legislative halls, and enforced in courts of justice. And, in short, let it become the political religion of the nation; and let the old and the young, the rich and the poor, the grave and the gay, of all sexes and tongues, and colors and conditions, sacrifice unceasingly upon its altars.[34]

Lincoln goes on to argue that even bad laws should be obeyed. He is calling for the support of the law, even in its shortcomings. This includes, for instance, a Constitution that countenances the injustice of slavery. Lincoln preaches the rule of law as a moderating influence on the passions of the people. While it is possible to see the rule of law as just one good among many, Lincoln is holding it up as a good by which other goods are secured. A danger of democratic politics, as noted above, is the passion of the people. The rule of law channels those passions so they conform to previously agreed-upon procedures. This prevents democracy from acting arbitrarily, which is the seed of tyranny. Indeed, Lincoln seems to be arguing that the rule of law makes democratic governance possible by keeping people secure in their rights, which, according to the Declaration of Independence, is the purpose of government in the first place.

The danger of not abiding by the law is the demagogue. The founders, Lincoln contends, created the nation in an extraordinary time when public spirit overcame private ambition. But the truly ambitious man scorns the following of old ways and may seek to subvert the founding order. Some may aspire merely to public office, "but such belong not to the family of the lion, or the tribe of the eagle. What! think you these places would satisfy an Alexander, a Caesar, or a Napoleon? Never! Towering genius disdains a beaten path."[35] Both the mob and the dictator are kinds of tyranny, and tyranny is characterized by immoderation. For Lincoln a characteristic trait of democracy is a tendency toward a lack of order. The statesman has to remind the demos that it too must live within limits.[36]

The desires of the public must be moderated and the people must be taught the best way to achieve just ends. The rule of law both moderates the people's demands and channels those demands through a process of law that approximates prudence. Jaffa writes,

> A law is foolish which does not aim at abstract or intrinsic justice; and so is it foolish to attempt to achieve abstract justice as the sole good by succumbing to the fallacy to which the mind is prone, which regards direct consequences as if they were the only consequences. Those who believe anything sanctioned by law is right commit one great error; those who believe the law should sanction only what is right commit another.[37]

Moderate statesmen must take the long view, seeing the consequences of their actions beyond any immediate application to abstract justice. The task for the leader is to temper the people's demand for abstract justice. This includes the abolitionist who would rather throw away the Constitution than make any concession to slavery.

Lincoln made supporting arguments in an address to the Washington Temperance Society in 1842. Temperance, along with antislavery agitation, was part of a broader reform movement largely led by evangelical Christians. Lincoln was not a Christian in any conventional sense, but he did share many of the goals of the reformers. He was against slavery and was himself a teetotaler. But regarding the abolitionists and the more fervent temperance advocates, Lincoln opposed their methods despite sharing their goals.

The Temperance Society address is a tour de force of political rhetoric, ranging from the coldly rational to the wildly demonstrative to the devastatingly comedic. Lincoln begins by indicating that temperance has gone from theory to practice: "The cause itself seems suddenly transformed from a cold abstract theory, to a living, breathing, active, and powerful chieftain, going forth 'conquering and to conquer.'"[38] This is a theme to which Lincoln will return, but the notion of going from theory to practice tells us from the start that Lincoln's speech is at least in part about prudence.

Lincoln poses the all-important question that could be used for any moral inquiry: Given a morally desirable goal, such as reduction of alcohol consumption, how do we properly pursue that goal? "Proper" here has two meanings. First, how do we get what we want? Second, how do get what we want in a just manner?

Lincoln suggests that the old method of fierce condemnation was not effective.

> Either the champions engaged, or the tactics they adopted, have not been the most proper. These champions for the most part, have been Preachers, Lawyers, and hired agents. Between these and the mass of mankind, there is a want of approachability, if the term be admissible, partially at least, fatal to their success. They are supposed to have no sympathy of feeling or interest, with those very persons whom it is their object to convince and persuade.[39]

The preacher can be too fanatical, the lawyer too pompous, and the hired gun too greedy. These methods were imprudent. "But, had the old school champions themselves, been of the most wise selecting, was their system of tactics, the most judicious?" Lincoln argues it was not. "It was impolitic," says Lincoln, "because, it is not much in the nature of man to be driven to any thing." Lincoln states, "If you would win a man to your cause, *first* convince him that you are his sincere friend."[40] He believes the way to win a man over is to first win his heart. This is not to say that reason has no place. Still, the beginning of persuasion is through emotion. People are not likely to be convinced after being bitterly denounced. Speakers who show empathy with their opponents are much more likely to have their more reasoned arguments given a sincere hearing. This is a lesson often forgotten by contemporary politicians.[41]

For just this reason, the Washington movement used rehabilitated drunkards rather than pure teetotalers like Lincoln to convince people to reform. Employing those who might have once been alcoholics may offend the pure temperance advocate, but Lincoln contends this is the proper strategy. The reformed alcoholics "are practical philanthropists; and they glow with a generous and brotherly zeal, that mere theorizers are incapable of feeling."[42] Lincoln is interested in "practicality" rather than "mere theorizing." To be sure, some theorizing is needed. But abstract theory divorced from the actual world does not attain results. Lincoln advocates symmetry of prudence and moderation. Because some temperance advocates will not moderate their views, they are stuck in the "mere theory" that intoxication is an evil to be denounced at every turn. "Lincoln believes this poses one of the greatest political dangers for a republic," posits Lucas Morel, "the creation of a faction within the community that becomes entrenched in the claim to sole possession of the truth."[43]

Lincoln warns against the temptation toward denouncing our political opponents as merely evil. This is the tendency of ideologues, so sure are they that they have sole and complete possession of the truth. They have nothing to learn from those who disagree. Because ideologues are certain of their rightness, and because rightness seems obvious to them, only stupidity or malice can explain any divergence from their opinion. Those on the other side must be arguing in bad faith; they must have malign motives or wicked intent. Therefore they can be dismissed without a fair hearing. Lincoln, in contrast, is teaching us to try to see the validity of other arguments, even those with which we deeply disagree.

In the Temperance Society address, Lincoln sets out many themes that would dominate his antislavery rhetoric in the 1850s. First, because totally eradicating drinking is not possible, it is not a meaningful goal. Second, those who do not drink are not morally superior to those who do. Abstinence is not usually a sign of virtue, Lincoln says, but an absence of appetite: "In my judgment, such of us as have never fallen victims, have been spared more from the absence of appetite, than from any mental or moral superiority over those who have."[44] So temperance advocates must control feelings of moral superiority. Finally, before changing the laws the statesman must change public opinion. In the Temperance Society address, Lincoln humorously asks his audience to consider why men do not wear bonnets to church:

> Let me ask the man who would maintain this position most stiffly, what compensation he will accept to go to church some Sunday and sit during the sermon with his wife's bonnet upon his head? Not a trifle, I'll venture. And why not? There would be nothing irreligious in it: nothing immoral, nothing uncomfortable. Then why not? Is it not because there would be something egregiously unfashionable in it? Then it is the influence of fashion; and what is the influence of fashion, but the influence that other people's actions have [on our own?] actions, the strong inclination each of us feels to do as we see all our neighbors do?[45]

Why don't men wear bonnets in church? Not because Scripture or natural law condemns it. Rather, it simply is not fashionable. A statesman must work to make sure that good things are fashionable and bad things are unfashionable. He or she must take care of public opinion. Most people have neither the time nor the capacity to think through all arguments from the bottom up. We accept any number of opinions based on prejudice.

That does not mean that no principles underlie the prejudice but that most people do not take the time to investigate those principles. To take one simple example, most Americans believe that hereditary monarchy is an unjust form of government while democracy is just. But few have seriously considered arguments in favor of the former or against the latter. Surely such arguments exist. The preference for democracy, therefore, is a prejudice for most. It is the statesman who must, through his or her education, know the principles behind various alternatives and then guide the prejudices of the people in the direction of the better arguments. Lincoln holds that it is hard to change opinion when "backed by interest, fixed habits, or burning appetites."[46] As we shall see, Lincoln argued that the opinion in favor of slavery was backed by all three of these things.

How do these addresses exemplify Aristotle's theories of prudence and moderation? Lincoln defends the rule of law as a great moderating principle. The will of the people and their pursuit of equality and justice are balanced with the need for order and the protection of rights. The law is a moderating force as it allows the people to rule, but their rule is just only if it follows preordained procedures, what we typically call due process. So the desire for justice or equality must be balanced with the good of law. In this manner, rule of law protects against the demagogue that Aristotle and Lincoln clearly fear. Appeal to passion and the yearning for quick, decisive justice is the road to injustice.

It is similar with prudence. The Temperance Society address, with its focus on "practical philanthropy," calls on the statesman to "calculate well," in Aristotle's words, how to achieve a good end. In the bonnet example, Lincoln teaches that a democratic statesman must account for public opinion but also lead it. The manner in which the statesman talks to the people matters. One must avoid fiery denunciations. Rather, sound statesmen convince even their opponents that they mean them well. In this way moderation is the handmaiden to prudence for democratic statesmen. By recognizing the legitimate claims of all, they open more ears to their message, making their own success more likely. Lincoln also warns against ideology, letting "mere theory" guide our actions. A good leader does not "push to extremes," as Aristotle warns, but recognizes that one must adapt abstract notions to practical realities.

The Prudent and Moderate Approach to Slavery

The Lyceum and Temperance Society speeches are remarkable in their thoughtfulness. This is all the more remarkable given that as a neophyte politician, Lincoln's reputation was of one who willingly engaged in highly partisan, personal, and sometimes vulgar rhetoric, often anonymously or pseudonymously, to the point of getting involved in a duel. Only later in life with some maturity did Lincoln consistently rise to the rhetorical level that we would call statesmanlike.[47]

Almost from the beginning of his political career Lincoln positioned himself as a moderate opponent of slavery. In light of the discussion above, "moderate" here does not necessarily mean a middle ground between abolitionists and the "positive good" school of slavery. More profoundly, Lincoln's approach to the political and philosophical problem of slavery is one that took into account the many competing goods in the American democratic order, of which the natural equality of man is only one.

In 1837, as a legislator in Illinois, Lincoln, along with his colleague Dan Stone, objected to a resolution denouncing abolitionism. The grounds on which they objected are curious. First, they wanted to iterate what the rest of the legislature had neglected, that "the institution of slavery is founded on both injustice and bad policy." But interestingly they immediately added that "the promulgation of abolition doctrines tends rather to increase than to abate its evils."[48] Lincoln and Stone did not indulge us with reasons why those abolition doctrines contributed to the evil of slavery.

A window into that thinking can be seen in an 1845 letter by Lincoln to Williamson Durley. Durley, an abolitionist, had supported the Liberty Party ticket in the hotly contested 1844 presidential election in which the Liberty Party arguably cost Whig candidate Henry Clay the White House, throwing the election to the overtly proslavery James Polk. The "Liberty men" would not support the slaveholder Clay, despite Clay's basic antislavery sentiments. Lincoln tells Durley that Durley is correct that "we are not to do evil even that good may come," but even more true, "By the fruit the tree is known. . . . If the fruit of electing Mr. Clay would have been to prevent the extension of slavery, could the act of electing him been evil?" Instead, the Liberty men had thrown the election to Polk, and the fruit of their labor was the annexation of Texas as a slave state and the Mexican War that expanded the territory open to slavery. Lincoln gives Durley a counterstrategy: "I hold it to be a paramount duty of us in the free states, due to the Union of the states, and perhaps to liberty itself (paradox though it may seem) to let the slavery of the other states alone; while, on the other hand, I hold it to be equally clear, that we should never knowingly lend ourselves directly or indirectly, to prevent that slavery from dying a natural death."[49] Lincoln believed that if slavery was contained to the states where it currently existed, the social, economic, and educational progress of the nation would render slavery untenable and the slave states themselves would choose to end the injustice. This would allow for the end of slavery without violence and within the confines of Southern constitutional rights. The Liberty men had acted in error. By holding on to mere theory, they had facilitated the extension, not the curtailment, of slavery. Also, by insisting on their position as the only just one, they unnecessarily heightened sectional conflict and refused to recognize the rule of law as it pertained to legitimate legal rights of slaveholders.

Lincoln's appeal to prudence and moderation was on display in 1854 in his famous speech in Peoria, Illinois, against the Kansas-Nebraska Act. Much as in the Temperance Society address when Lincoln asked his listeners to identify themselves with the drunkard, at Peoria Lincoln states that if Northerners were in the same position as Southerners, they too would hold slaves.

> Before proceeding, let me say I think I have no prejudice against the Southern people. They are just what we would be in their situation. If slavery did not now exist amongst them, they would not introduce it. If it did now exist amongst us, we should not instantly give it up. This I believe of the masses north and south. Doubtless there are individuals, on both sides, who would not hold slaves under any circumstances; and others who would gladly introduce slavery anew, if it were out of existence.[50]

Lincoln asks those in his audience to identify with their political opponents, attempting to show that neither side has a monopoly on justice. By seeing themselves in their political adversaries, walking in the skin of another, the populace moderates its passions, recognizing that each side has its own just claims. Lincoln encourages his listeners to look inside themselves to their own prejudices and prods them to curb their passionate opposition to slavery. Further, in promoting limited sympathy with the South, he reminds them that slavery, with over two hundred years of history in the South, could not be eradicated without substantial turmoil. The statesman must balance the good of equality with the prevention of the evil of social turbulence.

Lincoln establishes in the speech the injustice of slavery. But what to do about it? He suggests some options; one is colonization.

> My first impulse would be to free all the slaves, and send them to Liberia,—to their own native land. But a moment's reflection would convince me, that whatever of high hope, (as I think there is) there may be in this, in the long run, its sudden execution is

impossible. If they were all landed there in a day, they would all perish in the next ten days; and there are not surplus shipping and surplus money enough in the world to carry them there in many times ten days.[51]

Whatever his listeners might think of colonization, it is not a practical solution. Within the discussion Lincoln shows some concern for the potential freed slaves, recognizing that most would not survive colonization.

What other options does he suggest? "Free them all, and keep them among us as underlings? Is it quite certain that this betters their condition?" What good does it do to free the slaves and keep them in subservience? Or,

free them, and make them politically and socially, our equals? My own feelings will not admit of this; and if mine would, we well know that those of the great mass of white people will not. Whether this feeling accords with justice and sound judgment, is not the sole question, if indeed, it is any part of it. A universal feeling, whether well or ill-founded, can not be safely disregarded. We can not, then, make them equals.[52]

This is one of the most important passages in Lincoln's public speaking career. Many critiques of Lincoln use it and others like it to claim his seeming egalitarianism was a charade, giving credence to Lerone Bennett's assertion that we should honor the ardent abolitionists over Lincoln. So let us give this passage a close reading. First, note Lincoln's famously equivocal language. He states that his own feelings will not admit of total political and social equality. But he leaves open a possibility; "if mine would . . . ," he says. The rest of the passage clarifies Lincoln's stated opposition to total equality. He recognizes that the "great mass of white people" oppose such equality, so advocating it is pointless. This might explain why Lincoln chose to reject total equality. What is the use of advocating something that not only cannot succeed but will alienate the majority of one's constituency?

Lincoln continues by stating that whether this view "accords with justice and sound judgment, is not the sole question." Again, despite his own stated opposition to total equality, he leaves open the possibility that complete equality actually is the just position. But what to make of the notion that justice is "not the sole question"? Lincoln is teaching the people that there are various components to justice, of which equality is one. There are other goods to be considered. Primarily, as his reference to the "great mass of white people" suggests, he is concerned with the good of consent. He must get the majority to go along with his desire to stop the extension of slavery. Alienating white voters over the issue of social and political equality does nothing for the cause of defeating the injustice of slavery. As Lincoln puts it, when an opinion, even an ill-founded one, is universally held, prudent statesmen cannot discount it. This does not mean they have to stoke it, as a demagogic leader might, but they can try, as Lincoln does, to diffuse it—in this case, to get to the more fundamental injustice of slavery. Lincoln "neither denies moral principles nor considers them sufficient to meet the demands of practical politics."[53] The moral principle of justice serves as a light to guide the ship of state, but the precise route the captain might use to reach the goal of justice must take into account many variables. Sometimes the most direct path is not the wisest.

In this light, consider Lincoln's December 1856 speech in Chicago in which he calls equality the "central idea" of the republic. To Lincoln's mind, slavery and the indifference to it represented by Stephen Douglas's promotion of popular sovereignty were a graver and more immediate threat to that central idea than the question of civil rights.[54] Lincoln was disparaged by Douglas in their 1858 senatorial race as a "Black Republican" who favored complete equality. To drive the people away from Lincoln, it was Douglas's strategy to play on the people's worst racial fears.[55]

Lincoln's battle with Stephen Douglas, reaching its apogee in the 1858 senatorial race, illustrates well Lincoln's prudent and moderate approach to the slavery question. A key part of Douglas's strategy was to portray Lincoln as a radical while Douglas presented himself as the true moderate. It has been said of Douglas that he "prided himself as being a practical man of the world in contrast to rigid idealists such as Lincoln, and so he readily let Lincoln define him as a person not guided by moral considerations. That which Lincoln intended as a criticism, Douglas accepted as an unintended compliment."[56] This is why Douglas was so quick to make the "Black Republican" attack on Lincoln, attempting to align Lincoln with those who truly had radical views regarding racial equality. Appealing to the widespread prejudices of his age, Douglas stated plainly that the American system was of, by, and for the white man alone:

> For one, I am opposed to negro citizenship in any and every form. (Cheers.) I believe this government was made on the white basis. ("Good.") I believe it was made by white men, for the benefit of white men and their posterity for ever, and I am in favour of confining citizenship to white men, men of European birth and descent, instead of conferring it upon negroes, Indians and other inferior races.[57]

Lincoln played into Douglas's hands somewhat when, on accepting the Republican nomination for the Senate in 1858, he spoke of America as a "house divided" that could not exist half slave and half free. While one cannot quarrel with Lincoln's assessment of the likely trajectory of American slavery as of the late 1850s, Lincoln himself later admitted that the "house divided" rhetoric was needlessly vituperative, allowing Douglas to portray Lincoln as literally advocating division. Lincoln said of this language, "I made a prediction only—it may have been a foolish one perhaps."[58] Indeed, one Douglas supporter noted, "I had thought until recently that the Little Giant was dead in Illinois—until I saw the speech Mr. Lincoln made to the Republican Convention in Springfield."[59]

Douglas claimed that the language of a "house divided" ran counter to the teaching of the founders. If the founders created a nation that was half slave, half free, who was Lincoln to say such a partition was untenable? In contrast, Douglas rendered himself as the sincere moderate. If there were Radical Republicans who wanted full "negro equality" and also slaveholders who argued for slavery as a positive good, then Douglas's position of simply letting voters of new territories decide the slavery issue themselves within the context of a national "don't care" policy was the true middle course.

Lincoln's argument against Douglas will be considered in full when we examine Lincoln's moral case against slavery in its entirety. For now, Lincoln's view of the role of the prudent, moderate, responsible statesman is highlighted. In part, he diffused the "Black Republican" argument by acceding in part to the age's more noxious racial views. Lincoln would say,

> I have no purpose to introduce political and social equality between the white and the black races. There is a physical difference between the two, which in my judgment will probably forever forbid their living together upon the footing of perfect equality, and inasmuch as it becomes a necessity that there must be a difference, I, as well as Judge Douglas, am in favor of the race to which I belong, having the superior position.[60]

While to the modern ear this reeks of injustice, as we have seen for Lincoln justice is not the sole question. Realizing the association with the more radical abolitionist movement would doom his chances and would do nothing to advance the antislavery position as a matter of policy, Lincoln chose to defuse this prejudice in order to combat a more insidious one, namely the moral indifference to slavery represented by Douglas's "don't care" policy.

Lincoln's argument was that Douglas's seeming moderation masked a real radicalism. First, Douglas had to deny what everyone knew to be true, namely that slavery was a cause of deep discord in the nation. "I leave it to you to say whether, in the history of our government, this institution of slavery has not always failed to be a bond of union, and, on the contrary, been an apple of discord and an element of division in the house," stated Lincoln.[61] While he may have regretted giving Douglas rhetorical ammunition with the "house divided" rhetoric, Lincoln was analytically correct that slavery served as an instrument of division in the nation and always had.

If Douglas was right—that the nation could survive half slave, half free—then was he not by implication arguing for the perpetual nature of slavery? As Lincoln put it, "I wish to return Judge Douglas my profound thanks for his public annunciation here to-day, to be put on record, that his system of policy in regard to the institution of slavery contemplates that it shall last forever."[62] In addition, as "Bleeding Kansas" had proven, Douglas's popular sovereignty did not erase slavery agitation; it only heightened it into violence. Popular sovereignty was more a recipe for war than a recipe for democracy.

Douglas was acting as the immoderate statesman by valuing consent, as represented by elections, above justice. Here we see Lincoln moderating his stance that abstract justice is not the "sole question." Justice is surely *part* of the question. Lincoln was arguing in the Lyceum and Temperance Society addresses that a statesman must take care of public opinion. While rhetorically supporting self-government, Douglas was undermining true self-government by declaring himself indifferent as to whether an entire class of men and women could legitimately be bound into slavery. Douglas took "consent of the governed" to an extreme, supporting it even when it brought about manifest injustice.

Lincoln's policy was to point continually to the moral injustice of slavery while recognizing the practical problems of immediate abolition. He did so, for instance, in his debate with Douglas at Alton: "I look upon it as a great evil and deeply lament that we have derived it from the parental government, and from our ancestors. I wish every slave in the United States was in the country of his ancestors. But here they are; the question is how they can best be dealt with?"[63] It would be best if slavery never existed, yet here it is. What shall we do about it? Southerners were correct that in certain ways the Constitution recognized a right to slave property. The national government could not legally, nor wisely in Lincoln's view, simply end slavery. Lincoln likened the problem of slavery to finding a snake in the bed of one's children:

> For instance, out in the street, or in the field, or on the prairie I
> find a rattlesnake. I take a stake and kill him. Everybody would
> applaud the act and say I did right. But suppose the snake was
> in a bed where children were sleeping. Would I do right to strike
> him there? I might hurt the children; or I might not kill, but only
> arouse and exasperate the snake, and he might bite the children.
> Thus, by meddling with him here, I would do more hurt than
> good. Slavery is like this.[64]

This example explains the prudential take on slavery that typifies Lincoln's statesmanship. For Lincoln, the existence of slavery necessitated certain compromises with that injustice. It is not good that the snake is in the bed, but to strike at it too directly would create even more harm.

Prudent and moderate statesmen must use their rhetoric to mold the opinions of the people toward justice. The Lyceum address in particular is Lincoln's warning that public opinion, free from all restraints, can set the stage for democratic tyranny. As we have seen, it is precisely the lack of restraint, whether of one person or of the many, that is the root of tyrannical government. The "Caesar" or "Napoleon" might cater to that natural desire to avoid limits in order to lay the path to his own tyranny. Or, by undermining the rule of law, the unprincipled politician sets the stage for mob rule by falsely claiming that the people should get whatever they want. As the bonnet example from the Temperance Society address implies, people do tend to go with what is fashionable, fashion being a kind of public opinion. So a statesman must use rhetoric to shape the architecture of the democratic soul toward accepting certain limits and by making fashion and justice coexistent. Virtue comes not just from knowing what is right but by doing it. This is the democratic statesman's job, to teach the people to moderate their own passions in the name of justice.

As Lincoln put it, "Our government rests in public opinion. Whoever can change public opinion, can change the government, practically just so much." Further, "That 'central idea' in our political public opinion, at the beginning was, and until recently has continued to be, 'the equality of men.' And although it was always submitted patiently to whatever of inequality there seemed to be as matter of actual necessity, its constant working has been a steady progress towards the practical equality of all men."[65] Douglas, by opening up this central idea to dispute, was undermining the very bedrock of the American order. While one could argue that Lincoln's own willingness to entertain some concepts of racial inequality also is inconsistent with this central idea, it is not hard to see that moral indifference to slavery is far more fundamental to the very idea of the republic. Lincoln maintained that logic of "the Nebraska doctrine" of popular sovereignty "is to *educate* and *mould* public opinion, at least *Northern* public opinion, to not *care* whether slavery is voted *down* or voted *up*."[66] Lincoln summarizes his views thusly: "With public sentiment, nothing can fail; without it, nothing can succeed. Consequently, he who molds public sentiment, goes deeper than he who enacts statutes or pronounces decisions."[67] So while one might argue that Douglas's approach to slavery might get to the same policy outcome as desired by Lincoln, namely the non-extension of slavery, it does so at the cost of undermining the people's dedication to the noble principle of equality. To this extent, Douglas's seeming prudence is revealed to be dangerously revolutionary in the sense of undermining bedrock principles of the regime.

Lincoln's prudential and moderate take on slavery influenced his actual policy advocacy. As a member of Congress, Lincoln voted for the Wilmot Proviso, a provision excluding slavery from territory acquired from Mexico after the Mexican-American War but against banning slave trade in the District of Columbia without allowing District citizens a vote. The *New York Tribune* said that Representative Lincoln was "a strong but judicious enemy of Slavery."[68] We have seen how Lincoln wished to avoid what he saw as the extreme and sometimes lawless opinions of abolitionists. A report on a Lincoln speech from 1848 says, "He scored with the most scathing language, that 'consistency' of the Abolitionists, which, while they professed great horror at the proposed extension of slave territory, they aided in the election of Mr. Polk; for which, and its disastrous consequences, they were responsible, as they held the balance of power."[69]

Lincoln continued this moderate and prudent course as president. After his election as the chief executive, he instructed Illinois senator Lyman Trumbull, "My dear Sir: Let there be no compromise on the question of extending slavery. If there be, all our labor is lost, and, ere long, must be done again. . . . Have none of it. Stand firm. The tug has to come, & better now, than any time hereafter."[70] If Lincoln was merely ambitious, why not give in, now that he had the power? Some claim that he did not want to compromise with the South.[71] Yet, in his first inaugural speech Lincoln indicated support for a constitutional amendment recognizing the right of slavery where it currently existed.[72] So Lincoln could make a stand on the non-extension of the injustice of slavery while making concessions to it where it already existed.

Lincoln's approach to emancipation also reflected an attempt at prudence and moderation. Once the Civil War started, Lincoln countermanded emancipation orders from Generals John C. Frémont and David Hunter, disclaiming their authority to permanently free slaves, as opposed to temporarily liberating them as a war measure.[73] Lincoln notably wrote to Horace Greeley,

> My paramount object in this struggle is to save the Union, and is not either to save or to destroy slavery. If I could save the Union without freeing any slave I would do it, and if I could save it by freeing all the slaves I would do it; and if I could save it by freeing some and leaving others alone I would also do that. What I do about slavery, and the colored race, I do because I believe it helps to save the Union; and what I forbear, I forbear because I do not believe it would help to save the Union.[74]

Lincoln already knew that he would choose the third stated course (free some slaves while "leaving others alone"). So to some extent Lincoln's discussion of saving the Union was for public consumption, preparing the public for the emancipation that he knew was coming. Also, this letter expresses Lincoln's moderation. The immediate abolition of slavery everywhere was desirable, but not as desirable as saving the Union.

A thorough analysis of Lincoln's approach to slavery indicates that for him, preservation of the Union was the surest way to bring about the end of slavery. For one thing, a truly independent Confederate States of America would be almost totally free of antislavery sentiment. Also, Lincoln believed that a union based on the natural equality of the Declaration of Independence undermined the institution of slavery. So saving the Union was a prior good to the elimination of slavery. The central conflict of the Civil War, as Lincoln described in his first inaugural and at Gettysburg, was whether free government is possible. The idea of secession attacked that notion by being contrary to law and also by rendering majority rule impossible. Saving the Union was tantamount to saving democracy. Only after the Union was secured could the nation continue with the project of making that democracy decent, namely through a further vindication of the principles of the Declaration.

The actual Emancipation Proclamation was justified merely as a war measure, which Lincoln issued as part of his commander-in-chief power.[75] The proclamation reached only those parts of the nation in rebellion as of January 1, 1863 (the date of the proclamation). Secretary of the Treasury Salmon Chase, one of Lerone Bennett's heroes, protested at the limited nature of the measure. Lincoln responded that the proclamation had no "constitutional or legal justification, except as a military measure."

What defense was there of an extension of the proclamation to new areas "except the one that I think the measure politically expedient, and morally right? Would I not thus give up all footing upon constitution or law? Would I not thus be in the boundless field of absolutism? Could this pass unnoticed, or unresisted?"[76]

Perhaps the crowning achievement of Lincoln's statesmanship is his second inaugural address. Again Lincoln takes time to recognize the legitimacy of the Southern concerns, but this time remarkably during warfare. He states, "Both read the same Bible, and pray to the same God; and each invokes His aid against the other. It may seem strange that any men should dare to ask a just God's assistance in wringing their bread from the sweat of other men's faces; but let us judge not that we be not judged." Here Lincoln draws an analogy between the North and the South, showing their similarities. He does note the Southern defense of slavery but quickly pulls back lest the accusation sting too much. His conclusion is memorable:

> With malice toward none; with charity for all; with firmness in the right, as God gives us to see the right, let us strive on to finish the work we are in; to bind up the nation's wounds; to care for him who shall have borne the battle, and for his widow, and his orphan—to do all which may achieve and cherish a just, and a lasting peace, among ourselves, and with all nations.[77]

In his last major speech Lincoln again illustrates the virtues of prudence and moderation. First, with the Union clearly victorious, the prudent move was to attempt to heal wounds and bring the nation back together with minimal rancor. Notice that Lincoln does not discriminate between North and South when advocating helping the war veteran and the widows and orphans. Lincoln also recognized that punitive measures directed toward the South as advocated by Radical Republicans would be treating Southerners as foreign aggressors rather than as misguided countrymen. As one scholar puts it,

> Lincoln in fact was a quite unusual war leader, mostly in what he did not say. He led one side in a bloody war not by arousing the aggressive tribalism, the assertive collective will, that war leaders often summon and that war publics often display, but by rather reasoning and eloquence. He gave careful arguments for his position, implying that he and his followers and their adversaries—their "dissatisfied countrymen"—were all part of a universal community of human reason.[78]

The Liturgy of Democratic Statesmanship

Harry Jaffa gives four criteria by which to judge a statesman. He first asks whether that statesman pursues worthy goals. Second, the statesman should "judge wisely as to what is and what is not within his power." Next, he must use means that are "apt" to gain the desired result. Finally, a statesman should act in such a way as not to hinder future statesmen from going beyond him and achieving greater justice.[79] Lincoln appears to have succeeded on all these counts. The desire to see slavery eliminated was a worthy goal. Both legally and within the constraints of opinion, Lincoln adjudicated what was within his power and what was not. Further, Lincoln chose means to his end that he thought likely to achieve the desired result. And finally, none of Lincoln's more limited policies regarding slavery hindered future statesmen from further pursuing equality. Almost by definition, prudence belies the application of a formula, leaving Lincoln's actions open to criticism. There is no formula or checklist one can produce to determine precisely whether Lincoln acted well or poorly or whether what he proposed was proper or improper. What is at issue is not whether Lincoln is above reproach, which surely he is not, but whether he perceived correctly the competing claims regarding the goal of ending slavery and made a good faith effort to adjudicate among those claims.

Personifying Aristotle's theory, Lincoln sets an example for other democratic statesmen and at the same time instructs us on the true meaning of prudence and moderation. Harry Clor writes, "More clearly than Douglas, Lincoln squarely confronted and wrestled with the two crucial imperatives: fundamental human equality and the preservation of the republican Union."[80] Lincoln pursued justice in a way that sought to maximize justice given various limits and also took into account the balancing of various competing legitimate claims. Primarily he recognized that the good of equality must be tempered by the good of consent. As Jaffa notes, "To insist upon more equality than men would consent to have would require turning to force or to the arbitrary rule of law."[81] To please the more abolitionist sentiment, Lincoln would have had to either lose elections or become a despot in a pursuit of perfect racial equality. Among the many things one could say about the various abolitionist heroes Bennett praises (Chase, Sumner, and the like) is that none of them ever had a reasonable chance of becoming president and putting their beliefs into practice. Had the Republican Party nominated Chase in 1860, it is a surety that the South would still have seceded, and had Chase pursued his desired policies, it is almost certain that Missouri, Delaware, Kentucky, and Maryland would have left the Union, giving the Confederate States of America a much greater chance of success. Clor states, "There is an outlook we may refer to as 'rationalism' which supposes that cognitive enlightenment alone, liberated from tradition, religion and civic bonds, is a power sufficient for the resolution of society's troubles. This outlook is utopian and unsafe."[82] The abolitionist position favored by Bennett and others was both immoderate and imprudent. It was imprudent for the reason just stated: abolitionism went beyond what public opinion was willing to accept and therefore had no chance at persuading a sufficient percentage of the population to enact its beliefs. Abolitionism was immoderate in that it confused a partial truth, the injustice of slavery as a violation of natural equality, for the whole truth. The various slavery camps—the slaveholders, the abolitionists, the popular sovereignty Democrats—all had some truth or good in their outlooks. Lincoln was aware of this and sought to give each its due without violating any fundamental of justice. Slaveholders, Lincoln noted, did have the Constitution on their side, in part, as the law gave some protections to slave property. Popular sovereignty advocates correctly held that popular consent was central to the democratic regime. Abolitionists were quite right that slavery violated a chief tenet of justice. Moderate statesmanship entailed the balancing of all these legitimate claims.

While the focus here has been on slave policy, Lincoln personified moderation in other ways as president. He welcomed people of various competing views and ambitions into his cabinet, knowing that each had his own constituency that needed some representation in the executive branch. His disposition toward Great Britain during the Trent Affair avoided extremes of capitulation and overt hostility.

Lincoln's careful examination of evidence against Native Americans sentenced to death after a massacre in Minnesota demonstrates his devotion to the moderating effect of the rule of law. William Lee Miller, who directs our observation toward Lincoln's actions in this respect, suggests the commutation of numerous death sentences stemming from the massacre is evidence of Lincoln's tenderheartedness.[83] Perhaps this is true, although one is reminded of Flannery O'Connor's condemnation of tenderness separated from a higher dedication.[84] Like O'Connor, Lincoln does not seem impressed by tenderness in and of itself. His actions regarding the commutation of sentences in this instance seem more like a dedication to the rule of law. As Miller himself makes clear, the trials of the convicted Natives were highly irregular, violating principles of due process. Lincoln was not simply being tender. He pored over trial transcripts so as to ensure due process of law was followed, not the indiscriminate rule of the mob.

Lucas Morel, discussing Lincoln and "political religion," argues, "Lincoln developed a public approach to religion that would certainly draw upon its beneficent qualities for political ends, but that was also consistent with religion's own reason for being. . . . Government protection of religious liberty requires of the people a religious devotion to the principles and practices of government."[85] In his work on religion and violence, William Cavanaugh notes that the premodern conception of religion was not simply a set of internal dispositions and beliefs. In the same vein as Aristotle, religion was a virtue that required the perfection of habit: "As a virtue, *religio* is a type of *habitus*, a disposition of the person toward moral excellence produced by highly specific disciplines of the body and soul. *Religio* is not so much a matter of learning certain correct universal propositions about the world, but of being formed in bodily habits."[86] If Lincoln preached a political religion, and Morel is convincing in that respect, that religion could not be simply a set of interior dispositions assented to in the mind. It required practice. Being courageous does not only mean a mental affirmation of the good of courage; being generous does not only mean agreeing that generosity is a good thing. Rather, a courageous person acts courageously, a generous person generously. Similarly, the political religion of Lincoln needed its own habits. Among those habits was the habit of abiding by the law, including due process for Natives accused of murder and rape.

Lincoln's actions teach a valuable lesson in moderating the passions of the people and taking care of public opinion in such a way as to promote justice without playing the demagogue. The moderate statesman sees the legitimacy underlying various competing claims. Behind every political platform, even the most unjust, is some element of justice, albeit incomplete justice. If a political opinion is ascribed to by even a small number of people, it is likely speaking to some truth. Almost all political opinions operate in the gray, meaning they are a mixture of white and black, truth and falsehood. To be sure, some opinions are more white than black, and others more black than white. The moderate statesman, who seeks to balance legitimate claims, recognizes the legitimacy of the views opposed to his or her own. Akin to Augustine's claim that sin is simply disordered love, even odious political opinions are likely taking something good and misconstruing or misapplying it. In Lincoln's case, he openly accepted the partial justice of his opponents' claims. Yes, the Constitution gave slavery some protections. The rule of law being valuable, those protections had to be recognized. Popular sovereignty was just another way of saying that government must rule by the people's consent. This is true. Lincoln conceded this truth but then attempted to show how it did not apply to slavery in the territories.

It is a pathology of our time that our politicians regularly fail to rise to Lincoln's level of statesmanship. Our political debates habitually sink to the level of crude accusation. Such rhetoric is pleasing to fanatics of all stripes and motivates activist donors to whom such rhetoric is often directed. It is a sad fact that people are more likely to donate to a cause out of fear or anger than from any altruistic motive. Democrats accuse Republicans of wishing the death of the poor because Republicans prefer to limit social welfare spending. Republicans accuse Democrats of a lack of patriotism because Democrats generally have a less militaristic foreign policy and are more open to immigration. The remarkable fact is that little of our political debate is actually geared toward persuading anyone who is not already in total agreement. Contemporary political speech is designed to motivate activist or partisan voters by demagogic appeals to fear or anger. Our politicians accuse each other of the most heinous motivations and then seem puzzled at the lack of bipartisanship. If Congressman A publicly accuses Congressman B of the basest motives and calls B the most vicious of names, how likely is B to vote for A's proposals?

The immigration debate is illustrative. On the one hand, there is concern, with some good reason, that extensive immigration, legal and illegal, lowers wages, causes unemployment among native-born Americans, and upsets the stability of communities. On the other hand, in some cases there is an economic need for immigration, and the history of the United States and common decency suggest we should be welcoming to people from all around the world. Our debate should be about how to balance community stability, acceptance of all peoples, and the legitimate claims of low-skilled workers and employers. But Republicans, including and especially President Donald Trump, all too often appeal to fears and anxieties over lost jobs and the influx of new immigrants who may look or think differently from the majority.[87] In contrast, Democrats regularly accuse Republicans of racism due to Republican skepticism toward immigration.[88] A moderate approach, in the Aristotelian sense, to the subject of immigration would recognize the genuine claims of those who fear for their jobs and wages along with the reasonable worry that a large and sudden influx of immigrants may upset community stability, at least in the short run. Once the moderate statesman notes these concerns, he or she can then talk about being accepting of difference and the American tradition of welcoming people from abroad. Moderation is not necessarily characterized by particular policy stances but more by a rhetorical approach that avoids appeals to fears and anxieties and shows appreciation for the concerns and interests of one's political opponents.

A study of Lincoln's prudent and moderate approach to slavery can serve as a guide to how a democratic statesman engages in debate over even the most divisive of matters. Lincoln prudentially gave concessions to public opinion while at the same time teaching the public that there are some things that are unjust, even if opinion is for them. He also showed genuine appreciation for the reasonable arguments made by those with whom he was in deepest disagreement. His prudence taught the public to limit their policy desires and avoid the error of the ideologue. His moderation likewise taught them to limit their rhetoric and appreciate balance of many different claims, which is at the heart of statesmanship. Lincoln's example has never been more essential.

2

Lincoln and the Defense of Natural Rights

The previous chapter detailed Lincoln's dedication to two essential political virtues, prudence and moderation. These are virtues for any statesman but especially, it seems, for the democratic statesman. Precisely because these virtues help mitigate the vice to which democratic government is most prone, namely the blind worship of majority rule, the democratic statesman must cultivate these virtues to a high degree. Lincoln understood that a democratic statesman cannot safely ignore public opinion; rather, it was that leader's task to shape that opinion toward justice. True statesmen must be one step ahead of public opinion, but not ten steps. They must take opinion into account while not being obsequious to it. This is an art form that eludes most politicians, especially in our day when the plebiscitary nature of our politics makes deliberation and reasoned argument difficult to sustain, so prone are we to indulging in the politics of spectacle, sound bite, and entertainment. The poll-driven nature of contemporary American politics, stoked by media that require constant "news" to fill the twenty-four-hour cycle, makes it difficult for politicians and citizens alike to be patient and deliberate when assessing any particular controversy.[1] The emphasis on polls only enhances the notion that public opinion must rule, whether that opinion is well or ill considered. No one typifies these pathologies more than Donald Trump, who runs his presidency more like the professional wrestling television shows he used to frequent than as the head of the executive branch of the American government. Always leave them wanting more!

Lincoln's political teaching regarding prudence and moderation includes the lesson that the public must learn to limit itself, and the statesman as a political educator must encourage the public in this direction. As we have seen, Lincoln believed that close attention to the rule of law was essential in forming the habits of the people toward a moderation of their desires. Another limit on the public is that of natural rights, and to this subject we now turn.

The discussion in chapter 1 regarding the 1854 Peoria speech on the Kansas-Nebraska Act illustrated that Lincoln did not think that justice is the "sole question" when it comes to politics. In that address, Lincoln delicately considers the interplay between abstract justice and public opinion, believing that a political leader cannot safely ignore an opinion universally held by the people. But what was the Peoria speech if not an attempt to mold that opinion, in addition to recognizing the practical effects of this strongly held attitude? Why engage in political rhetoric if one is not trying to form opinion while also giving opinion its due consideration? Indeed, the central point of that Peoria speech argues against the notion that there is "no right principle of action but self-interest."[2]

What other principle is there, then, if not self-interest? Presumably a majority of people desire a certain thing because they believe that thing to be in their interest. That is the very definition of democracy, namely that individuals organize with like-minded citizens so as to get the government to respond to their interests. The government should do what the people want, with "what the people want" being defined as the majority. But how is this good, majority rule, to be prevented from becoming majority tyranny? As was indicated in the previous chapter, it is precisely the absence of limits that is the very definition of tyranny. Tyranny includes unlimited majority rule as much as the rule of an autocrat. James Madison famously indicates in *Federalist* No. 51 that in the American constitutional order, separation of powers represents the fundamental protection against majority tyranny. Put more positively, separation of powers is the ultimate protection of minority rights. But Madison also indicates the need for virtue on the part of the people.[3] In the end, says Madison, should tyranny arise, it will be up to the people to stop it. In *Federalist* No. 44, within a discussion of the manner in which separation of powers and federalism help protect against majority abuses, Madison is left to conclude that "in the last resort a remedy must be obtained from the people who can, by the election of more faithful representatives, annul the acts of the usurpers."[4] At the end of the day, if the American people want something bad enough for long enough, they will get it. If they consistently choose to elect those who will violate rights, there is little that institutional protections can offer. Statesmanship is required to buttress institutional protections of rights.

Lincoln's defense of natural rights was intended to shape public opinion and rededicate the American people to the proposition of natural rights expounded in the Declaration of Independence. A thorough explication of Lincoln's views on natural rights is in order. The exposition begins with a discussion of Lincoln's grounding in the Declaration. Next, Lincoln's basic natural rights critique of slavery is considered. Finally, central to the history of Lincoln's natural rights theory is his rivalry with Stephen Douglas. Throughout, it shall be seen that Lincoln's defense of natural rights serves as an argument for limiting the role of opinion in government, insisting that the voice of the people is just only when in conformity with natural rights.

Lincoln on the Declaration of Independence

On his way to Washington, D.C., in February 1861 to be inaugurated the sixteenth president of the United States, Abraham Lincoln stopped at Independence Hall in Philadelphia. As luck would have it, it was the twenty-second day of February, George Washington's birthday. But it was a different founder whom Lincoln had on his mind when he stated there, "I have never had a feeling politically that did not spring from the sentiments embodied in the Declaration of Independence."[5] This does not seem to be simply a piece of overblown political rhetoric, for since Lincoln's reentry into political life in 1854, slavery had been the central issue on his mind, and the propositions articulated in the Declaration inspired his most eloquent words. Lincoln argued regularly over the last decade of his life that the principles of the Declaration were true— not just for the time they were written but for all time and for all peoples. Among his primary critiques of the pro-slavery South and Stephen Douglas's less odious popular sovereignty position was the notion that both arguments undermined the Declaration.

Part of Lincoln's dedication to the Declaration of Independence was its age. An important aspect of Lincoln's political thought is the notion that ancient bargains should not be overthrown for light and transient reasons. This is at least part of his argument against Douglas and the Kansas-Nebraska Act that overturned the Missouri Compromise. The Missouri Compromise, in Lincoln's mind, had served the nation well and, unless it had been shown to have substantial failures, should be respected. This is not to say that Lincoln opposed innovation in principle. He said at Cooper Union in New York in February 1860,

Now, and here, let me guard a little against being misunderstood. I do not mean to say we are bound to follow implicitly in whatever our fathers did. To do so, would be to discard all the lights of current experience—to reject all progress—all improvement. What I do say is, that if we would supplant the opinions and policy of our fathers in any case, we should do so upon evidence so conclusive, and argument so clear, that even their great authority, fairly considered and weighed, cannot stand; and most surely not in a case whereof we ourselves declare they understood the question better than we.[6]

In the case of the Cooper Union address, Lincoln was arguing that the founding fathers—he uses the term "fathers" thirty-two times in the speech—had supported the policy of allowing the federal government to regulate, even proscribe, slavery in territories. This dedication to old agreements extends to the Declaration. Douglas and others were doing a great disservice by undermining the people's faith in a document that had served the nation well. The principles of the Declaration were true and, what is more, were what Lincoln often called an "ancient" truth. So it had the benefit of time to give its truth added support.

"All honor to Jefferson," said Lincoln, "to the man who, in the concrete pressure of a struggle for national independence by a single people, had the coolness, forecast, and capacity to introduce into a merely revolutionary document, an abstract truth, applicable to all men and all times, and so to embalm it there, that to-day, and in all coming days, it shall be a rebuke and a stumbling-block to the very harbingers of re-appearing tyranny and oppression."[7] We see here Lincoln's argument that the rights expressed in the Declaration of Independence are natural, coming to a person simply through the fact of one's humanity. These are not rights that derive from history (or History), from a culture, or from a particular place but are ascribable to all people in all places in all times. Rights stand as claims against authority, particularly that of government. Indeed, these would seem to limit even one's own authority, as the idea of natural rights suggests there are some things to which an individual cannot justly consent, such as being bound into slavery.

Lincoln compared rights to the axioms of Euclid. "One would start with great confidence that he could convince any sane child that the simpler propositions of Euclid are true," claimed Lincoln, "but, nevertheless, he would fail, utterly, with one who should deny the definitions and axioms. The principles of Jefferson are the definitions and axioms of free society."[8] Like Euclid's geometrical principles, natural rights are not things to be proven but "self-evident" truths, truths that carry their evidence within themselves. And just as one cannot then proceed to express the claims of geometry if one is ignorant of the basic axioms, so one cannot have a free society if one rejects the notion of natural rights.

It is not surprising, then, given Lincoln's high view of the Declaration, that he was dismayed at the attack on the Declaration by slavery's defenders. Even more insidious was the undermining of the Declaration by Douglas. Douglas at least had the patina of being a moderate when it came to slavery. At their 1858 senatorial debate in Alton, Illinois, Douglas declared,

> But the Abolition party really think that under the Declaration of Independence the negro is equal to the white man, and that negro equality is an inalienable right conferred by the Almighty, and hence, that all human laws in violation of it are null and void. With such men it is no use for me to argue. I hold that the signers of the Declaration of Independence had no reference to negroes at all when they declared all men to be created equal. They did not mean negro, nor the savage Indians, nor the Fejee Islanders, nor any other barbarous race.[9]

Douglas avowed that when the Declaration declared "all men" to be equal, it had only meant that the British citizens in America were equal to the British citizens actually living in Great Britain. In that sense there was nothing grandiose about the Declaration. It was merely a legal document announcing the separation of the Americans from Great Britain but making no claims about abstract justice. One could say of Douglas's view of the Declaration of Independence that it had all the moral grandeur of a bill of lading.

Lincoln jumped on Douglas's argument for a truncated view of the Declaration, stating, "Why, according to this, not only negroes but white people outside of Great Britain and America are not spoken of in that instrument. The English, Irish and Scotch, along with white Americans, were included to be sure, but the French, Germans and other white people of the world are all gone to pot along with the Judge's inferior races."[10] Lincoln achieved two goals with this line of argument. First, politically it allowed Lincoln to appeal to more recent immigrants such as Germans who were generally predisposed to vote for Democrats. More philosophically, Lincoln was demonstrating Douglas's inadequate view of rights. Douglas's scant care for the natural rights teaching of the Declaration put not just the rights of black Americans at risk but the rights of the great majority. Lincoln held that the Declaration presented the promise to immigrants that regardless of their place of origin, they too could find full freedom in the United States. While unable to trace themselves back to the nation's founding based on blood lineage, immigrants could do so by adoption through dedicating themselves to the Declaration's propositions. To that extent, immigrants "have a right to claim [the Declaration] as though they were blood of the blood, and flesh of the flesh of the men who wrote that Declaration."[11]

Lincoln made rhetorical use of the Declaration in two other ways. First, he took the natural rights teaching of the Declaration to enhance his argument that slavery should be kept out of the territories. Lincoln latched onto the liberal "state of nature" philosophy that undergirds the Declaration, implying that the territories, as they were imperfectly organized under any governmental system, approximated such a state of nature. While one might tolerate slavery where it currently existed and had some protection of law, one should not violate justice by introducing it in a virgin territory unspoiled by slavery. Tying himself to the memory of Henry Clay, Lincoln stated, "In our new free territories, a state of nature does exist. In them Congress lays the foundations of society; and, in laying those foundations, I say, with Mr. Clay, it is desireable that the declaration of the equality of all men shall be kept in view, as a great fundamental principle; and that Congress, which lays the foundations of society, should, like Mr. Clay, be strongly opposed to the incorporation of slavery among its elements."[12] In this case Lincoln is using the Declaration's statement of natural equality to defend his basic policy regarding slavery, namely that of non-extension to the territories.

Also, discussing the Declaration allowed Lincoln to explain precisely what he meant by equality. Here it is worth quoting Lincoln at length:

> I think the authors of that notable instrument intended to include all men, but they did not intend to declare all men equal in all respects. They did not mean to say all were equal in color, size, intellect, moral developments, or social capacity. They defined with tolerable distinctness, in what respects they did consider all men created equal—equal in "certain inalienable rights, among which are life, liberty, and the pursuit of happiness." This they said, and this meant. They did not mean to assert the obvious untruth, that all were then actually enjoying that equality, nor yet, that they were about to confer it immediately upon them. In fact they had no power to confer such a boon. They meant simply to declare the right, so that the enforcement of it might follow as fast as circumstances should permit. They meant to set up a standard maxim for free society.[13]

Once again Lincoln is setting up the Declaration as the "standard maxim for free society." It is the star by which a free people should sail. But more to the point, what does Lincoln mean by "equality"? It is obvious to anyone that there are various inequalities in society. Some are rich while others are poor. Some are wise while others are fools. Some are virtuous while others are vicious. Yet whatever these inequalities are, they do not translate into the right to rule another without that other's consent. Nor do these inequalities mean that some possess "more" natural rights than others.

The problem of slavery is that it takes something indifferent, an inequality in "color" for example, and says that this creates a right of the "right" color to rule those of the "wrong" color. The Declaration articulates axioms that limit majority rule. By suggesting a standard outside of majority rule, the Declaration proposes limits on that rule that protect the minority from majority tyranny. As will be illustrated in greater detail below, Lincoln's advocacy of natural rights was part of a conscious attempt to shape the opinion of the people in the direction of limiting their own rule. Preaching a veneration for the Declaration was part of that rhetorical project.

Lincoln's Natural Rights Argument: A Rebuttal to Stephen Douglas

Let us now turn to Lincoln's basic argument regarding the immorality of slavery. While Lincoln did not focus on slavery early in his political career, we have seen evidence—such as the resolution he cosponsored in 1837 with Dan Stone in Illinois—that he was antislavery from near the start. A few years later, in 1841, Lincoln made a trip to Kentucky with his friend Joshua Speed; it was there that he witnessed the selling of slaves at market. Lincoln left two accounts of this experience in letters. While the earliest letter has something of a lighthearted tinge to it, both carry a clear denunciation of slavery.[14] Lincoln's law partner William Herndon indicated that he too had heard Lincoln refer to this incident as an illustration of his disgust with slavery.[15]

Lincoln would continue to speak against slavery over the years. In 1848, as a member of Congress, he traveled to New England to speak in favor of the Whig candidate for president, Zachary Taylor. Lincoln told of the harmony in the thinking of those from Illinois and New England: "All agreed that slavery was an evil, but that we were not responsible for it and cannot affect it in States of this Union where we do not live. But, the question of the extension of slavery to new territories of this country, is a part of our responsibility and care, and is under our control."[16] Shortly after, he would introduce in Congress a compensated emancipation bill for the District of Columbia. This bill did not amount to much but reiterated Lincoln's belief that in areas under federal control, Congress had the power to ban slavery. In this case, because slavery already existed and was in federal land, Lincoln thought that emancipation should be gradual and that slaveholders deserved compensation.[17]

Indications of Lincoln's use of natural rights as a limiting principle for democracy are observable in this brief history of Lincoln's attitudes toward slavery and natural rights. Lincoln unfailingly held up natural rights as a standard of free government, condemning slavery as wrong. However, given the existence of slavery, Lincoln understood the prudent policy was to contain the cancer where it was rather than simply excising it in one fell swoop. He also believed in limiting the evil of slavery by rejecting its expansion. Lincoln taught that slavery is a wrong and should be treated as such. Thus Stephen Douglas's "don't care" policy of popular sovereignty was particularly insidious.

It was in 1854 that Stephen Douglas offered up the Kansas-Nebraska Act, an act that allowed slavery into territories where the Missouri Compromise of 1820 had previously forbidden it. An explicit repeal of the Missouri Compromise was part of the legislation. To Lincoln, with his now long record of non-extension, this was anathema. Douglas proposed to replace the federal ban on slavery in the territories covered by the Missouri Compromise with what he called "popular sovereignty," by which he meant that each territory should organize itself as either free or slave based on a vote of residents. But to Lincoln this was a breach of faith and represented a new aggressiveness in proslavery forces. Allen Guelzo writes, "He had long disliked the hedonism associated with slaveholding, but this was a criticism limited to the slaveholders themselves rather than the slave system. He needed a morality with which to embarrass popular sovereignty's appeal to selfishness—not the chilly morality of duty, but the morality of natural law, even of natural theology. And so, for the first time, Lincoln began to speak, not in terms of motives, but in terms of certain moral relationships, which slavery violated."[18]

For Stephen Douglas, agitation over slavery had the potential to thwart his grandest plans. Douglas was keenly aware of the power of the railroad. As the mileage of rail expanded, the eyes of the nation turned west and discussions of a rail line to the Pacific Ocean began. Douglas was eager that such a line would cross his state of Illinois. This was problematic in that the natural passage to the Pacific would be to the south, as the route over the Rocky Mountains was easier in that direction. One action that might encourage the more northerly route would be to organize, and thus populate, federal land possessions in the north, making this land more attractive to railroad developers. Douglas, as chair of the Senate Committee on Territories, was in a position to make this plan a reality. But he had a problem: a goodly portion of the lands that needed legal organization was covered by the Missouri Compromise. He deduced that organizing these territories, with inevitable statehood to follow, would cause him problems with Southern votes for his plan. Introduction of new free states would likely be opposed by Southern slave interests, who would already be none too pleased with Douglas's railroad plot. So Douglas had to find a way to placate both Southern and Northern interests.

Popular sovereignty was the answer. This was a reasonable course of action for Douglas. Popular sovereignty already had precedent in federal action, as this was part of the 1850 compromise. New Mexico and Utah Territories, not being covered by the Missouri Compromise, had been organized under the popular sovereignty rule.[19] So Douglas, with good reason, believed he could apply the same concept to the Kansas and Nebraska Territories. But these territories had been deemed free by the Missouri Compromise, so Douglas's proposal would overturn an antislavery policy. Douglas initially tried to pass his popular sovereignty bill without reference to the Missouri Compromise but eventually was forced to include its explicit repeal. Douglas plainly did not anticipate the firestorm he would raise by these actions.

The debate over the Kansas-Nebraska Act and the repeal of the Missouri Compromise triggered a six-year battle between Lincoln and Douglas, highlighted by their epic races for the Senate in 1858 and for the presidency in 1860. Some have argued, as does James Randall, that Lincoln and Douglas only "seemed to differ" on the question of slavery.[20] The argument is that both had an interest in keeping slavery out of the territories and differed only on tactics. But Merrill Peterson seems correct when he says that one can argue Randall's position only "if one found no difference between careless indifference to whether slavery was voted up or down and a fulfillment of the promise of freedom and equality for all people, black and white."[21] There were distinct and important distinctions between Douglas and Lincoln. At the core of these was the dedication of Lincoln to natural rights and Douglas's principled but flawed rejection of natural rights. I say "flawed" in that Douglas could appeal to no standard outside of public opinion, making politics the realm of pure power. Lincoln, by contrast, believed public opinion should be constrained by limits of natural rights.

A fair consideration of Douglas would grant him this: he consistently argued that Lincoln's moral argument against slavery would only heighten sectional tension and lead the country to a bitter conflict that might end in war. He was not wrong. This is why he took such offense at Lincoln's "house divided" rhetoric, which Douglas saw as baiting the South. Douglas misconstrued Lincoln's metaphor, but Douglas was obviously correct to worry about a potential break in the Union and any rhetoric that might increase the likelihood of such a break. So we should do Douglas the courtesy of taking his argument seriously.

After passage of the Kansas-Nebraska Act, Douglas went home to Illinois only to find his political position deteriorating. He gave various speeches explaining his views, including one to a packed House of Representatives chamber in Springfield in early October 1854. In the lobby was Abraham Lincoln announcing that he would speak the next day in opposition.[22] How did Douglas defend his position?

Part of Douglas's argument was a crude appeal to racism. As has been noted, during the Lincoln-Douglas debates of 1858 Douglas consistently referred to "Black Republicans" in an attempt to tarnish Lincoln as an advocate of total political and social equality of all races. Fifty-nine times he used this term in their seven formal debates. Douglas said during the debates, "If you desire negro citizenship, if you desire to allow them to come into the State and settle with the white man, if you desire them to vote on an equality with yourselves, and to make them eligible to office, to serve on juries, and to adjudge your rights, then support Mr. Lincoln and the Black Republican party, who are in favor of the citizenship of the negro."[23] Undoubtedly Douglas was stroking white supremacist prejudices. He was not above playing to the prejudices of the audience in invoking the fear that total equality would mean black men targeting white women. The most famous example of this is the reference to black abolitionist Frederick Douglass at the Freeport debate. Douglas said,

> I have reason to recollect that some people in this country think that Fred. Douglass is a very good man. The last time I came here to make a speech, while talking from the stand to you, people of Freeport, as I am doing to-day, I saw a carriage and a magnificent one it was, drive up and take a position on the outside of the crowd; a beautiful young lady was sitting on the box seat, whilst Fred. Douglass and her mother reclined inside, and the owner of the carriage acted as driver. (Laughter, cheers, cries of right, what have you to say against it, &c.) I saw this in your own town. ("What of it.") All I have to say of it is this, that if you, Black Republicans, think that the negro ought to be on a social equality with your wives and daughters, and ride in a carriage with your wife, whilst you drive the team, you have a perfect right to do so.[24]

The clear intent of Douglas in this speech is to play on the fears of the public regarding racial amalgamation and the perceived threat black men posed to white women. Lincoln's vision, Douglas slyly suggests, is one where black men ride in carriages with white women. The audience is left to draw the conclusion as to what that means. While no state at that time could claim to be a seat of racial egalitarianism, Illinois was a state with particularly deep-seated racial prejudice. By Illinois law, black people were not able to legally migrate to the state. Also, the closer one got to the southern border of Illinois, the more the state's political culture took on a Southern tinge. Douglas used this bigotry to his advantage.

While this was the least honorable tactic of Douglas, it was connected to a less dishonorable one, namely tagging Lincoln and his fellow Republicans as extremists. Part of that approach was to identify Lincoln with total racial equality. Another part was to tie Lincoln to the politically unpopular abolitionist movement and the more extreme elements of the antislavery position. While Illinois was not a slave state, abolitionism was disliked by a majority of citizens, so in defending abolitionism, or at least in refusing to denounce it, Lincoln was on the wrong side of public opinion. Douglas tried to depict the Republican Party as a stalking horse for abolitionism. Referring to Illinois's other U.S. senator, Republican Lyman Trumbull, Douglas said, "In 1854, Mr. Abraham Lincoln and Mr. Trumbull entered into an arrangement, one with the other, and each with his respective friends, to dissolve the old Whig party on the one hand, and to dissolve the old Democratic party on the other, and to connect the members of both into an Abolition party under the name and disguise of a Republican party."[25] He would make the same point using nationally known abolitionists as his examples: "[Lincoln] came up again in 1854, just in time to make this Abolition or Black Republican platform, in company with [Joshua Reed] Giddings, [Owen] Lovejoy, [Salmon P.] Chase, and Fred Douglass for the Republican party to stand upon."[26]

While Douglas attempted to associate Lincoln with unpopular antislavery extremists, he portrayed himself as the voice of reason and moderation. We have seen in the previous chapter how Douglas viewed himself as the middle ground between antislavery radicals and pro-slavery Southerners. He showed how he had resisted the more militant elements of his own party by defying the Buchanan administration on the Lecompton Constitution that came out of Kansas. And the whole idea of popular sovereignty was to stake out a middle ground. Rather than force slavery upon the territories, as Southerners and their sympathizers might desire, and rather than forbid it, as Lincoln desired, why not simply let the citizens of the territory decide for themselves?

Part of Douglas's method in presenting his own moderation was to tie himself to the widely respected figure of Henry Clay. Clay was a man who, with his many compromises, had shown himself able to bring Democrats and Whigs together for a common purpose. Douglas associated himself with this tradition in the seventh and final debate in Alton:

> Such was the case in 1850, when Clay left the quiet and peace of his home, and again entered upon public life to quell agitation and restore peace to a distracted Union. Then we Democrats, with Cass at our head, welcomed Henry Clay, whom the whole nation regarded as having been preserved by God for the times. He became our leader in that great fight, and we rallied around him the same as the Whigs rallied around old Hickory in 1832, to put down nullification.[27]

This was a clever maneuver by Douglas. Not only did he ally himself with the Whig Clay, but by invoking Lewis Cass, a Democrat from Michigan who was the party's presidential nominee in 1848, he showed how people of both parties had come together in 1850 for the common good. He did the same with the Andrew Jackson "old Hickory" reference, pointing out how Whigs and the Democrat Jackson worked together to defeat a sectional attack on the Constitution in the nullification crisis of 1832. Douglas portrayed himself as the individual who could unite Democrat and old Whigs, North and South. Meanwhile, the Radical Republicans were relegated by Douglas to a merely regional party that heightened sectional tension.

More programmatically, Douglas maintained that Lincoln, by defending the federal government's power over slavery in the territories, was trying to nationalize a matter that could best be dealt with locally. Douglas's refutation of the "house divided" claim was in this vein. Not only did Douglas object to what he saw as the extremism of that phraseology, he also thought it was false as a matter of policy. Douglas noted that the nation had begun divided on slavery and had continued that way for decades.

Douglas believed sectional peace could best be maintained by letting the people in their local capacity decide the slavery matter for themselves. There was no need for uniformity. "At the time the Constitution was formed, there were thirteen States in the Union, twelve of which were slaveholding States and one a free State," pointed out Douglas. "Suppose this doctrine of uniformity preached by Mr. Lincoln, that the States should all be free or all be slave had prevailed and what would have been the result?"[28] While Lincoln might make moralistic claims regarding equality of individuals, Douglas believed the only equality that mattered was the equality of states: "I hold it to be a fundamental principle in our republican form of government that all the States of this Union, old and new, free and slave, stand on an exact equality. Equality among the different States is a cardinal principle on which all our institutions rest."[29] This, Douglas argued, was the way to peace. "If each State will only agree to mind its own business, and let its neighbors alone," he stated, "there will be peace forever between us."[30] For Douglas, conflict was caused by one side advancing its sectional view of the good through national policy. This was true whether the view was proslavery or antislavery and was the root of his "don't care" policy about whether slavery was voted up or down, only that local majorities be respected. For Douglas, justice was letting these majorities rule.

This leads to the final aspect of Douglas's argument, namely that popular sovereignty was the path to sectional comity. "Now, my friends," argued Douglas, "if we will only act conscientiously and rigidly upon this great principle of popular sovereignty which guarantees to each State and Territory the right to do as it pleases on all things local and domestic instead of Congress interfering, we will continue at peace one with another. Why should Illinois be at war with Missouri, or Kentucky with Ohio, or Virginia with New York, merely because their institutions differ?"[31] This is associated with the argument over the founders and whether the nation could exist with different laws regarding slavery. The founders created a republic that was half slave and half free. Why cannot we continue this practice?, asked Douglas. While slavery might have been outlawed in the Northwest Ordinance, the founders allowed it in the South. Why not continue this, allowing each state to abolish or sustain slavery as it sees fit?

The abolitionists and Lincoln wanted to upset the apple cart, in Douglas's view. Douglas argued that the nation had compromised in the past, as in 1820 and 1850, and there was no reason why that tradition of compromise could not continue. "I then said, have often repeated, and now again assert, that in my opinion this government can endure forever, divided into free and slave States as our fathers made it,—each State having the right to prohibit, abolish or sustain slavery just as it pleases."[32] In Douglas's view, popular sovereignty was the position favored by the founders.

Douglas maintained that popular sovereignty had worked so far. Many states on their own had emancipated slaves without having to be told by the federal government. Further, Douglas argued that the North was populous enough to elect a president on its own, as was to be shown in 1860 much to Douglas's disappointment. Still, from the point of view of 1858, Douglas asserted that slavery was not going to spread wild, making the entire nation proslavery, as Lincoln had intimated was possible in the "House Divided" speech. "If the people of any other territory desire slavery let them have it," said Douglas. "If they do not want it let them prohibit it. It is their business not mine." Slaves are property, argued Douglas, and the states and territories should treat them as they do other property. It is the radical abolitionists who are trying to upset sectional peace.

The Supreme Court's *Dred Scott* decision complicated matters for Douglas by calling into question whether citizens of territories had the right to exclude slavery. Douglas argued that police regulation would keep slavery out of the territories. "Those police regulations can only be established by the local legislature, and if the people are opposed to slavery they will elect representatives to that body who will by unfriendly legislation effectually prevent the introduction of it into their midst. If, on the contrary, they are for it, their legislation will favor its extension," he stated. Perhaps, for example, they could tax that property putatively so that no slaveholders would move there.[33] This gives some credence to the position that Douglas legitimately expected that slavery would not advance into the West. While *Dred Scott* made it difficult for new states to explicitly ban slavery, Douglas thought states could and would do so by other means.

Before we turn to Lincoln's claims, a summary of Douglas's argument is useful. First, Douglas believed that Congress was not the proper legal forum for slave decisions and therefore should not be the locus for the slave debate. Thus his "don't care" policy. Douglas did not think Congress should raise an issue that it could not legally or prudently settle. Second, Douglas often argued that the West was naturally free-soil territory. The kind of agriculture practiced there, namely the growing of grain crops and cattle ranching, was not conducive to slave labor. Slaves were a large capital expense, but these forms of agriculture were less labor intensive than was cotton farming. There would be little to no economic incentive upholding slavery. Next, Douglas seemed to believe that historical trends were against slavery and that if the West was organized and populated quickly, the free-soil position would prevail and liberty would extend. Douglas's faith in progress led him to suppose that slavery was on its way to extinction. This is related to a fourth argument, namely that the massive foreign immigration to the North was already politically isolating the South. If current developments were allowed simply to take their course, slavery was likely on the road to annihilation anyway. Fifth, Lincoln's position was contrary to the Constitution, as, in Douglas's view, the federal government had no power over slavery in the territories. The final two arguments are closely aligned. Douglas promoted himself as the only candidate trying to make appeals that might attract votes of both the North and the South, and this would allow the Union to be preserved. Conversely, Lincoln was driving a moral argument that could only lead to war.

Let us turn then to Lincoln's rebuttal of Douglas. In Lincoln's case, there seems to be three core arguments. First, Lincoln made an argument from the authority of the founders regarding slavery. Ancillary to this argument is the accusation that Douglas, in breaking with the founding, was the true innovator and revolutionary. Second, Lincoln stressed his "state of nature" argument regarding expansion of slavery to the western territories. Since slavery was not there, it would be a grave moral wrong to allow for its introduction. It is within this argument that Lincoln addressed Douglas's attempted appropriation of Henry Clay. Finally, and certainly the heart of Lincoln's antislavery convictions, was the belief that popular sovereignty taught a dangerous indifference toward natural rights by failing to treat slavery as a wrong. As Guelzo puts it, "It was as though Douglas had exposed the dark side of Lincoln's liberalism, 'insisting that there is no right principle of action but self-interest,' that in its effort to gain the maximum exercise of rights, liberalism could allow no single version of truth or the good to rule. Lincoln's struggle was now the ultimate struggle of all Whig liberals, to find some kind of moral containment to right run amuck."[34] While any democrat believes in the concept of the people making their own laws, Lincoln made the argument that democracy must be limited, particularly by natural rights.

The first argument considered is the argument regarding the founders. Recall that Douglas's assertion was that the founders created a nation part free and part slave, an indication that they were content with the arrangement. Lincoln was needlessly stoking anxiety regarding the status of slavery in western territories, in Douglas's view. In a rare point of agreement between Lincoln and Douglas, both contended that the beliefs of the founders should be held in great esteem. Lincoln explained,

> I entertain the opinion upon evidence sufficient to my mind, that the fathers of this Government placed that institution where the public mind did rest in the belief that it was in the course of ultimate extinction. Let me ask why they made provision that the source of slavery—the African slave trade—should be cut off at the end of twenty years? Why did they make provision that in all the new territory we owned at that time slavery should be forever inhibited? Why stop its spread in one direction and cut off its source in another, if they did not look to its being placed in the course of ultimate extinction?[35]

Lincoln offers here an interpretation of the founding that essentially says that given that slavery existed at the time and could not be safely eradicated, the founders prudently made certain concessions, but that should not be taken to mean that they endorsed slavery. Lincoln notes that the Constitution provided for the abolition of the international slave trade, which Congress did abolish at the earliest practicable time. He could have further noted that the word "slavery" is conspicuous by its absence in the Constitution. Indeed, the Constitution refers to slaves as "persons." One sees again the use of the "father" motif. Joseph Fornieri points to the language of the Gettysburg Address as continuing this rhetorical pattern of appeal to paternity. Lincoln reminds his listeners at Gettysburg of the narrative of "birth, sin, sacrifice, death, rebirth and redemption."[36] The founding need not be pure of all sin to be a useful guide to what is ultimately just.

Douglas, in order to justify his position, had to take a novel view of the Declaration of Independence that did violence to the plain language of the document. Douglas was forced to argue that the phrase "all men are created equal" did not really mean "all." Lincoln pounced on this not merely for the fact that Douglas's argument put the rights of all at risk but also because Douglas was clearly making inventive arguments that dishonored the founding fathers. Douglas contended that the Declaration meant that only the citizens of Great Britain who happened to live in America in 1776 were equal to those then actually living in Great Britain. Lincoln countered, "I think I may defy Judge Douglas to show that [Jefferson] ever said so, that Washington ever said so, that any President ever said so, that any member of Congress ever said so, or that any living man upon the whole earth ever said so, until the necessities of the present policy of the Democratic party, in regard to slavery, had to invent that affirmation."[37] It is Douglas and the Democrats who are the innovators, asserted Lincoln. Lincoln could with some justification note that Douglas was breaking with the founding and expounding radical ideas to advance his agenda: "But I say, with a perfect knowledge of all this hawking at the Declaration without directly attacking it, that three years ago there never had lived a man who had ventured to assail it in the sneaking way of pretending to believe it and then asserting it did not include the negro."[38]

Not merely on the issue of the Declaration was Douglas innovating. Regarding congressional power over slavery in the territories, Lincoln went to some lengths to demonstrate that the pervasive opinion of the founding was in favor of Lincoln's position that Congress did have such power. Most persuasively in the Cooper Union address of early 1860,

Lincoln painstakingly went through public positions and congressional votes of various members of the Constitutional Convention. Lincoln showed that of those who had taken a position on the issue of congressional power over slavery in the territories, the vast majority had supported such a power.[39] Lincoln rhetorically attached his position to that of the founding. Thirty-two times in the speech he uses the word "fathers," such as "Who were our fathers that framed the Constitution? I suppose the 'thirty-nine' who signed the original instrument may be fairly called our fathers who framed that part of the present Government."[40] Lincoln emphasized the extent to which his own position was simply restating that of the founding generation:

> But you say you are conservative—eminently conservative— while we are revolutionary, destructive, or something of the sort. What is conservatism? Is it not adherence to the old and tried, against the new and untried? We stick to, contend for, the identical old policy on the point in controversy which was adopted by "our fathers who framed the Government under which we live;" while you with one accord reject, and scout, and spit upon that old policy, and insist upon substituting something new.[41]

Lincoln presents his own views as harmless and "conservative," directly rebutting the accusation of radicalism. It was Douglas and his supporters who were the radicals in their rejection of the wisdom of the founding. This both shows disrespect for "our fathers" and gives compelling evidence that Douglas was wrong on the constitutional question regarding federal power over slavery in the territories. Lincoln's position, he asserted, had the dual virtue of being both true and well-grounded in the nation's traditions.

Moving on to Lincoln's "state of nature" argument, one can see how the legal status of the territories is implicated in this theory. The whole point of a bill like the Kansas-Nebraska legislation was to take an unorganized piece of land and create a government ex nihilo. In this sense the land was pure. Lincoln's position was that it was one thing to tolerate slavery where it already existed, as when the nation was founded, but it was another to introduce it where it did not already exist;[42] new countries were formed in "moral and abstract right."[43] Lincoln often used simple examples to illustrate his point, such as the snake analogy discussed in chapter 1. One would not put a snake into a child's bed, but if one found a snake already in a child's bed one might simply leave it alone for fear of agitating it and making matters worse. To the point, "The new Territories are the newly made bed to which our children are to go, and it lies with the nation to say whether they shall have snakes mixed up with them or not. It does not seem as if there could be much hesitation what our policy should be!"[44]

This is the heart of Lincoln's contention regarding the fight over the legacy of Henry Clay, whom Lincoln referenced forty-one times in the course of his debates with Douglas in 1858. Douglas may have been right that Clay made some concessions to slavery (and was a slave owner himself), but Clay had called slavery an evil and said that if he were starting a society he would not have it. In the first debate of 1858, in Ottawa, Illinois, Lincoln argued that Clay himself defended the Declaration against novel interpretations that would eliminate liberty and justify slavery.

> Henry Clay once said of a class of men who would repress all tendencies to liberty and ultimate emancipation, that they must, if they would do this, go back to the era of our Independence, and muzzle the cannon which thunders its annual joyous return; they must blow out the moral lights around us; they must penetrate the human soul, and eradicate there the love of liberty; and then and not till then, could they perpetuate slavery in this country![45]

Again, while Clay may have countenanced some deals with slavery, the goal should be "ultimate emancipation." Douglas's proclamation that he was indifferent to this laudable goal was damnable to Lincoln. In the debate at Alton, Lincoln quoted Clay at length:

> And what is the foundation of this appeal to me in Indiana, to liberate the slaves under my care in Kentucky? It is a general declaration in the act announcing to the world the independence of the thirteen American colonies, that all men are created equal. Now, as an abstract principle, there is no doubt of the truth of that declaration; and it is desirable in the original construction of society, and in organized societies, to keep it in view as a great fundamental principle. But, then, I apprehend that in no society that ever did exist, or ever shall be formed, was or can the equality asserted among the members of the human race be practically enforced and carried out. There are portions, large portions, women, minors, insane, culprits, transient sojourners, that will always probably remain subject to the government of another portion of the community.[46]

While there is some equivocation here by Clay as to whether a pure state of nature ever existed, Lincoln's interpretation of Clay was precisely that Clay believed that in the abstract all are equal, and if one was starting a society anew, one would want to recognize that in law to the largest extent possible.

So far we have presented legal and historical arguments in favor of limitations on slavery. But these arguments, no matter their strength, are not quite principled arguments. They have not yet demonstrated that Lincoln thought slavery inherently wrong. The "state of nature" argument draws nearest to this point. If that argument is valid—that we should not introduce slavery where it does not currently exist—it must be asked why that is the case.

Here we come to Lincoln's core argument regarding natural right. Douglas's defense of popular sovereignty is compelling precisely because it appeals to the instinct of Americans that the people's will should rule. In this sense, Allen Guelzo is correct when he points to the "dark side of liberalism." As was argued in the previous chapter, the notion of choice without limits, whether choices of individuals or of majorities, is the root of tyranny. This tyranny is particularly seductive in a democracy precisely because the concepts of choice and individual autonomy are so durable.

There is within democracy, as Tocqueville noted, a critique of authority that in some sense is salutary in that authority is often unjust, but this critique runs the risk of undermining all authority, leaving the individual to choose without guidance. In fact it is the emphasis on individualism, along with an overemphasis on equality and a deterioration in the influence of religion, that causes Tocqueville to argue that despotism is more to be feared in a democracy than in other regimes.[47] Democracies must find some common authority, outside of mere opinion, to which all can appeal. This comes naturally to aristocracies, as the authority of class and tradition is part and parcel of that regime. In Lincoln's view, natural rights presented precisely that authority to which democracy could justly submit. Natural rights served the aims of democracy by suggesting that each person is endowed with a certain dignity. That dignity puts limits on what the government and private citizens can do to an individual, even on what the individual can do to himself or herself (for example, one cannot justly consent to enslavement). Natural rights are an authority that can be defended on democratic grounds.

By arguing for popular sovereignty and dismissing the claims of natural rights, Douglas was flattering democratic prejudices but ultimately undermining the very grounds of democracy, namely the natural equality and dignity of all. While Douglas declared popular sovereignty to be the quintessential democratic option, Lincoln argued that the true import of popular sovereignty was "that if any one man, choose to enslave another, no third man shall be allowed to object."[48]

Because slavery is naturally unjust, Lincoln was incensed by Douglas's "don't care" policy and his preaching of indifference toward it. This lack of concern, Lincoln maintained, was logically no different from outright advocacy, as it signified a common ground between Douglas and proslavery forces, namely that slavery is not a wrong. Lincoln stated, "The difference between the Republican and the Democratic parties on the leading issue of this contest, as I understand it, is, that the former consider slavery a moral, social and political wrong, while the latter do not consider it either a moral, social or political wrong."[49] Thus Lincoln famously opined,

> This declared indifference, but as I must think, covert real zeal for the spread of slavery, I can not but hate. I hate it because of the monstrous injustice of slavery itself. I hate it because it deprives our republican example of its just influence in the world—enables the enemies of free institutions, with plausibility, to taunt us as hypocrites—causes the real friends of freedom to doubt our sincerity, and especially because it forces so many really good men amongst ourselves into an open war with the very fundamental principles of civil liberty.[50]

This lowering of sights from the natural rights of the Declaration to the mere expedience of self-interest is contrary both to natural justice and to the real interests of democracy, as these two are entwined. When Lincoln proclaimed that "right makes might" he was arguing against the crude notion of majority rule in which the majority, due merely to its superior might in numbers, is always right.[51]

While Douglas's "don't care" mentality gave the impression of neutrality, it was in fact picking a side. In other words, there is a moral content to the seeming indifference of Douglas. Lincoln argued,

> If you will take the Judge's speeches, and select the short and pointed sentences expressed by him—as his declaration that he "don't care whether Slavery is voted up or down"—you will see at once that this is perfectly logical, if you do not admit that Slavery is wrong. If you do admit that it is wrong, Judge Douglas cannot logically say that he don't care whether a wrong is voted up or voted down. Judge Douglas declares that if any community want Slavery they have a right to have it. He can say that logically, if he says that there is no wrong in Slavery; but if you admit that there is a wrong in it, he cannot logically say that anybody has a right to do wrong.[52]

Lincoln made a similar argument in Alton during the last debate of the 1858 contest. This passage from Lincoln is worth quoting at length as it contains, I believe, Lincoln's fundamental argument against Douglas:

> And if there be among you anybody who supposes that he as a Democrat, can consider himself "as much opposed to slavery as anybody," I would like to reason with him. You never treat it as a wrong. What other thing that you consider as a wrong, do you deal with as you deal with that? Perhaps you say it is wrong, but your leader never does, and you quarrel with anybody who says it is wrong. Although you pretend to say so yourself you can find no fit place to deal with it as a wrong. You must not say anything about it in the free States, because it is not here. You must not say anything about it in the slave States, because it is there. You must not say anything about it in the pulpit, because that is religion and has nothing to do with it. You must not say anything about it in politics, because that will disturb the security of "my place." [Shouts of laughter and cheers.] There is no place to talk about [it] as being a wrong, although you say yourself it is a wrong. . . . Try it by some of Judge Douglas' arguments. He says he "don't care whether it is voted up or voted down" in the Territories. I do not care myself in dealing with that expression, whether it is intended to be expressive of his individual sentiments on the subject, or only of the national policy he desires to have established. It is alike valuable for my purpose. Any man can say that who does not see anything wrong in slavery, but no man can logically say it who does see a wrong in it; because no man can logically say he don't care whether a wrong is voted up or voted down. He may say he don't care whether an indifferent thing is voted up or down, but he must logically have a choice between a right thing and a wrong thing. He contends that whatever community wants slaves has a right to have them. So they have if it is not a wrong. But if it is a wrong, he cannot say people have a right to do wrong.[53]

The "don't care" policy of popular sovereignty reduces a question of deep moral significance to one of mere taste, resorting to the sophistic argument of "if you don't like slavery, don't own a slave." Some people are for slavery, some are against, so what is the difference?

Let us consider a modern illustration. Some people like Coca-Cola, while others prefer Pepsi. The Coke partisan does not judge a Pepsi drinker as morally inferior nor advocates legal restrictions on Pepsi consumption. The difference between Pepsi and Coke is literally one of taste. Thus the choice between them contains no moral significance, and the public is indifferent to that choice. We "don't care" what soft drink people prefer. But is this the kind of choice that is involved in slavery? Lincoln's point is that one must call a thing by its rightful name. He said in Peoria in 1854,

> The doctrine of self government is right—absolutely and eternally right—but it has no just application, as here attempted. Or perhaps I should rather say that whether it has such just application depends upon whether a negro is *not* or *is* a man. If he is *not* a man, why in that case, he who *is* a man may, as a matter of self-government, do just as he pleases with him. But if the negro *is* a man, is it not to that extent, a total destruction of self-government, to say that he too shall not govern *himself*? When the white man governs himself that is self-government; but when he governs himself, and also governs *another* man, that is *more* than self-government—that is despotism. If the negro is á *man*, why then my ancient faith teaches me that "all men are created equal;" and that there can be no moral right in connection with one man's making a slave of another.[54]

If the "negro" is a man, then he has moral status. The public cannot be indifferent toward his natural rights. The "ancient faith" says that he has these natural rights equal to all others. Further, it declares that "to secure these rights governments are instituted among men." While the practical policy the government pursues to secure the rights of the people may be up to dispute, one cannot justly say that government and the people it represents can be indifferent toward this thing that the Declaration says is the very purpose of government, the securing of rights. Indifference is not neutrality. The position of indifference is laden with moral content. Douglas's position is akin to believing such evils as slavery, as matters of public policy, are no more morally compelling than the difference between Pepsi and Coke.

In this sense the "sacred right of self-government" is a secondary good to the primary good of securing rights. One can see this articulated by James Madison in *Federalist* No. 51.[55] The very point of his famous discussion of angels and men speaks to Lincoln's argument. "If men were angels," Madison theorizes, "no government would be necessary." Why? Because angels are incapable of doing wrong. Because angels never violate each other's rights, there is no reason to have a government. Recall that according to the Declaration, the purpose of government is to secure rights. Since angels never violate each other's rights, they would not need government. But unfortunately humans are not angels, so humans need government. Madison continues by saying, "If angels were to govern men, neither external nor internal controls on government would be necessary." Why? Government exists to protect rights, but in the state of nature, men, who are most definitely not angels, violate each other's rights. So government must be a neutral arbiter to mete out punishment for violating another's rights. If that government was made up of angels, one would not need to set any limits on it because one could always trust the angelic rulers to make the correct choice. One need not put limits on angelic beings. But, "in framing a government which is to be administered by men over men, the great difficulty lies in this: you must first enable the government to control the governed; and in the next place oblige it to control itself."

In framing a government of men over men, which one might rewrite as "sinners over sinners," there is difficulty. The first thing government must do is to stop the people from violating each other's rights. That is, we must emerge from the state of nature to a condition where rights are more secure. But the difficulty is that government itself may violate rights as it is also made up of fallible, sinful human beings. Thus, limits are placed on government to heighten the chance that when government acts it is acting consistent with the people's rights, not contrary to them. What limits government? "A dependence on the people is, no doubt, the primary control on the government," argues Madison, "but experience has taught mankind the necessity of auxiliary precautions." The best control on government is some form of democracy. Typically through election, democratic government is dependent on the people who are naturally jealous of their rights. But, says Madison, while democracy may be necessary to the securing of rights, it is not sufficient. Ancient republics had shown the framers that democracy itself can be a threat to rights. This was the fundamental task of the framing of the Constitution. The history of political thought had been skeptical of democracy as it seemed to always degenerate into mob rule inconsistent with a decent public order. Lincoln's Lyceum address expresses much the same concern. The auxiliary precautions to which Madison refers largely consist in the separation of powers. This is similar to Lincoln's invocation of the rule of law. In both cases, though, we can see that democracy is the secondary good that serves the primary good, the protection of rights. Once democracy ceases to serve the higher purpose, it is despotic, little better than the autocratic tyrant with whom escapees from the twentieth century are more familiar.

Even if successful in keeping slavery out of the West, Douglas's position taught a terrible lesson: natural rights can be trumped by self-interest and the power of numbers. Douglas seemed to believe that original sin had skipped Americans. There was no need for statesmanship, as the people needed no improvement. Thus any appeal to a standard beyond the aggregate interests of the people would be unjust. Douglas was teaching the people not to care about natural rights, to think only about what was convenient or in their interest. This is rule of the mob, a majority that confuses justice with whatever the majority wills.

Lincoln's six-year argument with Douglas had five components. First, the founders had put slavery on the road to extinction. They and others (such as Henry Clay) saw the error/evil of slavery and treated it as such. Douglas twisted the history of the founding to justify jettisoning that founding. Second, Lincoln argued that the Kansas-Nebraska Act solved nothing. Rather than introduce democracy into the slavery question, it simply turned Kansas Territory into a battleground. If Douglas claimed that Lincoln's "house divided" language might someday inspire violence, Lincoln could accurately argue that Douglas's solution had already instigated violence and a kind of civil war in Bleeding Kansas.

Next, Lincoln rejected Douglas's argument that slavery was already on the way toward extinction. Lincoln offered various pieces of evidence that Douglas was wrong. First, he pointed toward the *Dred Scott* decision. If the Supreme Court could invent the notions that Congress had no power over slavery in the territories and that the black man had no rights that the white man was bound to respect, then how long would it take before that same court claimed that slave property was a right that *states* had to respect? This would nationalize slavery. Further, Lincoln argued that the climate north of the Wabash and Ohio Rivers was not that different from that below, so Douglas could not argue that the Northern climate was inconducive to slavery.[56] Slavery appears to have been economically viable outside the South. Slavery existed not just in agriculture but in mining and factories as well. There was no economic incentive to eliminate slavery. So Douglas was simply wrong in thinking that self-interest would limit the expansion of slavery.

Fourth, Lincoln was insistent that the Declaration of Independence includes all people. All men may not be equal in all matters (wealth, intelligence, color, birth, and the like), but they are equal in possession of certain natural rights. Lincoln did not claim *reality* of equality but the right. It was the task of Americans to turn that right into a greater reality. Douglas, in his perversion of the Declaration, made that task difficult if not impossible as he undermined the noble aspiration of the equality of man.

Fifth and finally, Lincoln insisted that it was bad statesmanship to treat matters of natural rights indifferently. If the halting of slavery was mere expediency, then by what principle other than expediency prevented anyone's enslavement? As Lincoln argued in what appears to be a private rumination on slavery,

> You say A. is white, and B. is black. It is color, then; the lighter, having the right to enslave the darker? Take care. By this rule, you are to be slave to the first man you meet, with a fairer skin than your own. You do not mean color exactly?—You mean the whites are intellectually the superiors of the blacks, and, therefore have the right to enslave them? Take care again. By this rule, you are to be slave to the first man you meet, with an intellect superior to your own. But, say you, it is a question of interest; and, if you can make it your interest, you have the right to enslave another. Very well. And if he can make it his interest, he has the right to enslave you.[57]

Douglas, with his preaching of self-interest and indifference toward natural rights, was not just undermining the argument against enslavement of Africans but was undermining democracy itself. Douglas could give no principled argument as to why any particular individual could not be justly enslaved by someone who could show himself either whiter, smarter, or more self-interested. In his unwillingness to submit public opinion to any sort of limit, Douglas was willing to countenance gross injustice.

Discoveries and Inventions: Technology and Natural Rights

In 1858 and 1859, at the same time Abraham Lincoln's battle against slavery was coming to a crescendo, Lincoln delivered a lecture on discoveries and inventions on at least four occasions.[58] These lectures, on the surface, deviate from Lincoln's project pursued in earnest since 1854 of defending natural rights in the face of the expansion of slavery. Instead, the lectures focus on the method of "discovery and invention" and the progress of technology over time. Intermingled with the Douglas debates and the Cooper Union speech of 1860, the "Lectures on Discoveries and Inventions" tend to go unexamined. In its day this speech was considered a failure. Douglas Wilson maintains that it contains "little coherence and no consistent theme."[59] "The lecture on inventions was a failure," says Richard Brookhiser, as it was "unharnessed from the great issues with which [Lincoln] had been engaged."[60]

This evaluation seems hasty. The "Lectures on Discoveries and Inventions" illustrate Lincoln's reflections on the nature of labor, technology, and progress and their relation to the slavery question. Far from being digressions from Lincoln's antislavery project, these addresses give a deeper insight into Lincoln's natural rights argument against slavery. As Fornieri points out, in this speech Lincoln "on the eve of the critical election of 1860" spoke "in defense of free labor" and "speculated both philosophically and theologically about the origins and development of human industry and enterprise."[61] In a period in which Lincoln was immersed in natural rights rhetoric, it is unlikely that the issue of slavery was far from his mind while he considered the issues of technology and progress. The lectures represent an imaginative approach to the greatest political issue of the day.

"All creation is a mine, and every man, a miner."[62] This is how Lincoln begins the "Lectures on Discoveries and Inventions." Lincoln depicts creation as a thing to be used for man's purposes. Miners take the material of the earth for their own purposes, to improve upon this material and make something more valuable of it than it is as raw material. Lincoln continues, alluding to the language of Genesis. "In the beginning," he remarks, "the mine was unopened, and the miner stood *naked*, and *knowledgeless*, upon it."[63] Adam in Eden did not need to labor and thus did not need any particular knowledge as to how one might extract a living from the "mine" of creation. But after the Fall, man must provide for himself. Labor "was imposed on the race," Lincoln says, "as a *penalty—a curse*" after the Fall.[64]

Man is not the only animal who manipulates creation to his own ends. But man is the only animal who improves what he manipulates.[65] Beavers have not come up with better ways to cut down trees; they fell trees the same way they have always done. Humans, by contrast, invent new and better ways of cutting down trees. Early humans easily found that a rock with a sharp edge could be used to chop wood. Put a handle on the rock and one has an ax. Put a metal head on the handle and one has a harder, more durable ax-head than mere rock. Shape that metal into a blade with a serrated edge and one has a saw.

Lincoln posits man as a creature who seeks to ease his burden in order to live a more commodious life. He offers transportation as an example:

> By his natural powers of locomotion, and without much assistance from Discovery and invention, he could move himself about with considerable facility; and even, could carry small burthens with him. But very soon he would wish to lessen the labor, while he might, at the same time, extend, and expedite the business. For this object, wheel-carriages, and water-crafts— wagons and boats—are the most important inventions.[66]

Man can move only so fast and carry so much with him on his own. So he invents tools, such as carriages and boats, which allow him to carry more than he can on his own. In this way he "lessens the labor" it takes to perform important tasks. He can also "expedite the business" before him, so he can do more in less time. Overall, invention makes his life much easier.

Lincoln uses most of the rest of this "first" lecture to discuss various inventions, using the Bible as his historical source. He discusses the use of animals as beasts of burden and the difficulty in harnessing the power of the wind and then concludes with the power of water, in particular steam.[67]

Importantly, Lincoln starts the "second" lecture with ruminations on "Young America." The invocation of Young America is a clear reference to Lincoln's archrival, Stephen Douglas. This should serve as an indication that these lectures were not a break from his argument with Douglas but a pursuit of that argument by other means. Douglas and various Democrats formed the Young America movement in the early 1850s to promote Douglas's ascension to the presidency. Young Americans were eager to expand the territory of the United States. Recall that Douglas chaired the Senate Committee on Territories, the committee charged with admitting new states into the Union. Stewart Winger argues that for Young America, "intellectually, politically, economically, and even spiritually, America was in the vanguard of world history, and world history knew only one direction."[68]

While Douglas favored rapid expansion of territory to facilitate railroads, other Democrats desired land for the expansion of slavery. With the faster growing population of the North, most Southern Democrats understood that the only way to protect the slave power was to increase the number of Southern states and keep the South in control of the U.S. Senate. Thus there was the push to annex Texas in the mid-1840s and in the late 1850s to write a slave code for the territory of New Mexico. Various Democrats advocated American expansion into Central America and Cuba in the late 1850s.

The desire for the expansion of territory also indicated a particular bias concerning the source of wealth. For a slaveholding plantation society, land was the source of wealth. The larger the possession of land, the wealthier the nation. For the agrarian South, ownership of land and the desire to expand slavery pushed it toward a quasi-imperialist strategy. The invocation of "Young America" is one hint that Lincoln means to remind his listeners of the slavery controversy and the difference of opinion between him and Douglas.

"We have all heard of Young America," says Lincoln. "He is the most current youth of the age."[69] Of Young America Lincoln states, "He owns a large part of the world, by right of possessing it; and all the rest by right of *wanting* it, and *intending* to have it. As Plato had for the immortality of the soul, so Young America has 'a pleasing hope—fond desire—a longing after' territory."[70] Young America "is the unquestioned inventor of 'Manifest Destiny.'"[71] Lincoln makes quite clear Young America's insatiable desire for land and the power that goes along with the possession of land. Young America seeks expansion, and thus power, without limit.

The thirst for land relates to Young America's comfort with slavery, despite his stated goal of expansion of freedom. Of Young America's imperialist tendencies, Lincoln sarcastically contends,

> He is a great friend of humanity; and his desire for land is not selfish, but merely an impulse to extend the area of freedom. He is very anxious to fight for the liberation of enslaved nations and colonies, provided, always, they *have* land, and have *not* any liking for his interference. As to those who have no land, and would be glad of help from any quarter, he considers *they* can afford to wait a few hundred years longer.[72]

Young America is interested in "liberating" nations, even those who "have not any liking" for his liberation. As for those who have no land, such as slaves, Young America is not interested in their liberation. As noted earlier, Lincoln did not think that slavery was incompatible with economic expansion. Douglas/Young America was perfectly happy to condone slavery if he thought it contributed to material wealth.

Young America also is arrogant about his possession of knowledge. Lincoln sardonically asks, "Is he not the inventor and owner of the present, and sole hope of the future?" Further, Young America "knows all that can possibly be known."[73] Young America has a zeal for innovation, disparaging "Old Fogy." The only old things that Young America respects are "old whisky and old tobacco."[74] Lincoln contrasts Young America with "father Adam," the original Old Fogy. What was Adam's condition? He was ignorant, and having no neighbors he had no one to teach him anything. It would seem as though Adam was in a very poor position. So what advantage does Young America have over the oldest of fogies? Lincoln asks "the Youngster" to "discard all he has learned from others" and then measure himself against Adam, for Adam possessed all the livestock and all of the land in the world. By Young America's own measure, "Adam was quite in the ascendant. He was in dominion over all the earth, and all the living things upon, and round about it."[75] Lincoln demonstrates that by Young America's reckoning, namely that prosperity and power come from ownership of land, Adam's position, even after the Fall, is actually one of untold wealth, as he "owned" all the world.

The difference between Old Fogy and Young America "is the result of *Discoveries, Inventions,* and *Improvements.* These in turn are the result of *observation, reflection,* and *experiment.*"[76] Old Fogy does not assume that he knows all. He seeks to gain more knowledge by scientific experimentation. The example Lincoln uses is steam power. He notes that man must have noted for generations that when water is boiled the lid of the container moves. Man began to wonder if he could harness this power for his own use. After "observation, reflection, and trial," he created the "now well known agent" of steam power.[77]

The inventor of steam power needed the help of those who had gone before him. Had he not learned from them, "he never would have succeeded—probably, never would have thought of making the attempt." In order to "be fruitful in invention," one must have the "habit of observation and reflection." This habit is acquired, "no doubt, from those who, to him, are old fogies." It is the learned habits of observation, reflection, and trial that separate Americans from other civilizations that do not make as much of the natural world as do "yankees."[78]

Lincoln returns to the miner metaphor that began the first lecture: "All nature—the whole world, material, moral, and intellectual,—is a mine."[79] All of creation is ripe for improvement. Education is necessary to make full use of the world. The scientific method that Lincoln advocates is itself a kind of education. Observing, reflecting, and trial are keys to modern scientific progress. Lincoln is pointing out that Young America gains what he wants by taking it. But Old Fogies learn from each other and gain wealth by ingenuity. For Old Fogy, wealth is not dependent upon ownership of land but upon resourcefulness.

Lincoln discusses specifically how this knowledge is transmitted from one Old Fogy to another. In order to begin the subduing of nature, Adam first had to invent invention. This is the importance of speech. Speech allows "different individuals to interchange thoughts, and thereby to combine their powers of observation and reflection," and "greatly facilitates useful discoveries and inventions." Using the powers of speech communication, two individuals can thus achieve a result "which neither alone would have arrived at."[80]

But speech is limited in its applicability. The spoken word does not pass through time. Lincoln proclaims that writing, "the art of communicating thoughts to the mind, through the eye," is "the great invention of the world." Writing, unlike speech, allows us to "converse with the dead." Lincoln uses the art of writing against Young America. "Suppose the art, with all conception of it, were this day lost to the world, how long, think you, would it be, before even Young America could get up the letter A." Young America, with its disdain for the past and acquired knowledge, would be helpless without knowledge handed down through the ages. Those who invented writing, Lincoln argues, "were very old fogies" indeed.[81]

Lincoln continues on to list the inventions that he thinks are most noteworthy in human experience. What these inventions have in common is the "great efficiency in facilitating all other inventions and discoveries." Lincoln first mentions "the arts of writing and printing" and also "the discovery of America, and the introduction of Patent-laws."[82] The latter two are odd inclusions in that they are not truly inventions in the usual technological sense, but they do allow for greater invention.

Lincoln continues his discussion of communication by considering printing in some detail. Putting one's ideas down on paper allows them "a better chance of never being forgotten."[83] Before the printing press, the possession of written material was extremely expensive, and thus only the aristocracy gained from its benefits. The mass of the people remained illiterate and ignorant. The printing press allowed for the mass production of less expensive books. Lincoln suggests, "Discoveries, inventions, and improvements followed rapidly, and have been increasing their rapidity ever since."[84] Printing, slowly at first, started the process of granting education to the greater populace. "The capacity to read," says Lincoln, "could not be multiplied as fast as the means of reading." While spelling books abounded, teachers did not. Without proper education, "the great mass of men, at that time, were utterly unconscious, that their conditions, or their minds, were capable of improvement. They not only looked upon the educated few as superior beings; but they supposed themselves to be naturally incapable of rising to equality."[85] Education is the great liberator in this scenario. "To immancipate the mind from this false and under estimate of itself, is the great task which printing came into the world to perform. It is difficult for us now and here, to conceive how strong this slavery of the mind was."[86]

Lincoln calls slavery to mind when he suggests a jarring final invention, "the invention of Negroes, or, of the present mode of using them, in 1434."[87] Lincoln crafts an analogy between the slavery of the "Negro" and the slavery of ignorance. For Lincoln, a lack of education is a kind of slavery. And as such, the possession of education allows one to break from the "shackles" of ignorance. Yet Lincoln's invocation of chattel slavery indicates that the desire for invention may have dire consequences, as one last piece of nature, human nature, is used to produce progress. As Eugene Miller puts it, "The Western traffic in slaves was crucial evidence, for Lincoln, that advancing technology could both stimulate and serve the human desire to master others."[88] Discovery and invention are liberating but have the potential of also creating new kinds of slavery.

According to Lincoln, invention enhances human freedom by making man more efficient in his labor. This means he does not have to spend inordinate amounts of time simply trying to raise the sustenance of life. He can exercise other skills he has, as Lincoln did with his lawyerly skills, rather than spend his life toiling in the soil. Importantly, the ease at which invention allows us to sustain ourselves reduces the temptation to exploit the labor of another to provide us with our daily bread.

The method of discovery ("observation, reflection, and experiment") requires education. This education provides the skills and habits that enhance the citizen's capacity for self-governance. Because he is literate, he can learn on his own. Further, his ability to analyze problems and arguments and to cultivate his higher mind and morals makes an educated man more fit for self-government. One can see here a critique of Southern plantation society, with a largely illiterate people tied to the land with no hope of improving their condition. This was the case for both black slaves and the mass of poor whites.

Lincoln also warns that liberation must have limits. The reference to "Negroes," or at least "the present mode of using them," suggests that humans might also be seen as mere tools for invention. As Stewart Winger puts it, "Lincoln meant either to imply that slavery ran counter to the most important currents of history or that the currents of history were not so swift and sure after all."[89] The spirit of progress, contrary to popular prejudice, can cohabitate with the grossest of injustices. The natural rights that men possess, grounded in their natural equality, do not allow for using other humans as instruments of discovery and invention. Lincoln cleverly adapts his argument against mere self-interest to address technology and progress. Just as economic self-interest does not justify slavery, neither does the desire for "progress." The aim of discovery and inventions seems to be the easing of the burdens of labor and the enhancing of material wealth. Viewing other human beings as mere material, as pieces of technology, tempts us into using some to advance the wealth and leisure of others. Slavery is one example of using people to this unjust end, unjust because reduction of the human person to mere utility ignores humanity's natural equality and dignity. The more poetic rhetoric of Lincoln's defense of natural rights is meant to remind people of this natural equality and teach citizens not to fall prey to the temptation toward despotism over our fellow man. The statesman has a key role to play in the moral education of the people. Happily, the literacy of an educated people such as envisioned by Lincoln makes dissemination of this moral education easier.

As Lincoln surmised, the slave South depended on keeping the masses ignorant and under the influence of the landed aristocracy. Lincoln's discussion of education calls to mind the differences on this subject between the slaveholding South and the more industrial North. In New England, for example, more than 95 percent of adults could read at midcentury, and three-fourths of children aged five to nineteen were enrolled in school. The South, by contrast, had an adult literacy rate of 80 percent, while only one-third of white children were enrolled in school. It is not surprising that 93 percent of the important inventions patented in the United States from 1790 to 1860 were created in free states. Said one Northern industrialist, "Intelligent laborers can add much more to the capital employed in a business than those who are ignorant."[90]

Read alongside Lincoln's more lyrical rhetoric, the "Lectures on Discoveries and Inventions" represents a sophisticated argument against slavery and for the liberating power of invention and education while reminding us of the limits posed by man's natural equality. These are useful warnings for those in a century ruled by technology, what some call a "technopoly." Such a society invents for the sake of invention, with the good of society being subsumed under the ideology of technology.[91] The mating of technopoly with advanced bureaucracy allows for the systematic abuse of human dignity in the name of progress. Contemporary questions concerning the good of genetic testing, cloning, artificial intelligence, and the ubiquity of technology in the guise of social media and mobile devices, just to name a few, make Lincoln's concerns more prescient than ever. Residents of twenty-first-century technopolies need reminding that all progress must be consistent with the dignity of the human person, as that is a good superior to the goods of comfort and ease.

Natural Rights as Democratic Poetry

We have argued here that Lincoln saw the defense of natural rights as central to this task of limiting majority rule and the desire to control. Lincoln offered no objection to the founders' methods, which famously sought to use the clashing of the multiple interests in the public and the ambition of officeholders to cobble together something that might approximate justice. But Lincoln seemed to believe that a community of mere self-interest was insufficient to the task of limiting the people's desires. Herbert Storing argues Lincoln harmonized the Federalist argument—that rights are best protected by well-designed institutions based on self-interest—with the Anti-Federalist argument for a "moral community" in which "the seat of that community must be the hearts of the people."[92] There must be something noble to which the people can aspire. Simply appealing to the private pursuit of interest, largely meaning economic progress, would not create a republic that could sustain a dedication to the propositions that are the very reason for the republic's existence.

The founders may have been correct that enlightened statesmen will not always be at the helm, and thus auxiliary precautions must be put in place if the rights of the people are to be protected. But a people that cannot regularly produce statesmen will not long maintain a free government. Stephen Douglas tapped into a strain of democratic thought that has powerful grounding in democratic theory. Precisely by appealing to our democratic instincts, the assumptions undergirding popular sovereignty distract us from the very foundations of democracy itself. If a people are left to indulge every whim, in due course corruption of democracy will be the result. All of us, if we look into our souls, will realize that there are things we want that we really should not have. Typically these are relatively harmless things, such as this unhealthy food item or that frivolous consumer product that represents a waste of money. But aggregated over a whole population and indulged by ambitious politicians, the notion that we should get something simply because we want it leaves the people little better than cows, creatures who are governed by animal wants rather than by higher ends.

Thus the argument for natural rights. Lincoln is renowned for his deft use of rhetoric. Never is he more poetic than in his defense of natural rights. Lincoln must make natural rights seem beautiful to make them appealing. If the job of political rhetoric is to rework the architecture of the soul, Lincoln's rhetoric concerning natural rights was designed to erect in the souls of Americans a beautiful cathedral, so to speak, rather than a shopping mall or garbage dump.

The purpose of natural rights rhetoric is to defend limits, yet there are those who argue that the notion of abstract natural rights undermines this very project. The classic modern critique of abstract rights is by Edmund Burke. Burke does not so much say that such rights do not exist as that they are irrelevant to society as actually practiced. For Burke, society has an organic quality made up of what Yuval Levin describes as an "array of layered obligations."[93] Burke's view of a polity is one that is more held together by "sentimental attachments and habits of affection," in Levin's description of Burke's thought, than by abstract philosophical ideals.[94] A healthy society is one in which people are bound to a series of obligations within the social structure as well as recognize obligations to ancestors and posterity. Burke rejects the social contract thinking that underlies much of liberal thought.

Rather than a collection of autonomous rights-bearing individuals coming together by consent under some system of government that will protect their rights, Burke's vision understands the individual in light of prior social obligations. In that sense political society "is a partnership in all science; a partnership in all art; a partnership in every virtue, and in all perfection. As the ends of such a partnership cannot be obtained in many generations, it becomes a partnership not only between those who are living, but between those who are living, those who are dead, and those who are to be born."[95] Given that our experience of political society necessarily entails obligations, Burke emphasizes duties as much as rights.

> Duty and will are even contradictory terms. Now though civil society might be at first a voluntary act . . . its continuance is under a permanent standing of covenant, coexisting with the society; and it attached upon every individual of that society, without any formal act of his own. . . . Men without their choice derive benefits from that association; without their choice they are subjected to duties in consequence of those benefits.[96]

Burke does have a concept of rights, but they are more conventional than abstract. Burke reinterprets rights to mean the benefit of a stable social order. As Levin puts it, "Burke essentially denies the relevance . . . of abstract, individual natural rights. He defines instead some practical rights to the benefits of society."[97] Far from advocating the abstract right to free choice, Burke is concerned with limiting choice for the good of society:

> Society requires not only that the passions of individuals should be subjected, but that even in the mass and body as well as in the individuals, the inclinations of men should frequently be thwarted, their will controlled, and their passions brought into subjections. This can only be done by a power out of themselves; and not, in the exercise of its function, subject to that will and to those passions which it is its office to bridle and subdue. In this sense the restraints on men, as well as their liberties, are to be reckoned among their rights.[98]

Burke is attempting to achieve through an emphasis on duty and public order what Lincoln wished to achieve through defending natural rights, namely limiting the people's options and directing them toward more socially beneficial beliefs.

Similarly, contemporary political theorist Robert Kraynak critiques natural rights thinking for undermining legitimate authority along with the illegitimate. Kraynak argues that Lincoln gives the "most plausible answer" to the question of why natural rights are so important. In Kraynak's view, Lincoln's natural rights defense suggested that "republican self-government is the ultimate test of human dignity." If the American republic could not meet this challenge, "then the logical conclusion would be that the people and their elected leaders needed a master of some kind to control them." The test of free government is the test of "the ability of the human race to progress to the point where people can take charge of their lives and act like mature adults rather than like children or slaves who were forever dependent on a self-appointed authority figure to govern them." Lincoln must be vindicated in order to vindicate the cause of democracy itself.[99]

Yet Kraynak dissents from this project. Kraynak objects to the notion that only modern thought and modern social structures are consistent with human dignity. This claim in fact seems facially false, as surely at least some people were able to live dignified lives before the advent of modern liberal democracy. Kraynak offers a biting critique of natural rights, or what he refers to as human rights:

> The central problem is that human rights are not only powerful weapons against tyranny; they also carry skeptical and subversive assumptions that undermine all authority. . . . The very same rights which help to protect people from tyrants—from the Hitlers and Stalins of the world—can also be used, and indeed have been used, to subvert good and just authority—such as the authority of parents, teachers, political rulers, canonical writings, and the church itself.[100]

Like Tocqueville, Kraynak fears that democracy may be dangerously subversive to legitimate authority.

Kraynak's critique of natural rights can be explained via example. Virtually all would agree that it is wrong for a parent to physically abuse a child. Why? From a rights perspective the child has a certain sphere of dignity that must be respected by all, including parents. To physically abuse a child is to violate that dignity and thus the child's rights. However, one can approach the subject from another direction. Parents, one could argue, have certain duties. They have the duty to care for their children in a loving manner so as to raise healthy, virtuous, and productive adults. The abuse of one's child runs contrary to the fulfillment of this duty by setting a poor example to the child regarding self-control and the use of violence, as well as concerning what kind of behavior is consistent with a loving, nurturing relationship. Both of these perspectives, that of rights and that of duty, get to the same point, namely it is wrong to physically abuse children. But they arrive at this point in two different manners that have serious implications for our view of the nature of the parent/child relationship. The rights perspective tends to start with the notion of limiting authority that is outside the self, while the perspective of duty is designed to educate parents as to the correct use of rightful authority. So we can see Kraynak's point, that "rights talk" serves to undermine all authority, not simply unjust authority. The question for natural rights thinkers, then, is whether natural rights must necessarily start from the individual autonomous chooser whom Kraynak describes. Does natural rights thinking have the tendency, perhaps unavoidability, of undermining all authority, even finally the authority of natural rights itself?

This is the root of Alasdair MacIntyre's critique of modern political thought, of which natural rights liberalism is a subset. MacIntyre famously argues that modern thought rejects the concept of ancient virtue. In doing so, moderns have been unable to come up with a moral scheme capable of replacing virtue ethics. The attempt to make abstract rules has failed. As moderns reject a teleological view of humanity as being inconsistent with human autonomy, morality now stems from emotivism, or "feelings." Skeptical of any hierarchy or authority, we struggle even to engage in moral argument.[101] MacIntyre specifically attacks the notion of natural rights, saying they are no more real than "witches and unicorns."[102] Based largely on our wants and desires, MacIntyre believes rights have no sound philosophical grounding. The concept of rights is just another attempt to set up abstract rules, and like all such attempts, rights-talk fails. "The concept of rights was generated to serve one set of purposes as part of the social invention of the autonomous moral agent," MacIntyre states. Originating from human desire, rights cannot serve as a useful limit on those desires. Thus, rights are a mask for "what are in fact the preferences of arbitrary will and desire."[103]

MacIntyre prefers a virtue ethics largely grounded in Aristotle. He directs our focus to virtues cultivated through habit and education rather than through obedience to abstract rules. As humans are relational creatures, these virtues can be cultivated only within political society. The notion of man as a rights-bearing individual in a state of nature is a fiction to MacIntyre. For him, virtue comes from inhabiting a role in society aimed at developing a moral excellence, such as being an excellent parent, an excellent neighbor, and so on. An authority or standard is needed by which to judge excellence. MacIntyre encourages his readers to see themselves as part of a narrative with a role to play. Like all narratives, the "story" of our lives has a point, an end, a telos. There is not one abstract story but various possible narratives that may be favorable to human flourishing. Not all stories are conducive to cultivating virtue, which is how MacIntyre saves himself from the charge of relativism. MacIntyre is much more concerned with how internal dispositions are cultivated through practice than with conforming to abstract speculative principles.[104]

Do these critiques fatally undermine Lincoln's argument for natural rights? Not necessarily. For one, we could argue that Lincoln's defense of natural rights was the prudential argument to make. It is worth noting that the thinkers discussed above—Burke, Kraynak, and MacIntyre—are not arguing out of the liberal tradition that undergirds the American regime. Burke is giving a defense of a more traditional, hierarchical, aristocratic society. Kraynak argues from the perspective of the Catholic intellectual tradition, a tradition that has an uneasy relationship with modern liberal thought. MacIntyre is attempting to resuscitate the classical concept of virtue. All three thinkers reject the liberal project. None of these viewpoints provides a perspective that would have served Lincoln well. Using MacIntyre, we can argue that irrespective of whether natural rights are true, they are part of the narrative of the American regime. Thus Lincoln the poet used what material his audience would find familiar and convincing. Even if Lincoln had some affinity for, say, medieval Catholic thought, it is hard to imagine how this take would have been rhetorically compelling to mid-nineteenth-century Americans. Lincoln, like Burke, believed in natural rights. Unlike Burke, Lincoln believed that natural rights language was useful in encouraging a just society. Natural rights are part of the American story, one might argue the noblest aspect of that story. Lincoln, drawing from Scripture, described the Declaration of Independence as an "apple of gold" framed by the "silver" of the Constitution.[105] Lincoln used his substantial rhetorical skill to rally the American people around the noble propositions of the Declaration, to turn the people's eyes toward something more principled than mere self-interest, and did so within the best of the American story.

It is worth noting that Lincoln does believe that nature should be the guide for judging the justice of an action or a society. Lincoln achieves his goal, and the goal of our three critics, in setting up a principle beyond the crude power of the majority by which to judge democracy's actions. While it is possible that rights-talk can be corrupting in the manner Kraynak and MacIntyre suggest, neither of them in their theory of rights takes into account the work of the statesman. What both MacIntyre and Kraynak fear, and what horrified Burke in the French Revolution, is the appeal to an abstract speculative principle that does not consider any tradition or societal narrative. A Lincolnian approach to rights would take into account prudence and moderation in addition to the appeals to abstract ideas. Recall that ideology is one of the enemies of a humane civilization. While the language of rights is important in limiting the excesses of democratic government, the statesman must also see where rights are less applicable or when the application of rights-theory might lead to obvious absurdities. The notion that "individual rights" must mean the right to consent to clearly destructive behavior such as slavery, prostitution, or use of hard drugs might be examples of absurd applications of natural rights. Looming controversies on polygamy, sexual identity, genetic manipulation, and cloning all touch on the notion of how much individual choice must be respected in light of other competing goods. In each of these cases, the "right" to individual choice must be balanced with personal dignity—perhaps consenting to prostitution is so undignified that it is itself a violation of natural rights—and the common good. We might ponder whether communities, such a families, have rights, as do individuals. Such a notion is easily reconcilable with Lincoln's defense of rights, as well as being characteristic of Lincolnian statesmanship, which has at its heart the search for balance. A statesman must ponder the point at which respect for individual choice must give way to the needs of the community and a decent public order. Such questions defy easy answers, but a statesman must ponder them, giving the people the context to allow for a proper balancing of competing goods.

Natural rights serve as a limit on democracy. Lincoln's defense of natural rights rhetoric suggests that when rights-talk is used to argue for autonomy without limit, such rhetoric ceases to serve its purpose. The problem then is not with rights language per se but with the lack of statesmen to teach the people the limits of the limit of natural rights.

3

★ ★ ★ ★ ★

Lincoln's Political Economy in
the American Tradition

A close inspection of the many monuments and statues in Washington, D.C., reveals a peculiarity. Of all the important founders—George Washington is known as the father of his country, Thomas Jefferson as the author of the Declaration of Independence, and James Madison as the father of the Constitution—Alexander Hamilton is perhaps given the least due. Considering Hamilton's indispensable role in establishing the economic system of the embryonic nation, it seems odd that he is relegated to one statue outside the Treasury Department building. Perhaps a best-selling biography by Ron Chernow, recently turned into, of all things, a hit Broadway musical, indicates a turn in gratitude toward Hamilton's contributions to the American republic.[1] Hamilton's role in defending the positive state, a strong presidency, and the commercial republic has been strangely underappreciated in a nation that at present embraces all of these ideals.

One reason why Hamilton's archrival, Thomas Jefferson, is more revered has to do with the fact that Jefferson's most notable achievement, the Declaration of Independence, was turned into the scripture of an American political religion by Abraham Lincoln. It is often argued that Lincoln owed his political philosophy to Thomas Jefferson. This is a more than reasonable inference due to Lincoln's reverence for the Declaration of Independence and the way he often hailed the name of Jefferson. Lincoln's admiration for the Declaration no doubt was on his mind when he wrote,

The principles of Jefferson are the definitions and axioms of free society. . . . All honor to Jefferson—to the man who, in the concrete pressure of a struggle for national independence by a single people, had the coolness, forecast, and capacity to introduce into a merely revolutionary document, an abstract truth, applicable to all men and all times, and so to embalm it there, that to-day, and in all coming days, it shall be a rebuke and a stumbling-block to the very harbingers of re-appearing tyranny and oppression.[2]

When articulating his position that slavery should not be extended to the territories under federal control, Lincoln, with some animation, brought Jefferson to his aid:

Mr. Jefferson, the author of the Declaration of Independence, and otherwise a chief actor in the revolution; then a delegate in Congress; afterwards twice President; who was, is, and perhaps will continue to be, the most distinguished politician of our history; a Virginian by birth and continued residence, and withal, a slave-holder; conceived the idea of taking that occasion, to prevent slavery ever going into the north-western territory.[3]

Language of this kind has influenced scholars to place Lincoln squarely in the Jeffersonian tradition. Noted Lincoln scholar James Randall explicitly rejects the idea of a Hamiltonian Lincoln in favor of Jeffersonian roots. "Among the nation's founders," writes Randall, "it is clear that Jefferson offered more of a cue for interpreting Lincoln than Hamilton."[4] Randall concludes, "It was in the bedrock of his beliefs that Lincoln was like Jefferson. The Declaration of Independence was his platform, his confession of faith. In those deeply sincere passages in which he expressed worshipful reverence for the Fathers, there was a Jeffersonian accent that was unmistakable."[5]

Richard Hofstadter concurs in Randall's judgment. "In Lincoln's eyes the Declaration thus becomes once again what it had been to Jefferson—not merely a formal theory of rights, but an instrument of democracy. It was to Jefferson that Lincoln looked as the source of his political inspiration."[6] Garry Wills writes that Lincoln was "unstinting in his admiration of Jefferson."[7] Thomas S. Engeman maintains that Jefferson and Lincoln stand together at the pinnacle of the American Mount Olympus: "Because of his revolutionary defense of democracy and his subsequent popularity, Jefferson was treated with the utmost respect by Lincoln. Lincoln made Jefferson not only the theoretical 'oracle' of the principles and axioms of democratic society, but the greatest practitioner of American practical statecraft as well."[8]

Yet many scholars draw a connection between the Whig Party, Lincoln, and Alexander Hamilton. Prominent Whig Henry Clay's "American System" of economics is called by Harry Jaffa the "lineal descendent" of Hamilton's *Report on Manufactures.*[9] Further, "Lincoln's policies were rooted in Hamilton and Clay's American System," writes Stephen F. Knott, "and his Hamiltonianism was evident in his support for internal improvements such as railroad and canal expansion and land-grant colleges. Most important, his celebration of the wage laborer as against the slave in an increasingly industrial America was decidedly Hamiltonian."[10] It was this "American System" that first attracted Lincoln to Whig politics and would later lead him to call Henry Clay his "beau ideal of a statesman."[11] Stephen Oates writes, "In between law books, [Lincoln] read American history again, paying particular attention to the Revolution and the Federalist era and applauding the nationalist programs of Alexander Hamilton."[12] John Patrick Diggins remarks that unlike Jefferson's romantic defense of the agrarian life, Lincoln could not wait to flee the farm that provided no future or advancement. Regarding Hamilton, Diggins writes, "Hamilton and Lincoln recognized that money is radically subversive in that it respects neither class, race, gender, nor ancestry."[13]

This chapter seeks to describe Abraham Lincoln's political economy and his view of the proper role of government, a role that should be central to any study of political statesmanship. One of the enduring questions of contemporary politics is the extent to which government should influence our economic lives. Citizens seek an economy that is at once productive but also just. This chapter begins a discussion of Lincoln's view of the role of government and of the president that will continue in the final three chapters. What does Lincoln have to teach us about the proper role of government, particularly in economic policy, and of the role of the president in promoting an economic vision? We shall see that Lincoln believed in a strong and active but limited government. He was not an advocate for a minimalist state, but his promotion of a robust central government was coupled with a profound respect for constitutional limits. This is particularly true of the office of the president, about which Lincoln was skeptical. Lincoln's statesmanship teaches the value of a sturdy, effective government while warning about the consequences of unlimited government and executive power.

Hamilton, the Powers of Government, and the Presidency

It has been stated that Lincoln owed a great debt to the ideas of Alexander Hamilton, so any discussion of Lincoln's view on the power of government must start here. Hamilton was one of the first to recognize certain shortcomings in the document governing the young nation, the Articles of Confederation. "The fundamental defect [in the Articles] is a want of power in Congress" and the jealous guarding of power by the states, Hamilton believed.[14] The Articles were based on the idea of state, not national, sovereignty. Hamilton wrote, "The idea of uncontrollable sovereignty in each state, over its internal police, will defeat the other powers given to congress, and make our union feeble and precarious." He concluded, "Nothing appears more evident to me, than we have a much greater risk of having a weak and disunited federal government, than one which will usurp the rights of the people." He lamented that in the case of the United States, "the common sovereign will not have power sufficient to unite the different members together, and direct the common forces to the interest and happiness of the whole." As early as 1780 Hamilton believed the leading lights of the burgeoning land should call a "constitutional convention" to create a governing document that would truly create a nation. This national government should have "complete sovereignty, except as to that of internal police."[15]

Hamilton argued his views regarding the powers of government most succinctly in *Federalist* No. 23. Hamilton declared that the "principal purposes" of the national government are "the common defense of the members . . . [;] the regulation of commerce with other nations and between the States; [and] the superintendence of our intercourse, political and commercial, with foreign countries." These are the three legitimate ends of the general government: national defense, regulation of commerce, and diplomacy. Hamilton argued regarding national defense, "The government of the Union must be empowered to pass all laws, and to make all regulations which have relation to [the army and navy]. The same must be the case with respect to commerce." Hamilton states, "The *means* ought to be proportioned to the *end*; the persons from whose agency the attainment of any *end* is expected ought to possess the *means* by which it is to be attained."[16] If the ends be legitimate, all means are assumed legitimate.

In his 1791 *Report on Manufactures*, Hamilton argued that the rise of commerce and manufacturing would furnish "greater scope for the diversity of talents and dispositions, which discriminate men from each other," and would afford "a more ample and various field for enterprise."[17] He envisioned a diverse society in which the opportunity to get ahead was available to all. The concept of the commercial society suggests that not all are best suited to work the land, as recommended by Jefferson's agrarianism. It was in the general public's interest that other avenues be made available to best allocate the variety of skills that existed among the people.

To encourage a commercial society, government aid might be needed for new industries or capital projects. Competition from other countries, particularly those already supporting their own domestic industry, presented an obstacle. Thus, tariffs on imported goods were necessary to promote and protect industry in the United States. Government moneys should be used for capital projects, as long as debt did not become excessive. Finally, a banking system was indispensable to extend the necessary capital for manufacturing.[18]

Hamilton argued for a broad federal spending power by the government. The government had power to raise money for "payment of public debts . . . providing for the common defense, and general welfare." He noted "general welfare" was "susceptible neither of specification nor of definition."

> It is therefore, of necessity, left to the discretion of the National Legislature to pronounce upon the objects which concern the general welfare, and for which, under that description, an appropriation of money is requisite and proper. And there seems to be no room for a doubt that whatever concerns the general interest of learning, of agriculture, of manufactures, and of commerce are within the sphere of the national councils, as far as regards the application of money.[19]

Hamilton also envisioned a vigorous and active executive as the centerpiece of his more energetic form of government. Famously in *Federalist* No. 70, Hamilton announced his conviction that "energy in the executive is a leading character in good government." To Hamilton, "A feeble executive implies a feeble execution of the government . . . and a good government ill executed, whatever it may be in theory, must be, in practice, a bad government." Especially in time of war is a vigorous executive recommended. Hamilton maintained that in "the conduct of war . . . energy of the executive is the bulwark of the national security." Only the executive, and a unitary one at that, possesses the "decision, activity, secrecy and dispatch" needed during the national crisis of war.[20] Hamilton's executive serves as a check on fickle public opinion, adding an element of deliberation to government. In *Federalist* No. 71 Hamilton writes,

> The republican principle demands that the deliberate sense of the community should govern the conduct of those to whom they intrust the management of their affairs; but it does not require an unqualified complaisance to every sudden breeze of passion, or to every transient impulse which the people may receive from the arts of men, who flatter their prejudices to betray

their interests. It is a just observation, that the people commonly *intend* the *public good*. This often applies to their very errors. But their good sense would despise the adulator who should pretend that they always *reason right* about the *means* of promoting it.[21]

The duration in office of the president allows the executive to oppose momentary public will and to have the time to explain presidential actions to the people. The distance of election will give the executive a "tolerable portion of fortitude" to resist unsound ideas while also allowing time for the president to "make the community sensible to the propriety of the measures he might incline to pursue."[22]

As Washington's Treasury secretary, Hamilton was able to advance his view of executive power. His influence was so great that he often acted as if he were the prime minister of the Washington administration.[23] Under Hamilton's leadership, the administration vigorously addressed issues such as public credit, finance, commerce, and domestic insurrection. Washington used Hamilton as his primary liaison to Congress to advance economic policy. Congressman Fisher Ames defended Hamilton's congressional activity, saying, "The very materials from which this knowledge is to be gleaned are not in the possession of this House—they are in the Treasury Department."[24] Hamilton was not averse to using Treasury officials for political work and was the de facto leader of about one-third of the Congress.[25] He sometimes would sit in the gallery during congressional debates.[26] During congressional debate on the Bank of the United States, Hamilton was in "regular consultation" with the Senate. John F. Hoadley argues that "distinct factions" began to form around Hamilton's economic program. These factions "were substantially different from those based on other issues." Hoadley reports that "many of the major legislative initiatives in the First Congress came directly from Hamilton" and that he was the "principal legislative leader on the Federalist side."[27] As in the modern executive, Hamilton acted much like a congressional party leader.

However, Hamiltonian energy should not be mistaken for the more clearly modern, potentially unlimited theories of national government and executive power developed by Woodrow Wilson and other Progressives, theories discussed below.[28] Unlike the twentieth-century Progressives, Hamilton was careful to respect the constitutional limits of executive power. Any action exceeding those limits must rely on prerogative—a power potentially inconsistent with republican government.

How then did Hamilton justify his actions taken on behalf of the National Bank or Washington's Neutrality Proclamation of 1793? The answer can be found in the careful language of the Constitution. Karl-Frie-drich Walling concludes, "Hamilton believed Article II was a complete grant of authority. Thus, the enumeration of specific executive powers in Article II, such as pardoning, receiving ambassadors, and so on was not a complete list. Since Article II contains no 'herein granted' qualification, the presumption is that every power in its nature executive belongs to this department."[29] As Hamilton put it, "The general doctrine then of our constitution is that the executive power of the nation is vested in the president, subject only to the *exceptions* and *qualifications* which are expressed in the instrument."[30] Walling suggests that these powers are the combination of John Locke's executive and federative powers.[31] By grounding these broad powers in the Constitution, Hamilton saw no reason to appeal to dangerous prerogative power. Perhaps more than any other founder, Hamilton appreciated the awesome responsibility and potential threats facing the president. Necessity often dictates that presidents act with broad power. Hamilton stated, "It is the province and duty of the Executive to preserve to the nation the blessings of peace."[32] Walling writes,

> Unfortunately, strict construction . . . leaves [presidents] no alternative but to invoke prerogative when extreme danger appears or great opportunity knocks, as Jefferson did in his defense of the Louisiana Purchase. For the sake of preserving the constitutional rule of law, however, one often wishes presidents would not only act but also speak like Hamilton, who preferred to act energetically within rather than outside the law.[33]

Having examined some basic principles of Alexander Hamilton's political science, let us turn to how that science was reimagined after Hamilton's passing, namely by the Whig Party.

Clay, Whigs, and an American System

"Of all the parties that have existed in the United States," wrote Henry Adams, "the famous Whig party was the most feeble in ideas."[34] This does not quite seem fair, though. The Whigs had a definite ideology concerning the ability of the government to aid economic progress, and thus economic mobility, and the formation of a unified nation based on economic ties. Daniel Walker Howe argues, "The chief reason for remembering the Whig party today is that it advanced a particular program of national development. . . . Taken together, the various facets of this program disclose a vision of America as an economically diversified country in which commerce and industry would take their place alongside agriculture."[35]

The Whig Party was born of a split in the Democratic Party, with the Whigs (or National Republicans, as they were at first called) differing with Andrew Jackson and other states' rights Democrats over such issues as the National Bank and internal improvement legislation. Originally led by John Quincy Adams, National Republicans gained the presidency in 1824 after Adams and Henry Clay made the "corrupt bargain" in the House of Representatives that threw the presidency to Adams.

Under the leadership of the second President Adams, the National Republicans, echoing Hamilton's nationalist vision, advocated tariffs, internal improvements, a national university, a national observatory, and a naval academy.[36] After Adams lost his reelection bid to Jackson in 1828, the National Republicans began to form a separate party organization to combat Jackson. Put off by Jackson's populist style and his opposition to the National Republican initiatives, Henry Clay, Adams's successor as leader of the anti-Jackson forces, concluded that Jackson must be fought from outside the Democratic Party. The new party was founded on two basic principles: opposition to the populist presidency and support for economic nationalism. It was the former position that gave the new party its name, the Whigs, referring to the eighteenth-century British party opposed to the Crown. Composed of National Republicans and the few remaining Federalists, such as Daniel Webster, they would form the anti-Jacksonian party.

When Jackson vetoed the rechartering of the Bank of the United States in 1832 and removed deposits from the bank (operating under the old charter) in 1836, the National Republican/Whig opposition resorted to denouncing this act as despotic and made opposition to executive power the center of its message. Clay protested, "We are in the midst of a revolution, hitherto bloodless, but rapidly tending toward a total change of the pure republican character of government, and the concentration of all power in the hands of one man."[37] While opposition to the Jackson presidency may have been the genesis of the party, the economic insecurity stemming from the Panic of 1837 turned the Whigs in a more programmatic direction. The Democratic Party, now headed by President Martin Van Buren, was radically laissez-faire. According to the Democrats, government promotion of economic growth would inevitably benefit some unequally.[38] Those business sectors that were the recipients of government largesse, at least in the short run, would gain unequally from the public coffers. This inequality was unacceptable to the Democrats. Michael Holt describes the Democrats' view: "The less government interferes with the private pursuits the better for the general prosperity. . . . Any positive government action created privilege. Government could best preserve equal rights by doing nothing."[39] The Jacksonians were inheritors of the Jeffersonian distrust of centralization.

Whigs, looking back to Hamilton, believed it was the government's responsibility to promote economic growth. Subsidizing capital projects, protecting American industry, and encouraging banking to expand credit helped achieve these ends. This was especially true in times of rudimentary transportation throughout much of the country. Cooperation being necessary for commercial activity, government help was indispensable. This government activity might benefit some unequally in the short run, but government action would promote general economic growth in the long term. It is not surprising that Whigs tended to get their support from the business and professional classes, as well as from wage earners who saw their interests tied up with those of business.[40]

The Whigs inherited Hamilton's rallying cry of economic nationalism. John Quincy Adams himself was a former Federalist. When the Federalist Party collapsed after 1815, many Federalists fled to the Democrats and strengthened the nationalist wing of that party.[41] While some who became Whigs had aesthetic problems with Federalist elitism, they bought much of the Hamiltonian project.[42] The Whig Party was "the party of small-scale urban businessmen and financiers and larger commercial (rather than subsistence) farmers."[43]

The man who embodied Whiggism, Henry Clay, developed a concept he called the American System in an attempt to unite the country after the bitter fight over the admission of Missouri as a state in 1820. Clay's American System was an amalgam of policies designed to link together the large republic through economic ties. Like Hamilton, Clay believed that the Union would be "invigorated by an intimate, social and commercial connexion between all parts of the confederacy." As binding the nation required ease of transportation, the national government must undertake the task of building and repairing roads and constructing canals to improve river travel. Clay foresaw a "chain of turnpikes, roads and canals . . . to facilitate intercourse between all parts of this country, and to bind and connect us all together." Also, as the end of European wars had lessened the demand for American goods across the Atlantic, the ensuing imbalance of trade should be alleviated by a protective tariff. Clay argued that the remedy for this imbalance was "a genuine American System" that would "naturalize the arts in our country" and provide "adequate protection against the otherwise overwhelming influence of foreigners. This is only to be accomplished by the establishment of a tariff."[44] The tariff would disincline business from entering into rivalries for European markets and would instead "transform these competitors into friends and mutual customers; and, by the reciprocal exchanges of their respective productions, to place the confederacy upon the most solid of all foundations, the basis of common interest."[45]

While starting his career as a Jeffersonian, Henry Clay drifted away from the anti-government strict constructionism that Jefferson represented. In contrast to the anti-bank Jeffersonians, Kentuckian Clay opened up his own bank in 1805 and began to defend the need for banking and commercialism. Robert Remini writes, "[Clay's] powerful efforts on behalf of the bank and his ideas and arguments sounded as they had come straight from the canon of Alexander Hamilton." Clay rejected the anti-banking stance of Jefferson as expressed in Jefferson's letter to George Washington against the First Bank of the United States. Instead, "Clay had formed an alliance with the entrepreneurial forces of the business and mercantile community against the individualist democratic forces of the countryside. That meant he favored the sound currency and credit facilities that a well-operated banking system could provide."[46]

Whigs believed in the "right to rise." By encouraging economic growth, eventually all citizens would benefit. To the Whigs, the Democrats made up the party of class warfare, pitting poor small farmers against the industrious and upwardly mobile middle class, while the Whig Party was for everyone.[47] Whigs believed that "all levels of the federal system should be used positively to elevate people economically, socially, and morally through the internal development of the nation's civic institutions and economic infrastructure."[48] While Andrew Jackson was lamenting "that the rich and the powerful too often bend the acts of government to their selfish purposes," Henry Clay was asking, "Is there more tendency to aristocracy in a manufactory, supporting hundreds of freemen, or in a cotton plantation, with its not less numerous slaves, sustaining perhaps only two white families—that of the master and overseer?"[49] This economic agenda was central to the Whig message through the Polk presidency, when fights over the Independent Treasury and tariffs were almost as important as the Mexican War and the annexation of Texas.

Lincoln's Political Economy and the Hamiltonian Tradition

The goal of the above discussion is not simply to lay out early nineteenth-century theories of political economy; the aim is to place Lincoln within the context of the American political tradition. Lincoln's quite distinctive political economy says something about his statesmanship. It is necessary to show the antecedents of his thought to gain a greater appreciation of his roots and also to see where he deviates from those roots. One of the central questions of Lincoln's time was should America "remain primarily agricultural with manufactured products imported, or should economic diversification and development be encouraged along with economic growth[?]"[50] Abraham Lincoln shared much of the view of economic vitality held by his Whig brethren, believing "industry and technology [were] the driving force of America's future."[51] Lincoln himself held no fondness for the yeoman farmer of Thomas Jefferson's dreams. Mark Neely points out that "Lincoln fought his entire political life for industrialization and there was not a pastoral bone in his body."[52]

Lincoln's broad view of the powers of government was similar to Hamilton's as expressed in *Federalist* No. 23 and the *Report on Manufactures*. In Lincoln's first (unsuccessful) run for the Illinois General Assembly in 1832, he noted the "public utility of internal improvements." He also promoted the "opening of good roads" and the "clearing of navigable streams," maintaining that the improvement of roads and waterways was necessary for commerce and communication.[53] After election to the state assembly, Lincoln backed numerous proposals for road improvements.[54] He also supported the distribution of profits from the sale of federal lands to the individual states to support internal improvements.[55]

In his career in the Illinois assembly, where he served as a member of the House Finance Committee, Lincoln clearly expressed his views on the power of government in a pamphlet from 1839 defending the National Bank.[56] Harkening back to Hamilton, Lincoln noted the many benefits of such a banking system, which fulfilled the government's duty to keep money circulating. In addition, when unhampered by the bureaucrats and politicians, the bank provided the people with a sound currency that instilled confidence. The National Bank also earned money for the government as investors paid for the privilege to borrow money. Lincoln reasoned that this money could be used "to pay for pensions of more than 4,000 Revolutionary soldiers, or to purchase 110 acre tracts of government land, for each one of 8,000 poor families."[57]

Lincoln's views were part of his generally broad interpretation of government power. Thomas Jefferson, Andrew Jackson, and James Polk had argued for a narrow interpretation of the constitutional powers of government. This limited view of power precluded government from funding internal improvements or sanctioning a national bank. Referring to the last clause of Article I, Section 8, of the Constitution, Lincoln argued that banks are "necessary and proper" to the power to "collect, safely keep, transfer and disburse a revenue." Using an "indispensable necessity" interpretation of the Constitution's "necessary and proper" clause, as Jefferson and Jackson did, could "exclude every sort of fiscal agency that the mind of man can conceive," Lincoln argued. *Some* fiscal agent is indispensable, even if no *specific* agent is indispensable.

As a member of the U.S. Congress in 1848, Lincoln made a similar defense of internal improvements in a speech before the House.[58] Many Democrats had argued that internal improvement projects were unconstitutional because they benefited the improved local area more than the nation in general, perhaps even to the exclusion of any general benefit. Echoing his broad constitutional vision in his banking pamphlet, Lincoln stated, "No commercial object of government patronage can be so exclusively *general*, as to be not of some peculiar *local* interest; but, on the other hand, nothing is so *local*, as to not be of some general advantage."[59]

Lincoln pointed out that the Illinois and Michigan Canal lay completely within Illinois, but by connecting the Mississippi to the Great Lakes, people from as far away as New York benefited. There was both a local and a general benefit from the project. Certainly the people of Illinois might benefit unequally, "but is every good thing to be discarded, which may be inseparably connected with some degree of [inequality]? If so, we must discard all government." Lincoln protested the contention of President Polk, delivered in a message vetoing an internal improvement bill, that states could pay for their internal improvements by charging tonnage duties. Lincoln argued that it was futile to expect states to raise enough revenue from tonnage duties to make the needed improvements. By this circular reasoning, the only way states could raise enough revenue to improve their rivers and harbors would be by improving their rivers and harbors so as to increase revenue. As Lincoln put it, this argument was akin to the Irishman who bought a new tight pair of boots and said, "I shall niver git 'em on till I wear 'em a day or two, and stretch 'em a little." For a Hamiltonian like Lincoln, internal improvements could legitimately be seen as regulating commerce and were of sufficiently general benefit.[60]

Lincoln had a clearly articulated vision of government activity in the service of economic growth. This vision appears so polished in Lincoln's thought because it was first quarried and cut by Alexander Hamilton. Both defended tariffs, internal improvements, and regulation of the money supply. Later in life, as a prominent Illinois lawyer, Lincoln would become a great defender of railroad interests in the court of law. Lincoln bought the Whig argument for government activity in the service of commerce and rejected the laissez-faire minimalism of the Democrats. Allen Nevins notes that lawyer Lincoln "and the state grew up together, their business becoming more complex, difficult, and important."[61]

But Lincoln's views on executive power were also distinctly Whiggish, seemingly wary of presidential power. Subsequent chapters will illustrate that the Whig theory of the presidency was one of deep suspicion, its genesis in part stemming from the perceived abuses of executive powers. The Whigs tended to extoll the virtues of congressional dominance at the expense of the presidency, and outside of prosecuting the Civil War, Lincoln tended to operate within this Whig view of the presidency. Yet when it came to prosecuting the war, Lincoln proved to be one of the strongest presidents in the nation's history. His strength came from a Hamiltonian conviction that the president is ultimately responsible for preserving the Union. He spent money out of the treasury and raised troops without permission of Congress. He took advantage of Constitutional ambiguities to suspend the writ of habeas corpus, again without Congress's permission. Lincoln inundated himself with books on military strategy so that he could better direct the war effort. While he agreed that these were unusual acts, the crisis of civil war necessitated extreme actions by the chief executive that would normally be unconstitutional. Lincoln asked, "Are all the laws, but one, to go unexecuted, and the government itself go to pieces, lest that one be violated?"[62] Lincoln believed that his oath to preserve and protect the Constitution might entail violating the letter of the Constitution in order to preserve the Union the Constitution created and maintained that the president had "broader powers conferred by the Constitution in cases of insurrection." While some of Lincoln's actions "were without any authority under the law," they accorded with constitutional design in that the Union was defended.[63] Here we see Lincoln arguing for a kind of federative power. Given certain necessities, it is appropriate for the president to exploit ambiguities in the law to defend the integrity of the Constitution and the Union it created. This is in line with Hamilton's own thinking on the subject. Lincoln acted with energy and dispatch in order to protect the Union, and his four-year term in office allowed him to convince the people he acted justly. This was the purpose of his famous July 4, 1861, address to Congress. Here he defended his forceful actions and declared that he acted in the belief that Congress, the people's representatives, would ratify what he had done.[64] Lincoln assumed the role of a strong Hamiltonian president regarding war prosecution, whether consciously or not. But, as we shall see, when it came to nonwar "domestic" policy, the Whiggish Lincoln was less prone to flex his presidential muscles.

The Whig Party was a combination of Hamiltonian nationalism coupled with a decidedly un-Hamiltonian view of presidential power. Lincoln's presidency shows that in spite of his distrust of executive power, there were certain circumstances that demanded presidential activism. Lincoln's activities as a war president obviously fit this category. Still,

Lincoln was never the advocate for the aggressive use of executive power to expand the American empire as was Hamilton.[65] Lincoln preferred American principles be expanded by example rather than by force. As Brian Danoff puts it, "Lincoln . . . thought that America should be admired not for its success in advancing its economic and territorial interests on the world stage, but rather for its success in demonstrating to the world that self-government is possible."[66] This is perhaps what Lincoln meant when he called the United States "the last best, hope of earth."[67] It is unlikely that absent the Civil War Lincoln would have tested the limits of executive power. In the aggressive use of executive powers in prosecuting the war, Lincoln could truly say, "I claim not to have controlled events, but confess plainly that events have controlled me."[68]

Yet, one can witness the practical effects of Lincoln's Hamiltonianism when considering the historic legislation passed during the Thirty-Seventh Congress, the first Congress of Lincoln's presidency. Innovative and nationalistic proposals such as the Homestead Act, the Pacific Railroad Act, the Legal Tender Act, and the National Bank Act were enacted by this Congress and were in perfect harmony with Lincoln's Hamiltonian and Whig roots.

Unlike his Democratic predecessors in the presidency, Lincoln did not frustrate the efforts of economic nationalists. Some seventy-five years after Hamilton announced his economic nationalism, a sympathetic Congress finally met a sympathetic president. Indeed, Lincoln was the first president since John Quincy Adams to fully embrace the economic nationalist argument. Once he was elected in 1860, the extent to which Lincoln would promote this agenda remained to be seen. Before the war, the Senate's disproportionate representation meant that the Southern agrarians could thwart a combined effort by Northern and Western interests.[69] Secession solved that problem for the nationalists and for Lincoln. Now that they were in complete control of Congress, it was only a matter of time before the nationalist bills became law. In some cases Lincoln would simply not oppose these bills as other presidents had. In other cases, Lincoln took an active role in promoting preferred policies. In the creation of a modern commercial republic, Hamilton and his Whig heirs were the indispensable prophets. While Lincoln may have owed much to the natural rights philosophy of Jefferson, in practice Lincoln was very much the Hamiltonian statesman in that he did not simply view the government's role as essentially negative in the promotion of liberty.

Lincoln as a Precursor to the Progressive Movement

Some argue that Lincoln's support for a nationalist economic agenda along with a broader definition of constitutional power means that

Lincoln would have been supportive of the modern Progressive government. There is some justification for this attempt. Compared with many politicians of his day, Lincoln (and the Whig Party from which he received his political education) was more comfortable with government activity in economic development, had a more elastic view of the Constitution, and, as president, oversaw a government that was vigorous in response to rebellion and may have set a "blue print for modern America."[70]

Some of the "founders" of the Progressive movement looked to Lincoln as a forerunner. For example, Woodrow Wilson wrote, "What commends Mr. Lincoln's studiousness to me is that the result of it was he did not have any theories at all. . . . Lincoln was one of those delightful students who do not seek to tie you up in the meshes of any theory."[71] Theodore Roosevelt, in his essay "Who Is a Progressive?," said of Lincoln's politics,

> [The Republican Party] is to decide whether it will be, as in the days of Lincoln, the party of the plain people, the party of progress, the party of social and industrial justice; or whether it will be the party of privilege and of special interests, the heir to those who were Lincoln's most bitter opponents, the party that represents the great interests within and without Wall Street which desire through their control over the servants of the public to be kept immune from punishment when they do wrong.[72]

In *The Promise of American Life*, influential Progressive Herbert Croly extolled Lincoln's virtues, saying, "He was the first responsible politician to draw the logical inference from the policy of the Republican party. The Constitution was inadequate to cure the ills it generated. . . . Thus for the first time it was clearly proclaimed by a responsible politician that American nationality was a living principle rather than a legal bond."[73] Finally, the Progressive Party platform of 1912 includes this statement: "We hold with Thomas Jefferson and Abraham Lincoln that the people are the masters of their Constitution, to fulfill its purposes and to safeguard it from those who, by perversion of its intent, would convert it to an instrument of injustice."[74]

There are contemporary examples as well. Former New York Democratic governor Mario Cuomo has written a book attempting to answer "What would Lincoln do?"[75] While Cuomo admits, "Politicians have twisted themselves—and Lincoln—out of shape to make it appear that they are standing next to the sixteenth president," it is not surprising that Cuomo thinks Lincoln would adopt many of the same positions as Cuomo does himself. Lincoln would, Cuomo argues, "find ways to provide education, food, employment, security from assault, and, most of all, equality of opportunity and the right to be treated with dignity for all people."[76] Similarly, former Democratic senator and presidential nominee George McGovern, in an otherwise straightforward biography of Lincoln, concludes with this analysis:

> The war that Lincoln fought gave rise to a new definition of liberty. Prior to the Civil War, liberty was thought to be the restraint of government from tyrannizing the individual. After the war, liberty was something that the government helped to provide.
> ... Gone forever was the South's concept of the Republic: a government of limited powers that worked primarily to protect (white) property owners, and a social order predicated on family, kinship, and tradition. In its place came a strong centralized government that promoted industrial development, competition, and free-labor capitalism.[77]

Both McGovern and Cuomo agree that Lincoln represented a departure from the American founding, and the leading characteristics of that departure were a rejection of individualism and a great acceptance for strong centralized action by the federal government to right society's wrongs. Harold Holzer and Norton Garfinkle's recent work, *A Just and Generous Nation*, represents a book-length attempt to show that the modern Democratic Party is the logical inheritor of the Lincoln label, while the contemporary Republicans have more in common with the Jacksonian laissez-faire mentality. According to Holzer and Garfinkle, there is near-perfect harmony in the belief in "the American Dream of a successful middle-class society, inspired by Lincoln and carried forward by Presidents Theodore Roosevelt, Woodrow Wilson, Franklin Roosevelt, Lyndon Johnson and more recently William Jefferson Clinton and Barack Obama."[78]

It is no accident that Barack Obama used Lincoln as a justification for his run for the presidency in 2008. Obama chose to announce his candidacy at the Old State Capitol in Lincoln's hometown of Springfield, Illinois (two days shy of Lincoln's birthday). In his address, Obama pronounced,

> As Lincoln organized the forces arrayed against slavery, he was heard to say: "Of strange, discordant, and even hostile elements, we gathered from the four winds, and formed and fought to battle through." That is our purpose here today. That's why I'm in this race. Not just to hold an office, but to gather with you

to transform a nation. I want to win that next battle—for justice and opportunity. I want to win that next battle—for better
schools, and better jobs, and health care for all.[79]

An assessment then is due for the claim that Lincoln was a forerunner
for Progressive politics.[80] The main differences between Lincoln and the
Progressives concern a belief in the power of centralized government,
advocacy of a strong presidency, and a rejection of the founders' basic
political science as inadequate for modern times. There is more to Progressive thought than this, but these are the areas where Progressives tend
to claim some allegiance with Lincoln. We have already seen this above
in part with Croly's claim that Lincoln believed that the Constitution was
an outmoded instrument and with McGovern's argument that Lincoln
embraced centralization of government power. By examining Lincoln's
commitment to the rule of law (and to the Constitution in particular),
his views on the presidency, his natural rights philosophy, and his actual
record as president, we can see that Lincoln's governing philosophy was
considerably divergent from that of Progressives. Overall, the discussion
allows us to better place Lincoln and Progressives in the history of American political thought and begins the application of Lincoln's economic
thought to more contemporary circumstances.

Principles of Progressive Political Thought

In the early twentieth century, a revolution occurred in American political thought: scholars and politicians influenced by those scholars
began to question the political science of the American founding. They
substituted a philosophy steeped in historicism and at odds with the constitutionalism and natural rights philosophy of the American founding.[81]

One of the essentials of Progressives' political theory was the notion
that modern industrialization had created a centralization of economic
power, which required a centralization of government. In his famous New
Nationalism speech, Theodore Roosevelt articulated this notion, saying,
"Combinations in industry are the result of an imperative economic law
which cannot be repealed by political legislation. The effort at prohibiting
all combination has substantially failed." Roosevelt thought that the government required a general just as an army does. "Let me again illustrate
by a reference to the Grand Army," he argued. "You could not have won
simply as a disorderly and disorganized mob. You needed generals; you
needed careful administration of the most advanced type."[82] The notion
here is that an economy must be regulated and guided by those with
advanced knowledge.

This was echoed by Roosevelt's distant cousin, Franklin Delano Roosevelt. In his 1932 Commonwealth Club address, FDR borrowed from Frederick Jackson Turner's frontier thesis to justify a stronger centralized government. Throughout most of American history, citizens who struggled to find economic success could always travel to the frontier and find land to cultivate and sustain themselves. But the frontier had closed, meaning that opportunities were now limited. This closing of the frontier created a political situation unanticipated by the founders, leaving their political science useless to modern government. "We were reaching our last frontier; there was no more free land and our industrial combinations had become great uncontrolled and irresponsible units of power within the state," said FDR. "Clear-sighted men saw with fear the danger that opportunity would no longer be equal; that the growing corporation, like the feudal baron of old, might threaten the economic freedom of individuals to earn a living."[83] The corporation had replaced the frontier. Because the average man was now dependent upon the corporation for his livelihood, the corporation must be regulated to serve the needs of democracy. FDR's conclusions were clear:

> All this calls for a re-appraisal of values. . . . Our task now is not discovery or exploitation of natural resources, or necessarily producing more goods. It is the soberer, less dramatic business of administering resources and plants already in hand, of seeking to reestablish foreign markets for our surplus production, of meeting the problem of underconsumption, of adjusting production to consumption, of distributing wealth and products more equitably, of adapting existing economic organizations to the service of the people. The day of enlightened administration has come.[84]

FDR's argument is that the closing of the frontier makes large industrial corporations the central organizing principle of the economy. Thus, the theory built around Jefferson's yeoman farmer is both inadequate and inappropriate for the circumstance. FDR further argues, "In other times we dealt with the problem of an unduly ambitious central government. So today we are modifying and controlling our economic units. As I see it, the task of government in its relation to business is to assist the development of an economic declaration of rights, an economic constitutional order."[85] What is needed is a strong central government to deal with the centralization of economic power. The essential task of "enlightened administration" is not to break up large conglomerations of capital but to manage them for the good of the people. The rise of industrial power has made the individual too weak to look out for his or her own interests; thus the founders' emphasis on individual political rights—that is, individuals protecting themselves against the state—must be jettisoned. Instead, the government becomes the champion of weakened and isolated individuals, protecting them against the real threat, that of corporate power. Franklin Roosevelt, like Theodore Roosevelt, was prone to the military metaphor. In his first inaugural speech, FDR argued that "we must move as a trained and loyal army willing to sacrifice for the good of a common discipline, because without such discipline no progress is made, no leadership becomes effective. We are, I know, ready and willing to submit our lives and property to such discipline, because it makes possible a leadership which aims at a larger good."[86]

Similarly, in his early work *Congressional Government*, Woodrow Wilson wrote, "There is plain evidence that the expansion of federal power is to continue. . . . The times seem to favor a centralization of governmental functions such as could not have suggested itself as a possibility to the framers of the Constitution."[87] In his "Study of Administration" essay, Wilson argues that "administration lies outside the proper sphere of *politics*. Administrative questions are not political questions. Although politics sets the tasks for administration, it should not be suffered to manipulate its offices."[88] Again, history has rendered the founders' political science moot. Instead, what is called for is centralization of governmental power, for centralization puts power in the hands of bureaucrats who will administer society based on the principles of social science. Wilson goes so far as to say, "To society alone can the power of dominating by combination belong. It cannot suffer any of its members to enjoy such a power for their own private gain independently of its own strict regulation and oversight."[89] A good and just society is one where the freedoms of the individual are controlled by an enlightened central government that regulates on behalf of the people while being only distantly accountable to the people. After all, a scientist does not put his or her findings up to a democratic vote.

Herbert Croly echoed these sentiments. "The new organization of American industry," wrote Croly, "has created an economic mechanism which is capable of being wonderfully and indefinitely serviceable to the American people." Like other Progressives, Croly saw the wealth of corporate America as a public resource to be managed by the central government. "If wealth, particularly when accumulated in large amounts, has a public function, and if its possession imposes a public duty, a society is foolish to leave such a duty to the accidental good intentions of individuals."[90] The property rights of business are secondary to the

97

public's claim on that wealth and the justice of managing that wealth by the government in the name of the people.

Coupled with the strong desire for a more vigorous central government and drawing generously from the military metaphor, many Progressives favored a strong presidency. Theodore Roosevelt famously advocated the "stewardship" theory of the office, usually contrasted with William Howard Taft's "constitutional" presidency.[91] Roosevelt, citing Abraham Lincoln as a source, argued, "The course I followed, of regarding the executive as subject only to the people, and, under the Constitution, bound to serve the people affirmatively in cases where the Constitution does not explicitly forbid him to render the service, was substantially the course followed by both Andrew Jackson and Abraham Lincoln."[92] It was Roosevelt's view that the Constitution gives presidents extremely wide latitude for making the most of the ambiguities in that document.

Woodrow Wilson is probably most famous among Progressives for his advocacy of a strong presidency. Early in his academic career, Wilson had indicated a frustration with the separation of powers theory embodied in the Constitution. Wilson, a great admirer of the British constitution, favored replacing the American constitution with a parliamentary/prime minister style of government. But as he matured as a scholar, Wilson began to see the presidency as accomplishing much the same task, namely the centralization of decision-making into a few hands, as a parliamentary government. Wilson's vision of the presidency deserves to be quoted at length:

> No one else represents the people as a whole, exercising a national choice. . . . For [the president] is also the political leader of the nation, or has it in his choice to be. The nation as a whole has chosen him, and is conscious that it has no other political spokesman. His is the only national voice in affairs. Let him once win the admiration and confidence of the country, and no other single force can withstand him, no combination of forces will easily overpower him. His position takes the imagination of the country. He is the representative of no constituency, but of the whole people. When he speaks in his true character, he speaks for no special interest. If he rightly interpret the national thought and boldly insist upon it, he is irresistible; and the country never feels the zest of action so much as when its President is of such insight and calibre. Its instinct is for unified action, and it craves a single leader. It is for this reason that it will often prefer to

choose a man rather than a party. A President whom it trusts can not only lead it, but form it to his own views.[93]

We see here how the belief in inevitable and desirable centralization influences Wilson's political science. The people are not a collection of factious interests for Wilson but instead have become a unified national interest. That unified interest is represented by a president, who supersedes faction. The people "crave" a single leader who can interpret and shape the will of the masses and translate that will into practical policy. Wilson is confident that the interests of a modern mass democracy can be safely represented by a single leader. There is no need for a division of power, either within the central government or between the central government and states. Indeed, this kind of division of power fatally weakens government's ability to direct society. Wilson believes, "For this democracy—this modern democracy—is not the rule of the many, but the rule of the whole."[94] Wilson clearly rejects separation of powers in favor of centralization of power into one or few hands. Wilson concludes, "You cannot compound a successful government out of antagonisms."[95] Richard J. Ellis concludes, "Mid-twentieth-century liberals believed . . . that the framers' elaborate system of checks and balances was a luxury that the nation could no longer afford."[96]

Finally, Progressives openly dissented from the founding political science, typified by a Jeffersonian dedication to natural rights and a Madisonian constitutionalism. The Progressive movement represents a rejection of the natural rights theory of the founding and of a government limited by a constitution. Wilson denounced what he called a "blind worship" of the Constitution, saying, "The divine right of kings never ran a more prosperous course than did this unquestioned prerogative of the Constitution to receive universal homage."[97] Wilson famously argued in favor of a "living constitution," one elastic enough to allow each generation to reinterpret the document to suit its needs. Wilson writes, "The government of the United States was constructed upon the Whig theory of political dynamics, which was a sort of unconscious copy of the Newtonian theory of the universe. In our own day, whenever we discuss the structure or development of anything, whether in nature or in society, we consciously or unconsciously follow Mr. Darwin; but before Mr. Darwin, they followed Newton."[98] The founders, by virtue of having lived earlier in history, were deprived of the knowledge of Darwin that Wilson possessed. "The trouble with the theory is that government is not a machine, but a living thing," Wilson writes. "It falls, not under the theory of the universe, but under the theory of organic life. It is accountable to Darwin, not to Newton. . . . Living political constitutions must be Darwinian in structure and in practice."[99]

Wilson also had qualms about the Declaration of Independence, rejecting the theoretical portions of the Declaration that lay out the natural rights foundation of the republic. He argued that "the rhetorical introduction of the Declaration of Independence is the least part of it. . . . If you want to understand the real Declaration of Independence, do not repeat the preface." Of the political thought of the Declaration's main author, Thomas Jefferson, Wilson wrote that it "was un-American in being abstract, sentimental, and rationalistic, rather than practical. That he held it sincerely need not be doubted; but the more sincerely he accepted it so much the more thoroughly was he un-American."[100]

Few were as harsh in their critiques of the American founding, especially the Constitution, as Herbert Croly. Croly derides the "undemocratic" Constitution as the tyranny of the "Word." Croly writes that the American republic relies more on the "supremacy of the Word rather than on that of a gradually educated and enlightened will." Croly rails against the notion that the outmoded theory of the founding era should still guide the nation in Croly's own time. By giving honor to the Constitution, we limit our ability to experiment and move democracy into modern times. Croly's analysis of the Constitution concludes, "The authority which the Higher Law ought to exercise, according to the political philosophy of the period, was reinforced by the authority which, as a result of its comparative independence, it actually did exercise. The Law in the shape of the Federal Constitution really came to be a monarchy of the Word." Croly finds the Constitution to be at the heart of an "essentially obnoxious political system."[101]

Croly also demonstrates a lack of comfort with the Jeffersonian philosophy of the Declaration. Jefferson, of course, argued in favor of a limited government, which left the citizens mostly alone to govern themselves in their local capacity and to exercise their natural rights. Croly, by contrast, argues, "The modern nation, particularly in so far as it is constructively democratic, constitutes the best machinery as yet developed for raising the level of human association. It really teaches men how they must feel, what they must think, and what they must do, in order that they may live together amicably and profitably." Croly does not see a regime in which individuals are left to pursue happiness as they see fit, largely free of governmental interference. Rather, it is precisely the job of government to control conditions and mold individuals into a new modern man, one superior in his selflessness and sociability to the Jeffersonian individualist. Also note that Croly does not argue from assumptions based on asserted truths about human nature. Croly seems to assume that humans can be shaped in any manner that reason dictates, irrespective of whether man's nature and natural rights might put limits on what government could or should do. Croly explicitly rejects the notions that democracy should concern itself with "certain existing political and civil rights" and that governments are instituted to allow individuals to "exercise" and "preserve those rights." Instead, government must help create a "higher type of individual and associated life."[102]

While this discussion clearly is not a complete treatment of the political thought of Progressives, it does describe certain key planks. Progressives were committed to historicism. They believed that truth is not fixed but is unique to each new historical circumstance. This is why they rejected both constitutionalism and the natural rights foundation for the American regime. The notions of natural rights and constitutionalism/limited government, they held, are outmoded and not relevant to modern industrial society. Also, natural rights and constitutions are themselves static (or mechanistic, as Wilson describes the Constitution) and miss the reality that human nature evolves. The evolutionary character of human institutions requires that we constantly adjust and experiment.

Thus, Progressives also held a commitment to scientific government. Here we might think of Franklin Roosevelt's call for "bold, persistent experimentation."[103] Woodrow Wilson, one of the founders of the field of public administration, and other Progressives, highly influenced by Max Weber, believed that bureaucracy staffed by those schooled in social science could govern a society better than elected officials. Progressives tended to see elected legislators as corrupted by special interests and the need for reelection. A healthy polity needed liberation from legislatures. This was to be done in two ways. First, put the people in direct control of their government via direct democracy (for example, recall, initiative, referendum). Second, give more power to bureaucrats. Just as the "hard sciences" were ever increasing their ability to master the physical world, social science was believed to be capable of mastering the social world, building up a progressive society managed by the scientific principles of public administration and ruled by objective, disinterested social scientist bureaucrats. A strong executive would lead by interpreting a kind of general will that would then be implemented into policy by scientific managers.

Lincoln and Progressivism: A Contrast

Given these basic commitments of Progressives, it remains to be seen whether Lincoln can be adequately described as a forerunner of Progressive politics. As indicated above, some Progressives, both early and more contemporary, drew on Lincoln as a source for their own political thought. Lincoln had his own vision of government that touched on the themes developed in Progressive thought. Throughout his thirty-year public life, Lincoln developed clear ideas about the purpose of government, its role in organizing society, and the president's role in that government. That governing philosophy deviates considerably from the Progressive vision.

We have seen previously in the discussion of the Lyceum address Lincoln's spirited defense of the law, in particular the Constitution, holding up reverence for the law as a kind of "political religion." Lincoln practiced this defense as president. When John C. Frémont used his authority as a military general to emancipate slaves, Lincoln countermanded Frémont's order. Lincoln argued against his own or a general's power to emancipate the slaves. He said, "What I object to is that I as president, shall expressly or implicitly seize and exercise the permanent legislative function of the government."[104] Lincoln objected to Frémont acting *politically* rather than *militarily* in issuing an emancipation order. Lincoln reserved for himself, as commander in chief, the military power for emancipation: "I think the Constitution invests its commander-in-chief, with the law of war, in time of war."[105] He felt this military power was also limited. Lincoln continued to hold throughout the war that the permanent eradication of slavery throughout the nation necessitated an amendment to the Constitution.[106]

When Lincoln finally did issue the Emancipation Proclamation on January 1, 1863, he justified it in terms of military necessity and applied it only to those parts of the United States currently in rebellion. The preliminary proclamation, issued the previous September, stated that the war would be prosecuted not to remake Southern society but to restore "the constitutional relation between the United States."[107] The actual proclamation was justified as "a fit and necessary war measure" by the commander in chief to "suppress" the "rebellion" in the South.[108] Not only was the action justified as a necessary war measure rather than some revolutionary scheme, but Lincoln asked all slaves freed by the proclamation to "to abstain from all violence, unless in necessary self-defense."[109]

Lincoln's defense of natural rights has been demonstrated. He frequently praised the Declaration of Independence and Jefferson, as we have seen. Lincoln markedly said that the Declaration was the "apple of gold" that made the Revolution worthwhile, with the Constitution serving as the "picture of silver" that framed the Declaration. The Declaration promoted "Liberty to all," Lincoln argued. "The expression of that principle, in our Declaration of Independence, was most happy, and fortunate. Without this, as well as with it, we could have declared our independence of Great Britain; but without it, we could not, I think, have secured our free government, and consequent prosperity."[110] Lincoln, unlike Woodrow Wilson, does not equivocate in this support of the Declaration.

Lincoln's theory of the presidency was incubated by the Whig Party, in which he received his political tutelage. The very birth of the Whig Party came in response to the presidency of Andrew Jackson, whom many saw as abusing the powers of the office. Whigs derided him, calling him "King Andrew the First." As noted above, at the core of Whig politics was opposition to presidential power (which might partially explain the party's terrible record in presidential elections). Daniel Webster had denounced Jackson's bank veto of 1832, arguing, "According to the doctrines put forth by the President [Jackson], although Congress may have passed a law, and although the Supreme Court may have pronounced it constitutional, yet it is, nevertheless, no law at all, if he, in his good pleasure, sees fit to deny it effect; in other words, to repeal and annul it."[111] The Whig platforms of 1848 and 1852 were platforms devoid of substance, but as Lincoln pointed out in 1848 while campaigning for Zachary Taylor, a specific platform could be seen as a sign of presidential influence and thus an imposition on Congress.[112] Lincoln argued that the president should trust the people and not interfere with Congress. A president cannot "know the wants of the people . . . coming from all the localities of the nation." If this were not the case, "where is the propriety of having a congress," as only Congress can know "with minuteness" the will of the people?[113] As much as Lincoln favored energetic government, he was wary of an energetic presidency. Lincoln believed there was a diversity of interests in America that defied representation in one man. Only a large and heterogeneous Congress could adequately represent the nation. This seems to suggest that during a Lincoln presidency, the initiatives would have to percolate up from the legislature rather than be dictated by a President Lincoln. It is no accident that upon winning election to the presidency in 1860, Lincoln refused to make any policy statements before his inauguration, simply referring interrogators to the Republican platform. In his first inaugural address, Lincoln refused to discuss "those matters of administration about which there is no special anxiety, or excitement."[114] As president, Lincoln felt it was unbecoming to someone of his station to make political speeches and take public positions on policy matters.[115]

Finally, it is difficult to say that the Lincoln presidency was the forerunner of a large, activist government. Lincoln scholar Allen Guelzo has analyzed the size of government before, during, and after the Lincoln presidency using various measures. One way to look at the matter is through spending. Guelzo finds that in 2010 dollars, "the 1865 federal budget would still translate into only $26 billion and would still account for only 1.8 percent of real GDP."[116] Even at the end of the Civil War, the government was spending a pittance compared with modern government, and by 1871 the federal budget had largely returned to prewar levels.

One might also consider the number of federal agencies as a measure of government's size. Again, Guelzo finds that government was extremely limited after the Lincoln presidency. "In the 1850s, the federal government included exactly 15 formally designated civilian agencies or bureaus (compared to 513 in 2010), including the Patent Office, the Pension Office, the Lighthouse Board, the Bureau of Weights and Measures, and the Mexican Boundary Commission. The federal government ended the Civil War with exactly 22, so the 'reach' of the federal government expanded by only *seven* agencies, commissions, or boards."[117] It is worth noting that Abraham Lincoln could serve as a president in wartime with a White House staff of exactly three secretaries. By contrast, a 2017 report on the White House staff to Congress lists 377 staff members. This includes 4 staff members assigned to the First Lady, one more staff member than Abraham Lincoln used to fight the Civil War.[118] One ponders what Mary Todd Lincoln would have done with four employees.

Finally, while some point to legislation such as the Homestead Act, the Pacific Railroad Act, and the Land-Grant College Act as evidence that Lincoln supported activist government, Guelzo notes that unlike much modern legislation, the Civil War–era laws did not set up permanent bureaucracies and, in fact, reduced the power of government as they largely consisted in giving away or selling government land at a favorable price. The government was divesting itself of landholdings in ways it considered beneficial to the public.

Lincoln famously articulated his view of the role of government in a "Fragment" dated to 1854. Lincoln says this:

> The legitimate object of government, is to do for a community of people, whatever they need to have done, but can not do, *at all*, or can not, *so well do*, for themselves—in their separate, and individual capacities.
>
> In all that the people can individually do as well for themselves, government ought not to interfere.
>
> The desirable things which the individuals of a people can not do, or can not well do, for themselves, fall into two classes:

those which have relation to *wrongs*, and those which have not. Each of these branch off into an infinite variety of subdivisions.

The first—that in relation to wrongs—embraces all crimes, misdemeanors, and non-performance of contracts. The other embraces all which, in its nature, and without wrong, requires combined action, as public roads and highways, public schools, charities, pauperism, orphanage, estates of the deceased, and the machinery of government itself.

From this it appears that if all men were just, there still would be *some*, though not *so much*, need of government.[119]

Lincoln seems to make the following claims about the role of government. First, government operates when people in their private capacity are incapable of acting as well as government. Lincoln argues that absent signs of failure by private individuals or groups, government should not act. One clear job of government is to provide basic public order, which relates to the "wrongs" he speaks of. Another task of government is precisely to do that which requires collective action beyond the capacity of private individuals. Roads and highways are obvious examples. Lincoln does expand this to schools and some sorts of charitable activity. It strains Lincoln's words to say that this is an argument in support of the Progressive state.[120] He does not suggest that there are no limits to government power. There is nothing here to imply that centralization of power in a national government is a priority for Lincoln. Indeed, the opposite seems to be the case. Lincoln begins with the notion that the people should be left to regulate their own lives. Only when failure is manifest should the government step in. The burden of proof seems to be on the government to justify its actions, not on individuals to justify their rights. Also, Lincoln never specifies which level of government he is discussing. For example, while Lincoln believes that government should operate schools, does that necessitate involvement of the *federal* government? Lincoln ends in a phrase reminiscent of Madison's ruminations on angels in *Federalist* No. 51, stating that if men were just, little government would be needed. What we can say authoritatively about Lincoln's claims is that he believes the basic task of government is maintenance of order and that he sees the necessity of something beyond the minimalist state.[121]

I argued above that three important features of Progressive political thought are advocacy of a robust, even unlimited, national government, a strong and largely unbounded presidency, and a drastic reinterpretation of the principles of the Declaration of Independence and the Constitution in order to achieve these goals. I have tried to show that Lincoln's political philosophy does not conform to that Progressive vision. Joseph Fornieri argues that for Lincoln, "progress" was measured against a standard, the Declaration of Independence. It was not the open-ended view of progress favored by Progressives. The Declaration gives democracy a telos, some standard by which to measure progress. Also, according to Fornieri, Progressives unsuccessfully made a distinction between an active government and presidency in time of crisis and the ordinary relationship between government and citizen: "The progressive interpretation of Lincoln's leadership also fails to distinguish between the temporary exercise of broad power during extreme circumstances like the Civil War and the routine or permanent exercise of such power for purposes of economic redistribution and social reform without principled limit."[122]

Modern government has routinized crisis. The governing strategy over the course of at least two generations is to call a thing a crisis and then declare war on it. Whether it is poverty, inflation, drugs, illiteracy, terror, lack of health insurance, or climate change, the stoking of a crisis mentality has been in service of regularizing government intervention and enhancing executive power. To be sure, sometimes a crisis really is a crisis, but it cannot be denied that often such rhetoric is purposefully overheated, its aim being the fueling of anxiety so as to justify the expansion of the scope of government. There is little in Lincoln's record that gives support to this regularizing of crisis. Lincoln had a vision of a presidency that was largely passive regarding domestic policy but clearly exercised considerable strength as commander in chief. He was devoted to the natural rights philosophy of the founding and made considerable effort to conform his presidency to the constitutional order.

Finally, while Lincoln favored a more vigorous government than did some of his contemporaries, the evidence suggests that he did not favor unlimited government, and as president he did not propose large increases in the role of government. Going back to Lincoln's Whig antecedents, Daniel Walker Howe cautions that there is danger in comparing the Whig idea of what he describes as a "positive liberal state" to what he calls twentieth-century liberalism. "Actually, the differences between the Whigs and the twentieth century liberals are more important than the similarities," suggests Howe. "Whig policies did not have the object of redistributing wealth or diminishing the influence of the privileged. Furthermore, the Whigs distrusted executives in both state and federal government... whereas twentieth-century liberals have endorsed strong executives more often than not."[123]

Lincoln has been used by some Progressives, both early and contemporary, as precedent for their governing philosophy. This theory is backed somewhat by historians who see Lincoln as leading a "second American Revolution."[124] Some on the libertarian right agree with Progressives that Lincoln's philosophy and presidency were harbingers of unlimited government.[125] This study suggests that these arguments are in error. Both Progressives and libertarians take the side of Jefferson and Jackson in viewing the Constitution in a narrow, clause-bound fashion that we often call strict constructionism. The difference is that libertarians see strict construction as a virtue, while Progressives see it as a vice. Progressives have felt the need to create a novel reinterpretation of the Constitution in the notion of the "living constitution" to justify the expansion of governmental power. Madisonian political science is uncomfortable with both strict construction and the "living constitution" as interpretive lenses. Madisonian theory does not accept the unlimited ends of government claimed by Progressives. Further, Madison argues in *Federalist* No. 49 that the living constitution deprives "the government of that veneration which time bestows on every thing, and without which perhaps the wisest and freest governments would not possess the requisite stability." Madison parts with the strict constructionist libertarians in that he believed rights are protected through proper construction of political institutions, not by limiting government thorough what he derides as "parchment barriers."[126]

There is no indication that Lincoln rejected this theory, and his well-known and sincere veneration of the founders' constitution make it unlikely he would have accepted the explicit rejection of the founders' political science, as seen in Progressives. In fact, his attacks on the Supreme Court after the *Dred Scott* decision indicate Lincoln similarly thought that rights were better protected by a vigorous separation of powers rather than, as we tend to think today, a Supreme Court applying specific clauses.[127] While Madison and Hamilton would go on to have their differences, they both agreed that the Articles of Confederation were inadequate to govern the nation and a stronger central government was needed. What they and Lincoln seemed to realize, and Progressives did not, is that there is a clear and important distinction between a strong but *limited* government and a strong and *unlimited* government.

Lincoln's place within the American political tradition is as someone attempting to fulfill the mission of the founding. In that sense he is a liberal statesman. Progressives, then, represent a break from Lincoln and the American founding.[128] We can see the Progressive movement for what it is, an innovation in American political thought that seeks to refound America on new and elevated grounds. Progressivism stands in contrast to Lincoln's defense of limitations. We have already established

Lincoln's belief in the role of prudence, moderation, and natural rights in limiting government for the goal of maintaining a just democratic regime. Here we see Lincoln arguing that limited government, including a more circumscribed notion of presidential power, is essential to the preservation of democracy. A strong central government is not inimical to free government, but an unlimited government is.

This is not to say that Progressive principles are not superior to the founding principles. Progressives may be entirely correct that the enormous shift from an agricultural economy to an industrial economy represented such a dramatic change in the republic that new governing principles needed to be sought and a new science of politics was necessary. Lincoln's thought itself may be indicative of this. Lincoln believed in a civilization defined by small businessmen and small freeholders who were free precisely because they were not reliant on anyone for their daily bread. He seemed not to have anticipated an age in which most people would have to rely permanently on hired labor status. Modern economic circumstances ensure that most of us will work not for ourselves but for someone else. This creates power relationships that Lincoln did not consider, or at least did not consider permanent enough for concern. In short, Lincoln did not worry about the concentration of power in a capitalist class because he assumed that class would consist of the great majority of Americans. However, the rise of the modern corporation and revolutions in agriculture that allowed the nation to feed itself with far fewer farmers rendered this moot. Progressives can reasonably argue, then, that Lincoln's principled defense of free labor, discussed below, now requires activist government on the behalf of labor to equal out the power relationship with capital. In an attempt to be provocative in the best sense, perhaps we can consider a third alternative, one beyond laissez-faire capitalism or socialism/welfare-statism. To do this we need to consider a radical alternative, namely the economic theory of distributism, and go further in explicating Lincoln's theory of labor. When we consider this theory, we will see that his views are much harder to pin down and apply to contemporary circumstances. Perhaps the modern economy has developed in ways that Lincoln would find fundamentally objectionable, and he would find both doctrinaire free-market capitalism and Progressive liberalism unequal to the task of defending free labor. To this we now turn.

Crowned-Kings, Money-Kings, and Land-Kings: Lincoln and Free Labor

While most arguments regarding political economy work within the parameters of capitalism and socialism, in the late nineteenth and early twentieth centuries a "third way" was discussed, largely but not exclusively within the confines of Catholic social thought. This alternative political economy, called distributism, was born of the papal encyclical *Rerum Novarum*, published by Leo XIII in 1891 and reinforced by Pius XI forty years later in *Quadragesimo Anno* in 1931. The ideas that lay nascent in Leo's encyclical were picked up by such English Catholics as G. K. Chesterton and Hilaire Belloc and in the American experience by the Catholic Land Movement. To this day the theory of distributism is upheld by certain traditionalists with an agrarian bent. Distributists have their own unique take on the relationship between labor and capital, advocating for a wide distribution of property that negates the necessity for centralized reallocation of wealth while also combating perceived evils of capitalism.

Roughly thirty-five years prior to Leo XIII's encyclical, Abraham Lincoln was also articulating a theory of labor and capital that bears remarkable similarity to distributist theories. Lincoln believed that the destiny of the worker was not to work for a wage paid by an employer but to own his own property and work for himself. He felt strongly that slavery was inconsistent with free labor and the role of wage earner was at least problematic. Particularly in an important speech given at the Agricultural Fair in Milwaukee in 1859, Lincoln contrasted his theory of "free labor" with what he called the "mud-sill" theory of labor that dominated the South.

There is a surprising congruence between the distributist vision and Lincoln's free-labor thinking. To show such a congruence, we first will consider the major features of distributism. This task faces an obstacle in the fact that distributism has been described as a "big tent" under which many interpretations and perspectives may find a home.[129] While a definitive description of distributism may be elusive, there are common themes that arise when the theory is considered broadly. Next, we will lay out Lincoln's theory of labor, focusing on the Milwaukee address and a digression on free labor that concludes his 1861 annual message to Congress. I contend that distributism corresponds with many (but not all) of the principles regarding labor and economy espoused by Lincoln and thus is a live option for those wishing to find a Lincolnian position on modern economics.

Lincoln thought deeply about the dignity of work and how it relates to free government. Lincoln would likely agree with Yuval Levin that work "buttresses dignity, inculcates responsibility, encourages energy and industry, and rewards liability."[130] Work is one of the central institutions that help shape the habits of citizenship. Lincoln strongly believed that work is about more than simply making money to provide for material needs, although it is at least that. How our economic lives are formed will go a long way in shaping us as citizens. Some economic arrangements are more appropriate for influencing free and decent citizens than others. Lincoln's notion of free labor was not just an economic theory but also a political theory. The job of an economic order is to promote the liberty of a free people as much as it is to make money. A statesman realizes that while economic growth and material comfort are goods, they are goods subservient to higher goods, and in the American regime liberty ranks first among those higher goods. A nation that forgets that will be impoverished in ways beyond the material.

Distributism Explained

This discussion of distributism includes two features. First, we will consider why distributists saw socialism as an inadequate solution to the problems of capitalism. And second, the positive argument for the distributist state is articulated and discussed.

Hilaire Belloc offers definitions of capitalism and socialism in his classic work *The Servile State*. According to Belloc, capitalism is where ownership "is confined to some number of free citizens not large enough to determine the social mass of the State, while the rest have not such property." Socialism, on the other hand, is an "ideal society in which the means of production should be in the hands of the political officers of the community."[131]

Taking the critique of capitalism first, which he describes as a "dreadful moral anarchy," Belloc writes that in that system people are "politically free" but are divided between capitalists and proletarians and that ownership is in the hands of a "small minority" of capitalists.[132] Leo XIII, in describing the industrialism of the late nineteenth century, argues that "working men have been surrendered, isolated and helpless, to the hardheartedness of employers and the greed of unchecked competition." The pope warns against "the greed of possession and the thirst for pleasure—twin plagues, which too often make a man who is void of self-restraint miserable in the midst of abundance" and says of laborers that "grasping employers too often treat them with great inhumanity and hardly care for them outside the profit their labor brings."[133] Leo's critique of capitalism is echoed by Pius XI, who argues, "Property, that is, 'capital,' has undoubtedly long been able to appropriate too much to itself. Whatever was produced, whatever returns accrued, capital claimed for itself, hardly leaving to the worker enough to restore and renew his strength."[134]

A fundamental problem of capitalism, say the distributists, is precisely that it tends to centralize property into the hands of the few. As Belloc puts it, in capitalism "you have private ownership; but it is not private ownership distributed in many hands and thus familiar as an institution to society as a whole." This creates an inequality of power. The capitalist may speak of the freedom of contract, but Belloc argues that in capitalism, contracts are not really free. While "one man was free to take or to leave . . . the other man was not free to take or to leave, because the second had for his alternative starvation."[135] John Médaille observes, "Ownership is increasingly concentrated in vast collectives known as corporations, even as production is distributed around the globe. . . . But mere size also brings great power, and it is this power that interferes with the free market and hides the inefficiencies." "In capitalist economies," declares Médaille, "the vast majority of men are not capitalists; that is, they do not have sufficient capital to make their own livings, either alone or in cooperation with their neighbors, but must work for wages in order to live."[136]

Capitalism separates labor from ownership by promoting absentee ownership of stockholders. Thomas Storck maintains, "Here ownership is entirely separated from work, for the stockholders are often unaware of the activities of the firms they legally own, of their products, labor policies, political activities, or foreign ventures." Stockholders are ignorant of and likely uninterested in the labor that produces the value of the stock. Such an economy is based not on "producing useful and well-made products to fulfill human need, but merely upon products that can be sold. Put succinctly, if a product is badly made and serves no real and useful purpose, but sells, then it will be pushed for all it's worth. . . . The corporation does not ask, 'Is this something useful and good that people need?' but rather, 'Can we convince people to buy this and thus make money?'"[137] Absentee ownership encourages shoddy workmanship. Ownership has no stake in the pride of craftsmanship but merely in making profit.

Capitalists will claim that their theory promotes the most efficient way to produce wealth and increase the material well-being of all. Thus state intervention should be kept to a minimum. But in the American experience, times of low regulation have been times of great economic uncertainty. "'Big' capitalism seems to require big government for its proper functioning," says Médaille. Capitalism is too chaotic. The solution is either distributive justice or "re-distributive justice, as in Keynesianism."[138]

This leads us to the discussion of the other end of the theoretical spectrum, namely some form of statist socialism. For Belloc, socialism theoretically puts property in the hands of "none," but in practice it "means to vest it as a trust in the hands of political officers."[139] This is part of the problem with socialism, according to the distributists. Socialism puts the lives of workers in the hands of bureaucrats and politicians. This is little better than having their lives in the hands of the capitalists. In either case, the labor of the workers is not owned by those workers. The good of the worker is secondary to the profit motive of the capitalist or the desire for power of the bureaucrat. The freedom of socialism "is a mere illusion, an illusion that will lead men back to the half-forgotten reality of ownership of man by man."[140]

Arthur Penty argues, "Without private property there can be no economic freedom, initiative, or sense of personal responsibility."[141] So socialism, in pure form, is unjust because the state controls property instead of putting it in workers' hands. Chesterton, in that way, smells a rat: "I think, that if some form of Collectivism is imposed upon England it will be imposed, as everything else has been, by an instructed political class upon a people partly apathetic and partly hypnotized."[142] While the "collectivists" will claim to use property in the name of the people, in fact they will inevitably use property in favor of the elite and well connected. So, as Belloc concludes, collectivism is "the servitude of the many."[143]

John Médaille sees five basic problems with the centralization of economic power in the state. First, "it encourages political centralization" and to that extent is the enemy of democracy. Second, "it encourages gigantism in business in two ways. . . . Small businesses must devote a proportionally larger share of their resources to meeting regulations [while] large entities are better at obtaining contracts, subsidies, tax exemptions, and privileges from the government." Next, the state distorts the economy by "reducing [business's] costs." Fourth, as an economy grows dependent on statist stimulation, like a drug addict, each stimulus must get larger. "Eventually, the cost of stimuli must exceed the effects, and the whole system collapses of its own weight." Finally, "the worst effect is that a giant government increases servility and dependence. More and more, we cease to be real citizens and become mere clients of the state, mere employees of the corporation. Our lives are suffocated between these two great powers."[144]

Collectivism, argues Belloc, does not do what the collectivists claim. It is, in a sense, neither collectivism nor capitalism but a third thing, the Servile State, "a State . . . in which the mass of men shall be constrained by law to labor to the profit of a minority, but, as the price of such constraint, shall enjoy a security which the old Capitalism did not give them." The capitalist may see collectivism as the enemy, but "it is an enemy which they understand and an enemy with whom they can treat in terms common both to that enemy and themselves."[145] In collectivism the laborers are kept materially secure and politically impotent, but the capitalist is allowed to use the state to protect his status.

So, given the critiques of both capitalism and socialism/collectivism, what do the distributists offer in return? We can see that distributists share with capitalists a belief in private property, albeit on different grounds. They also believe with the socialists in the necessity to mitigate the avarice stimulated by capitalism.

As mentioned, one of the conundrums of distributism is that there are various definitions of the theory. Thomas Naylor provides a useful summary: "Distributism called for broad-based, decentralized ownership of private property as well as small businesses, small factories, small schools, small farms, small crafts, and small towns. It advocated a return to farming, the primacy of the countryside, organic methods, environmental integrity, and human-scale enterprise of all sorts."[146] Kirkpatrick Sale defines distributism thusly: "It is a society based on small self-sufficient regions, empowered communities, vibrant neighborhoods, gainfully employed families, individual self-satisfaction, decentralized politics, local economies, sustainable organic agriculture, cooperative work, environmental humility, and careful nurturing of the earth."[147] Thomas Storck has his own summation of the distributist ideal:

> It is that economic system or arrangement in which ownership of productive private property, as much as possible, is widespread in a nation or society. In other words, in a Distributist society most heads of families would own small farms or workshops, or in the case of entities which are necessarily large, such as railroads, they would either be jointly owned in some manner by the work force (be it noted: workers of hand and brain).[148]

This last parenthetical statement is important, as we will see that Lincoln agreed that both physical and mental labor count as labor.

The commonality of these various definitions is the notion of a wide distribution of property ownership. Médaille writes, "In a distributed system of property, there are many owners. Ownership becomes the 'natural' condition of people in that society."[149] As Chesterton puts it, each man "wants an objective and visible kingdom; a fire at which he can cook what food he likes, a door he can open to what friends he chooses."[150]

It is not, though, simply about owning "one's own castle," that is, a house, but about ownership in the actual production of goods. Belloc states, "To control the production of wealth is to control human life itself. To refuse man the opportunity for the production of wealth is to refuse him the opportunity for life; and, in general, the way in which the production of wealth is by law permitted is the only way in which the citizens can legally exist."[151] Edward McPhail says that distributism seeks to "fundamentally alter the relationship by making the workers *into* owners, thus eliminating many of the 'bones of contention' that come up in modern economic life regarding the employer-worker relationship."[152]

Journalist Harold Robbins points to three benefits of a wide distribution of property. First, giving each worker property makes him or her "independent of the dominion of other wills." Workers are not solely dependent on an employer for their sustenance. Second, the egalitarianism of a wider distribution of property fosters a more stable society. Robbins contends that "great wealth and great poverty, both corrupters of good morals and order, are unlikely and rare" in a distributist system. Finally, Robbins argues for the material advantages of such a system. By "promoting harder and more intelligent work," the "best possible use is made of productive powers." As is often noted, people tend to take greater care of what they own. So if a laborer also has ownership in property, he or she is more likely to craft a better product.[153] Similarly, McPhail states, "From this perspective people can enjoy work and find it fulfilling, and they are willing to work hard when they feel that they have some control over their lives, when they respect those in authority over them, and when their work is emotionally and intellectually rewarding."[154]

Leo XIII echoes this notion when he calls for property to be "more equitably divided":

> If working people can be encouraged to look forward to obtaining a share in the land, the consequence will be that the gulf between vast wealth and sheer poverty will be bridged over, and the respective classes will be brought nearer to one another. A further consequence will result in the great abundance of the fruits of the earth. Men always work harder and more readily when they work on that which belongs to them.[155]

Pius XI lauds Leo's sentiments when he writes, "As We have already indicated, following in the footsteps of Our Predecessor, it will be impossible to put these principles into practice unless the non-owning workers through industry and thrift advance to the state of possessing some little property."[156] Thus, says Pius XI, "We consider it more advisable, . . . in the present condition of human society that, so far as is possible, the work-contract be somewhat modified by a partnership-contract."[157]

Leo XIII promotes two principles that have become fundamental to Catholic social thought: subsidiarity and solidarity. Tobias Lanz calls these principles "the very essence of Catholic economics."[158] Subsidiarity can be defined as the principle that social problems be solved at the level closest to the family as possible. As George Weigel has summarized, subsidiarity is the principle that "the community must not deprive individuals, nor larger communities deprive smaller communities, of the opportunity to do what they can for themselves."[159] Pope Leo states, "Hence we have the family, the 'society' of a man's house—a society very small, one must admit, but none the less a true society, and one older than any State. Consequently, it has rights and duties peculiar to itself which are quite independent of the State." "It is a most sacred law of nature," writes Pope Leo, "that a father should provide food and all necessaries for those whom he has begotten." This is where Leo grounds the right to property, namely in the right of a father to provide for his family. Further, "inasmuch as the domestic household is antecedent, as well in idea as in fact, to the gathering of men into a community, the family must necessarily have rights and duties which are prior to those of the community, and founded more immediately in nature." Thus in provisioning society, private associations should be used before the state: "especially as circumstances, times, and localities differ so widely, it is advisable that recourse be had to societies or boards . . . or to some other mode of safeguarding the interests of the wage-earners."[160] A system that undermines the family and local associations through centralization of power is an unjust system, argue the distributists.

Solidarity, which is typically linked to subsidiarity as a principle in Catholic social thought, calls on all to recognize the common good and work for it. Leo discusses this mostly in terms of workingmen's unions (related to but distinct from labor unions). Leo writes, "We may lay it down as a general and lasting law that working men's associations should be so organized and governed as to furnish the best and most suitable means for attaining what is aimed at, that is to say, for helping each individual member to better his condition to the utmost in body, soul, and property."[161] In Anthony Esolen's words, "Leo has in mind a society wherein the rich man and the poor man are friends; they live near one another; they celebrate at the same festivals; they kneel beside one another in church; they know one another's children."[162]

Pius XI is somewhat more detailed in how he envisions the place of workers' associations in an economy:

> Thus associations of this kind have molded truly Christian workers who, in combining harmoniously the diligent practice of their occupation with the salutary precepts of religion, protect

effectively and resolutely their own temporal interests and rights, keeping a due respect for justice and a genuine desire to work together with other classes of society for the Christian renewal of all social life.[163]

Again, these associations are distinct from what we typically see in labor unions. Pius has in mind an institution that combines the virtues of the labor union with that of fraternal organizations such as the Elks or Eagles. Still, says Pius, "Side by side with these unions there should always be associations zealously engaged in imbuing and forming their members in the teaching of religion and morality so that they in turn may be able to permeate the unions with that good spirit which should direct them in all their activity."[164] Subsidiarity protects the family and local arrangements, while the principle of solidarity calls on individuals to recognize a common good and to work for a common purpose.

Distributism starts from the assumption that the fundamental unit of society is the family and that sanctity of that unit must be protected by any economic system. The best way to protect that sanctity is by giving each laborer ownership in some form of property or capital. This is done primarily through what today we would call employee ownership or possibly through a guild-type system in which a democratic workers' association looks out for the good of the whole. Distributism seeks both economic and political decentralization. Distributists also maintain support for a "Just Wage," namely a wage sufficient "to support a frugal and well-behaved wage-earner."[165] The distributist system is more likely to achieve this wage, it is argued, as each employee is also a capitalist, in a sense, in that he or she has a share in ownership of the business entity. Employees are not simply wage-earners, subject to the whims of either the state or the capitalist, but owners of property themselves, giving them some say in how business runs and what their compensation is.

This presentation is not meant to be a brief for distributism. The aim is to present the major features of the theory and perhaps show it in its best light. There are many possible criticisms of distributism. To be sure, distributist descriptions of capitalism and socialism often border on caricature. Free market capitalists might point to the success of global markets in lifting the poor out of misery and note the inefficiencies inherent in small-scale local operations. Defenders of the free market would surely criticize the medieval guilds as kinds of cartels that served their own interests at the expense of the whole. On the economic left, one might argue that it is precisely distributism's rejection of revolutionary politics and affinity for medieval arrangements that make it a defender of unjust social orders. This is especially true given distributism's strong affiliation with the Catholic Church. And some on the left might point to examples of welfare-state liberalism that have thrived in producing material well-being along with social cohesion. This, such progressive liberals might argue, is the real "third way" between unfettered markets and socialism, demonstrating that a true democratic socialism is possible. Notably within Catholic social thought, particularly the thought of Popes John XXIII and Paul VI, welfare-state liberalism draws some support. Finally, observers of any stripe will note that distributism has been left largely untried in modern industrial/technological times. With some minor exceptions, distributism has remained more of a literary theory than a practical option.[166] The distributist emphasis on an economy that fulfills needs instead of wants is unlikely to be attractive to those used to a consumer-based economy.

Still, as a theory distributism offers a coherent alternative and corrective to the more dominant capitalist and socialist alternatives. As we shall see, various parts of this theory find significant analogs in Abraham Lincoln's theory of labor.

Lincoln on Free Labor

The first two decades of Lincoln's public life were far more concerned with economic matters than with slavery, which began to concern him in earnest only after the repeal of the Missouri Compromise in 1854. In Lincoln's formative years he "lingered longest over books on political economy."[167] Foremost among the economists he studied were Francis Wayland and Henry C. Carey. Lincoln's economic education convinced him that economics was as much a moral science as a science of efficiency or wealth creation.[168] From these two theorists Lincoln imbibed a belief that labor was the source of economic value while developing a strong support of the protective tariff. Lincoln believed that domestic production was more efficient because it limited waste due to excessive transportation; thus domestic production should be encouraged by a high tariff on imports.[169] Lincoln adopted other policy positions that he thought best advanced the laborer's cause. Among these policies was free soil, as Lincoln knew that slavery was the most direct assault on any decent concept of labor. But further, Lincoln's desire to help the laborer also led him to support a national banking system, internal improvement schemes, land grants for railroads and homesteaders, and other government policies designed to advance economic growth.

One could argue, however, that Lincoln failed to see the consequences of some of his favored economic policies. David Herbert Donald observes,

"Confident that advancement was open to all who worked hard, he was untroubled by the growing disparity of wealth between the poor and rich. ... In his analysis he gave scant attention to the growing number of factory workers, who had little prospect of upward social mobility."[170] Gabor Boritt says of Lincoln's economic ideas, "That an unbridled growth of large concentrations of capital might occur and either threaten or change the mode of the individual's chance to rise had not yet appeared as a *real* danger in Lincoln's eyes."[171] "Indeed his ideas about the factory system," continues Boritt, "like that of most of his generation, were hazy."[172] It might seem odd to say that the visionary Lincoln lacked the foresight to see the consequences of considerable industrialization, yet this seems to be the case. One is left to speculate how Lincoln would have reacted to the concentration of wealth and the inequality of the Industrial Revolution. Given that he died before the rise of mass industrialization in the United States, would distributism (or something akin to it) have been an approach to that phenomenon consistent with Lincoln's economic thinking?

Lincoln believed strongly, as did many economic theorists of his day, that labor was the source of value in a product. He stated in 1847, "No good thing has been, or can be enjoyed by us, without having first cost labour."[173] "Labor is the great source from which nearly all, if not all, human comforts and necessities are drawn," wrote Lincoln in a "Fragment on Free Labor" in 1859.[174] This is, in part, why he was steadfastly opposed to slavery. In addition to the natural rights argument against slavery, Lincoln saw the institution as an assault on free labor. In the concluding debate against Stephen Douglas in 1858, Lincoln stated, "Slavery hurts advancement because you base yourself on a system which perverts labor. People need places where they don't have to compete against slavery or have their view of labor warped by the presence of slavery."[175]

There are some that would enslave labor, stealing it in consequence. This stems from a false view of the origin of productive value. Lincoln states,

> Some men assume that there is a necessary connection between capital and labor, and that connection draws within it the whole of the labor of the community. They assume that nobody works unless capital excites them to work. They begin next to consider what is the best way. They say that there are but two ways; one is to hire men and to allure them to labor by their consent; the other is to buy the men and drive them to it, and that is slavery.[176]

While this appears to be a qualified endorsement of wage labor, as it is "labor by their consent," note that Lincoln says that even wage labor stems from a false view of the relation between labor and capital, namely the view that "nobody works unless capital excites them to work." This is not Lincoln's view. He states elsewhere, "One of the reasons why I am opposed to Slavery is just here. What is the true condition of the laborer? I take it that it is best for all to leave each man free to acquire property as fast as he can." Lincoln extends the connection to slavery, saying, "I want every man to have the chance—and I believe a black man is entitled to it—in which he can better his condition—when he may look forward and hope to be a hired laborer this year and the next, work for himself afterward, and finally to hire men to work for him! That is the true system."[177] Crucially, Lincoln's assumption is not that people will commonly work for another for a wage but for themselves with their own property.

This statement on the "true condition of the laborer" directly precedes Lincoln's famous avowal "I don't believe in a law to prevent a man from getting rich; it would do more harm than good. So while we do not propose any war upon capital, we do wish to allow the humblest man an equal chance to get rich with everybody else."[178] Lincoln, unlike more radical thinkers, does not propose a revolution against capital, but he does wish to defend labor as the primary source of wealth. This prolabor sentiment recurs in his 1861 annual message to Congress, wherein President Lincoln states, "It is assumed that labor is available only in connexion with capital; that nobody labors unless somebody else, owning capital, somehow by the use of it, induces him to labor."[179] While wage labor may not be the evil that is slavery, it does appear to be a second-best option to something else, namely free labor. It remains to be seen what the content is of "free labor."

Lincoln most thoroughly discusses his notion of labor in his "Address before the Wisconsin State Agricultural Society," presented in 1859. In this lecture Lincoln lays out the distinctions between the "mud-sill" theory of labor articulated by South Carolina senator James Henry Hammond and the theory of "free labor" advocated by Lincoln. "The world is agreed," he says, "that labor is the source from which human wants are mainly supplied."[180] Lincoln declares, "By some it is assumed that labor is available only in connection with capital—that nobody labors, unless somebody else, owning capital, somehow, by use of that capital, induces him to work."[181] This wording anticipates the 1861 annual message. Lincoln in Wisconsin argues that some say there is a part of the population fit only for laboring, either hired or slave. As Lincoln puts it, the owner of capital must decide whether to "induce [laborers] to work by their own consent; or buy them, and drive them without their consent." Whichever it is, there is some class of men who act as a permanent laboring class, unable to improve their condition. They serve as a "mud-sill" of society.

Lincoln instead promotes free labor by defending the "right to rise." In the Wisconsin address, Lincoln defines free laborers as a class of men who do not have their labor possessed by someone else. An individual may start as a hired laborer, but if he works hard and acquires knowledge and skill, he can be liberated from the condition of wage labor. Lincoln states, "There is no such thing as a freeman being fatally fixed for life in the condition of a hired laborer."[182] The man who labors at first can one day own his own property and, more importantly, his own labor. "It is not forgotten," says Lincoln, "that a considerable number of persons mingle their own labor with capital." That is, some people both labor and own capital, the farmer being the most conspicuous example. Again, the annual message of 1861 also articulates this idea. Lincoln there states that "it is naturally concluded that all laborers are either *hired* laborers, or what we call slaves. And further it is assumed that whoever is once a hired laborer, is fixed in that condition for life. Now, there is no such relation between capital and labor as assumed; nor is there any such thing as a free man being fixed for life in the condition of a hired laborer."[183] The right to rise suggests that although one may be a hired laborer today, one may rise someday to hire others to work for him or her—that is, be both a laborer and a capitalist. As he states in 1861 while discussing the relation of labor and capital, "The error is in assuming that the whole labor of community exists within that relation. A few men own capital, and that few avoid labor themselves, and, with their capital, hire or buy another few to labor for them. A large majority belong to neither class— neither work for others, nor have others working for them."[184] Most men, he is saying, are neither purely capitalists nor solely laborers. Because they own their own labor and work their own field or their own shop, they partake of both roles. "Men with their families—wives, sons, and daughters—work for themselves, on their farms, in their houses, and in their shops, taking the whole product to themselves, and asking no favors of capital on the one hand, nor of hired laborers or slaves on the other."[185] One is reminded of Naylor's identification of distributism as consisting in "small businesses, small factories, small schools, small farms, small crafts, and small towns." "Lincoln's America was the world of the small producer," argues Eric Foner.[186] Like the distributists, Lincoln believes that free labor induces a man to work harder. He states, "Free labor has the inspiration of hope; pure slavery has no hope. The power of hope upon human exertion, and happiness, is wonderful."[187]

Lincoln does not believe that only physical labor counts as labor. If that was the case, Lincoln himself would not be considered a laborer, as he was a lawyer by profession. Lincoln ran his own law office and "labored" at the practice of the law. He was both a laborer and a capitalist, a working lawyer and proprietor of his own firm. No doubt thinking of his own employment history, Lincoln in Wisconsin suggests, "Many independent men, in this assembly, doubtless, a few years ago were hired laborers. And their case is almost, if not quite, the general rule. The prudent, penniless beginner in the world labors for wages awhile, saves a surplus with which to buy tools or land for himself."[188] Lincoln concludes, "This, says its advocates, is free labor—the just and generous, and prosperous system, which opens the way for all—gives hope to all, and energy and progress and improvement of the condition of all."[189] Lincoln maintains that if someone stays in the wage category on a permanent basis, it is either because of a character flaw or bad luck. "If any continue through life in the condition of the hired laborer," he says, "it is not the fault of the system, but because of either a dependent nature which prefers it, or of improvidence, folly, or singular misfortune." Allen Guelzo contends, "Wage labor, in the Jacksonian imagination, created a relationship of dependency on the whims and fortunes of an employer little better than slavery, while subsistence agriculture was supposed to guarantee stability and well-nigh total independence. Lincoln saw wage labor, not as a relationship of dependence, but as a ticket toward the kind of mobility and prosperity that the agrarians could scarcely dream of."[190] Guelzo seems basically correct here but fails to grasp Lincoln's ultimate point. There is no doubt that Lincoln saw wage labor as superior to that of slave labor. And as we have seen, Lincoln believed that working for a wage could give valuable experience that would allow the laborer to improve his condition in life. But this is precisely the point. Wage labor for Lincoln is an intermediate stage that often occurs before actual free labor, but it is *not* free labor.

The society Lincoln describes appears to be made up largely of small farms and shops, rather than large plantations or industrial corporations. Advances in technology allow individuals to be productive with small capital outlays. According to Daniel Walker Howe,

> The relatively small scale of antebellum manufacturing often permitted master mechanics to become owners of a manufactory, perhaps by pooling capital with others. . . . Only in the largest enterprises was industrial management separated from ownership; more typical factories were operated by the same people

who owned them. The early industrial revolution in the United States permitted this kind of opportunity for social mobility and thus blurred the line between capitalist and working classes.[191]

Lincoln believes that "in a world less inclined to wars, and more devoted to the arts of peace," population will greatly increase. Before long "the most valuable of all arts, will be the art of deriving a comfortable subsistence from the smallest area of soil." This kind of self-sufficiency is a bulwark against despotism. Lincoln proclaims, "No community whose every member possesses this art, can ever be the victim of oppression in any of its forms. Such community will be alike independent of crowned-kings, money-kings, and land-kings."[192]

Lincoln's concept of freedom is not the same as that held by later free market purists. Note that Lincoln's defense of free labor is founded upon a moral argument. He is less concerned with economic efficiency or wealth production. This is why free labor is contrasted with slavery. Even if slavery were economically superior, it is inconsistent with human dignity. It is hard to reconcile Lincoln's economic views with the notion that "freedom has nothing to say about what the individual does with his freedom. . . . A major aim of the liberal is to leave the ethical problem for the individual to wrestle with."[193] Like Stephen Douglas regarding politics, some see the realm of economics as a value-free zone, being simply a realm where individual interests are aggregated. Lincoln applied moral thinking to both politics and economics.

In Lincoln's very first run for political office in 1832 he stated, "Upon the subject of education, not presuming to dictate any plan or system respecting it, I can only say that I view it as the most important subject which we as a people can be engaged in. . . . For my part, I desire to see the time when education, and by its means, morality, sobriety, enterprise and industry, shall become much more general than at present." Lincoln picks up the subject of education in the Wisconsin address. The advocates of the mudsill theory of labor believe that education is bad for the laboring class, at best a waste of time. Lincoln states that it was the "old general rule" that "educated people did not perform manual labor. They managed to eat their bread, leaving the toil of producing it to the uneducated." If one believes that there is a permanent laboring class that cannot better itself, there is no reason to educate that class. The members of that class cannot improve their condition or rise above it. "By the 'mud-sill' theory," Lincoln argues, "it is assumed that labor and education are incompatible, and any practical combination of them impossible. . . . According to that theory, the educating of laborers is not only useless, but pernicious and dangerous." Those who form the mudsill, be they wage laborers or slaves, do not need ingenuity or literacy. In fact, such intellectual skills will only make them dangerous to the established social order. "According to [the mudsill] theory, a blind horse upon a treadmill is a perfect illustration of what a laborer should be—all the better for being blind, that he can not tread out of place, or kick understandingly."[194] The laborer, from this perspective, is dehumanized and turned into a mere cog in the wheel, or what we might now call a "human resource," little different than a mule or a lump of coal.

On the other hand, the free laborer desires more education as it makes him more inventive. Lincoln notes that "especially in the free states," a great percentage of the people are now educated. Lincoln, again likely thinking of himself, draws the conclusion "that henceforth educated people too must labor." "No community can sustain, in idleness," he says, "more than a small percentage of its numbers. The great majority must labor at something useful—something productive."[195] For it is true that "as the Author of man makes every individual with one head and one pair of hands, it was probably intended that heads and hands should co-operate as friends."[196] Again, recall Storck's discussion of labor being property of "workers of hand and brain."

Lincoln believes that labor is the primary source of value. Also, he is uneasy with wage labor and clearly condemns slave labor. Both of these are inferior to a worker owning his own labor, to be achieved by widely distributing property among the laboring class, effectively making one both a laborer and a capitalist. This, Lincoln thinks, will encourage industry by giving the laborer a direct stake in the outcome of his endeavor. Lincoln, as we have seen in the "Lectures on Discoveries and Inventions," believes that education helps develop the technology that will make each individual more productive, lessening the need for massive accumulations of capital. All of this is in service of freedom. The free laborer is not beholden to anyone for his governance or sustenance.

Would Lincoln Have Been a Distributist?

There are various areas of general agreement between Lincoln and distributists. First, both Lincoln and distributists hold that labor is the central source of productive value. Lincoln is much more explicit in arguing that labor is prior to capital and that labor is justly privileged. Second, distributists invoke Middle Age guilds as an institutional defense of labor, while for Lincoln it is the right to strike and the organization of labor into unions. Lincoln says, "I am glad to see that a system of labor prevails in New England under which laborers can strike when they want to where they are not obliged to work under all circumstances, and are not tied down and obliged to labor whether you pay them or not!"[197] Both Lincoln and distributists favor some form of worker organization to regulate the relation between labor and capital. But it must be highlighted that for both Lincoln and distributists, the best protection for laborers is to work for themselves, not in a wage relationship with an employer.

Next, deriving from this theory of labor both Lincoln and distributists favor the ownership of capital by the laborer, creating a kind of mixed economic condition. While Lincoln, and one presumes distributists, prefers wage labor to outright slavery, both indicate a clear penchant for some kind of employee ownership. Lincoln, like distributists, believes that it is workers' destiny to own their own labor. Lincoln supported this theory as president by signing into law the Homestead Act, which provided land for small farmers; the Pacific Railroad Act, which would help the West develop economically; and the Morrill Act (also known as the Land-Grant College Act), to educate those who would run small agricultural operations. Fourth, distributists and Lincoln concern themselves with concentrations of power and wealth. When Médaille makes the connection between political and economic centralization, he echoes Lincoln's desire that each citizen be independent of both "crowned-king" and "money-king." Like distributists, Lincoln sees cultivation of the small landowner or independent craftsman as a bulwark of democracy. A hard-working, thrifty working class that comprises both laborer and capitalist is self-sufficient. This type of laboring class is not in need of government management nor beholden to capitalists. Self-governing in the ownership of their own labor, members of this class are also self-governing in a more holistic sense. Free labor is part of being a free people. In addition, distributist thinker Rupert Ederer finds some correlation regarding Lincoln's view of the role of government and distributism. Lincoln wrote, "The legitimate object of government, is to do for a community of people, whatever they need to have done, but can not do, *at all*, or can not, *so well do*, for themselves—in their separate, and individual capacities. In all that the people can individually do as well for themselves, government ought not to interfere."[198] This, argues Ederer, is akin to the notion of solidarity and subsidiarity, the notion that problems should be solved at the level closest to the family.[199]

Lincoln and distributists, while having strong affinity for the laborer, are alike in rejecting a war on capital and property as suggested in revolutionary socialism. And finally, while Lincoln seems much more comfortable with the pursuit of wealth for its own sake, both he and distributists value the higher ideal of liberty as defined as a kind of self-sufficiency.

Neither distributists nor Lincoln think a just society can be based on the pursuit of mere material self-interest.

One should be cautious about taking the comparison too far. The distributist theory arose in a religious tradition. The argument for the just wage and the status of the family, to take two examples, are firmly grounded in a religious conception of man that Lincoln did not share. Overall, distributists have a conception of a good life in which the amassing of material wealth plays a minor role. Tobias Lanz states, "A society awash in material goods could still be emotionally and spiritually poor."[200] Thomas Aquinas, not surprisingly much admired in distributist circles and whose theology was given pride of place by Leo XIII, argued that "business, absolutely speaking, is wicked, since it does not essentially signify a worthy or necessary objective."[201] Lincoln, as we have seen, said he did not believe in a "law to prevent a man from getting rich." There are those, though, who place Lincoln in a school of thought more critical of material wealth, such as Stewart Winger: "Lincoln's economic views were permeated with antimaterialistic, Romantic, and religious notions."[202] From this point of view, Lincoln's economic thought harmonizes with his antislavery philosophy in that both are critiques of mere self-interest.

Another tension between Lincoln and distributists is the fact that many distributists have great affinity with the Jeffersonian agrarian ideal, an ideal with which Lincoln was highly uncomfortable. John Sharpe, in his introduction to the distributist volume *Beyond Capitalism and Socialism*, consistently draws parallels between the Southern agrarians of *I'll Take My Stand* fame and the distributist ethos. Sharpe states, "The question of family ownership of property was not, and cannot ultimately, be separated from the question of rural life and ownership."[203] American distributist priest Vincent McNabb, part of the Catholic Land Movement, called for Americans to "flee to the fields."[204] It should be noted that there is not unanimity among distributists on this matter. As documented above, some distributists see mental labor as equivalent to physical labor in its rights. Anthony Cooney writes, "I will merely point out that there are many forms of private property—the doctor's, lawyer's, or accountant's practice for example. . . . There is all manner of private property proper to industry and town—from the corner shop to the family-owned factory."[205] Still, there is a strain of distributist thought that is firmly rooted in agrarianism. Lincoln's own relationship with the agricultural life was mixed at best, and he seemed dedicated to an economy that worked for people who did not have an agrarian calling. Lincoln rejected the notion that wealth was founded in land rather than in productivity.

Lincoln was a strong believer in a nationalized industrial economy at which the distributists would balk. He had a clearly articulated vision of government activity in the service of economic growth and embraced a sort of centralization with which distributists are uneasy. While I find in distributism no precisely articulated theory of localism versus nationalism in regard to economics, the clear predilection is toward localism. Lincoln favored a commercial republic that offered a diversity of economic opportunities and was comfortable with some government action and with banking. This is hardly the distributist sympathy for agrarianism.

But we have also seen that Lincoln did look to Jefferson with some affinity, albeit more in relation to natural rights thinking than in political economy. There are elements to Jefferson's agrarianism that complement Lincoln's economic vision. Jefferson's preference for the agrarian life is rooted in his belief that the self-sufficiency of the yeoman farmer is central to the definition of a free citizen. Within Jeffersonian thought is a concept that self-government is made up of both political and economic liberty. The yeoman farmer is truly free precisely because he does not depend on anyone else for sustenance. How many of today's urban or suburban residents could live a day without electricity? How many could last a week? In Jefferson's view this is an indication that the urbanized citizens are not really free while yeoman farmers are. The modern economy has made us dependent upon others for our food, clothing, shelter, and the like. We do not grow our own food, make our own clothes, or build our own houses, and few of us have the skill to do so. To this extent we are not free. This is akin to Lincoln's desire for the small proprietor and the belief that free labor makes one independent of crowned-kings, money-kings, and land-kings.

Further, one can take the nationalist vision of the Whigs too far. Daniel Walker Howe argues we should hesitate in presenting Whigs as prophets of mass industrialization. Whig industrialists wished to avoid the "grotesque urban sprawl" of English industrial cities. "There was to be an attractive town of controlled size, where working and living would form an integrated whole," Howe notes. The business operations favored by Whigs were "middle-sized" and "family controlled." "Truly big corporate business, impersonal and bureaucratic, did not arise until the middle of the nineteenth century," Howe observes.[206] Eric Foner suggests, "Many Republicans, of both Democratic and Whig antecedents, were deeply suspicious of corporations and of economic concentration." Maine Republican Israel Washburn protested against the danger "that the money-power will be too much centralized—that the lands and property of the country, in the course of time may come to be held or controlled by a comparatively small number of people."[207] Prominent Whig Edward Everett argued, "Society is in its happiest state when town and country act and react upon each other to mutual advantage, when the simpler manners and purer tastes of rural life are brought to invigorate the moral atmosphere of the metropolis, and when a fair proportion of the wealth acquired in the city flows back, and is invested in landed improvement."[208] "Because Lincoln and his generation did not have modern American life in mind when they unwittingly set its big industrial wheels in motion," notes Stewart Winger, "it is inappropriate to read them as cheerleaders of the American way of life as it came to be."[209] A decent polity is one built on a human scale. It should be big enough to offer a variety of opportunities to the diverse talents of citizens but should not be so large that citizens become strangers to one another or that they become divorced completely from the agricultural life.

We have historical reasons for rejecting a clean separation of Lincoln from Jeffersonian agrarianism. Take land policy as an example. The notion of selling unused public land to citizens to cultivate small farms started with agrarians. George Henry Evans argued that "everyone should be entitled to his own property, but instead of redistributing what already existed, he called for drawing upon the unclaimed national domain, giving away free homesteads of 160 acres to any actual settler over the age of twenty-one," Howe writes. Promoting his idea with the slogan "Vote Yourself a Farm," Evans was supported by eventual Republican leader Horace Greeley in Greeley's *New York Tribune*. "Although Evans himself died in 1856, his vision of free homesteads lived on," notes Howe. "The Free Soilers endorsed a moderate version of it in 1848, and so did the new Republican Party, which implemented it . . . in 1862."[210] This is a direct connection between the Republican Party and agrarian policy.

Lincoln is connected to such sensibilities. Above we noted the influence of economist Henry C. Carey on Whig thought, including that of Abraham Lincoln. The themes of the moderate-sized town and the balance between agriculture and urban life are also found in Carey's thought. Howe says of Carey, "A head of household with foresight, thrift, and conscientious application would have not only a variety of career choices but also the opportunity to rise from wage-earner to employer. . . . Carey's ideal was neither an arcadia of yeoman farmers nor a big city but a 'middle-state' between rural and urban life."[211] Again, one sees an antipathy toward the impersonal metropolis alongside the preference for self-employment over wage labor. "Though Carey and the

Whigs favored industrialization," writes Howe, "they were not generally enthusiastic about large-scale urbanization." "Swollen megalopolises" had a "proletariat . . . just as truly exploited as the distant laborers who produced the staples."[212] Carey was in favor, for example, of breaking up the industrial city of Lowell, Massachusetts, into "twenty or thirty little towns."[213] These approaches partially explain Carey's defense of protective tariffs. Carey believed that the tariff buttressed local industry and provided a disincentive to engage in commerce with distant, impersonal traders. Protectionism "enabled local people to organize their industry instead of being forced into dependence on distant monopoly capitalists."[214] Crucial for the argument here, Carey, unlike Lincoln, survived the Civil War and lived to see the arrival of mass industrial capitalism. Carey was an admirer of Scottish Enlightenment philosopher Adam Ferguson and the notion of the "small organic community made self-sufficient by its people's virtues and diverse talents."[215] At the end of his life Carey came to the conclusion that the form of capitalism evolving within the Industrial Revolution was not consistent with his philosophy. He blanched at the Gilded Age worship of efficiency and wealth at the expense of more humane concerns. Howe explicitly links Carey's philosophy to Lincoln. Lincoln's "objective . . . was to defend and extend the kind of free society he had known in Springfield. This was a society of small entrepreneurs, market-oriented farmers, young men working for others until they could save enough to set up for themselves, and striving professionals like himself. It was the same 'mixed' society that Henry C. Carey had celebrated."[216] Howe draws the same conclusion as is drawn here, namely that if Lincoln had lived, it is doubtful that he would have supported the crude capitalism that arose after the Civil War. "Within a generation after his death, the kind of society Lincoln loved was being superseded by urban-industrial capitalism, and nowhere faster than in his own state of Illinois. Henry C. Carey was horrified when he saw the new economy, and we may believe that Lincoln, too, would have been grieved by its oppression and sordid materialism."[217] It is worth recollecting that the advent of the notion of free labor as simply the right to contract is more a product of the Industrial Revolution, which Lincoln obviously did not live to see.[218] Given the sort of commitments at the heart of Whig economics, the political economy expressed by Lincoln, and the radical transformation of the Industrial Revolution, there is reason to believe that something like distributism would have been attractive to Lincoln.

Those who defend the "Hamiltonian Lincoln" against the "Jeffersonian Lincoln" have the better argument, but Lincoln's views on labor suggest enough tension to require reconciliation. The lens of distributism may allow us to reconsider Lincoln's economic thought. We should reevaluate Lincoln's relationship with both Jeffersonian and Hamiltonian traditions. Bearing in mind the shifts in economic power that occurred with industrialism, Lincoln may have seen more value in the Jeffersonian ideas as a response to that industrialization. There is an underappreciated harmony between Lincoln's foundational economic assumptions and a more decentralized, worker-centered economy and state. Further, Lincoln rejects the commodification of labor that is one of the hallmarks of modern capitalism.

Lincoln's political economy ties directly to his view of natural rights in regard to statesmanship. Lincoln argued regarding natural rights that mere self-interest or the raw power of the majority cannot in the end be the rule of a free and just people. There are principles outside majority opinion that should elevate opinion beyond that of interest or power. Lincoln's political economy is similar. To be sure, Lincoln had no problem with wealth. He was free of class envy. It is clear that Lincoln as a policy maker wished Illinois and the United States to pursue policies that would generate economic growth and help alleviate material poverty. But Lincoln is not interested in wealth for its own sake. An economy serves political ends, not the other way around. A people must limit their desire for material wealth, recognizing that the pursuit of wealth, economic growth, and efficiency at the expense of liberty is a fool's errand. As with popular sovereignty or the desire for mob justice, the lust for material gain speaks to something real, even good in its own way. It is not difficult to list the advantages of material wealth and comfort. The quest for wealth has given us better health care, easy transportation, access to entertainment, more abundant and healthier food. Surplus wealth has allowed the diversion of money to education, for example, which still eludes the poorest residents of Earth. But Lincoln is teaching us that material comfort is a limited good, not to be pursued to the point of losing ordered liberty. It is difficult to imagine Lincoln supporting an economy that sustained large GNP growth and allowed for a commodious living yet left people unable to pursue a virtuous and free life. Lincoln favored a Hamiltonian approach to economics because he thought that a diverse economy, rather than a simple agrarian one, gives the individual the greatest opportunity to make use of his or her talents. Someone like Lincoln who had neither interest nor talent for agriculture needed to have more options available in a dynamic economy that could produce plentiful opportunity to rise above one's station. Still, an economic vision that has material wealth as a sole criterion for success is akin to a political theory that sees majority rule as the only political good. Therefore a statesman does not simply desire the material well-being of the people, however good that is, but balances the very human desire for material comfort with the more noble ends of a free and democratic people. Lincoln's political economy said that material well-being is good, but not as good as being independent of crowned-kings, money-kings, and land-kings.

Part II

★ ★ ★ ★ ★

The Domestic Lincoln: Presidential Power and the Second American Revolution

4

★ ★ ★ ★ ★

Lincoln and the Second
American Revolution

P art 1 engaged in what might be called a theoretical discussion of Lincoln's political thought and statesmanship, albeit while connecting that thought to practical uses. Also, much of the argument up to this point has dealt extensively with Lincoln's pre-presidential years. The discussion now directs itself toward Lincoln's actions as chief executive, particularly his approach to the application of presidential power to what is typically called domestic policy. Consideration of Lincoln's presidency usually focuses on the man as a wartime leader. This is understandable. But it distorts the lessons of his presidency because Lincoln governed in a crisis, and crisis is by definition the exception, not the rule. There has been a dearth of scholarship on Lincoln's use of presidential power in regard to matters not connected with war and the president's role as commander in chief.

This chapter and the next two attempt to remedy this deficiency. Contemporary Americans live under a presidency-centered government, a presidency whose centrality to our political order extends far beyond the war powers, where executive action is on firmer constitutional ground. Woodrow Wilson's muscular approach to the presidency, namely that of a visionary who dominates the national government and is a singular interpreter of the national voice, defines the office to this day. Lincoln's presidency, as was seen in the discussion of Progressivism, is sometimes seen as a harbinger of today's activist government headed by a strong executive. Some go so far as to say that under Lincoln's guidance, a "second

American Revolution" occurred during the Civil War years, not just in the eradication of slavery but in the passage of historic nonwar legislation meant to promote economic growth. The ensuing chapters discuss this "revolution" thesis at length. The overall intent is to investigate Lincoln's view of presidential power as it pertains to matters that are less obviously executive in nature as war making. From Lincoln's use of executive power on noncrisis matters we learn lessons about presidential leadership that may help contemporary Americans evaluate the extent to which our presidency-centered government represents virtue or vice. Lincoln exemplifies a much more modest conception of the president's role in our political system, one that distrusts the notion that the desires of millions of Americans (now hundreds of millions) can be distilled into one person. The example of Lincoln's presidential statesmanship provides lessons for a nation now consistently frustrated by the gap between presidential promises and presidential actuality. In line with the theme of limits, the lesson of Lincoln's presidency, far from glorifying executive power, is that we should lower our expectations of presidential power and of government in general.

This particular chapter presents the claim that Lincoln was a revolutionary leader and then analyzes the sources of that contention. The evidence indicates that even those who promote the revolutionary thesis struggle to find support for it. I then lay out three different scholarly approaches within political science that might help us better assess the revolutionary thesis. These approaches, namely the study of realignment theory, of public policy, and of presidential theory, give us a unique insight by which to judge Lincoln's domestic presidency.

While the typical American will, with good reason, agree with Phillip Paludan that the two greatest accomplishments of Abraham Lincoln are saving the Union and ending slavery, historians and political scientists also take note that this period was the beginning of considerable activity concerning what I will call the domestic side of public policy, by which I mean "normal" public policy separated from war policy.[1] Yet, Lincoln's role in forming nonwar policy is usually ignored by biographers.[2] The United States government did more than fight a war from 1861 to 1865; it also passed sweeping new legislation in the areas of public lands, education, transportation, banking, currency, and other areas previously untouched by the federal government. The legislative output of the Civil War Congresses—the Thirty-Seventh and Thirty-Eighth—was the most numerous up to that time. Some scholars have noted this output but do not present evidence that Lincoln himself took any leadership role in domestic policy making.[3]

Was Lincoln a "revolutionary" who presided over a bold new domestic agenda, or a "conservative" figure who maintained the American order? From the first vantage point, Charles A. Beard and Mary R. Beard in 1927 labeled the Civil War era a "second American Revolution" because the American Revolution of 1776 produced no redistribution of wealth among the classes, whereas the triumph of the Republican Party in 1860 brought about "the unquestioned establishment of a new power in the government, making vast changes in the arrangement of classes, in the distribution of wealth, in the course of industrial development."[4] James G. Randall made the counterargument in 1947. If conservatism meant "caution, prudent adherence to tested values, avoidance of rashness, and reliance upon unhurried, peaceable evolution, [then] Lincoln was a conservative."[5] Randall's charge that Lincoln was conservative, grounded largely in the slave question, has support among other prominent historians.[6]

Historian James M. McPherson resurrected the Beards' thesis. It will be useful to reprint his detailed summary of the 1861–62 legislative achievements in order to outline the important questions that will guide ensuing discussion. McPherson points to these enactments:

> The second American Revolution, as Charles Beard viewed it, involved not only this destruction of the southern plantation gentry but also the consolidation of the northern entrepreneurial capitalist class in national power, supported by its rural and urban middle-class allies. Legislation passed by the Union Congress during the war promoted this development. The Republican Party had inherited from its Hamiltonian and Whig forebears a commitment to the use of government to foster economic development through tariffs to protect industry, a centralized and regulated banking system, investment subsidies and land grants to high-risk but socially beneficial transportation enterprises, and government support for education. By 1860 the Republican Party had also pledged itself to homestead legislation to provide farmers with an infusion of capital in the form of free land. Before 1860, the southern-dominated Democratic Party that controlled the federal government had repeatedly defeated or frustrated these measures. During the war, Republicans passed them all: a higher tariff in 1861; a homestead act, a land-grant college act, and a Pacific railroad act providing loans and land grants for a transcontinental railroad in 1862; and a national banking act in 1863, which, along with the legal tender act of

the previous year authorizing the issuance of a federal currency, the famous greenbacks, gave the national government effective control over the nation's currency for the first time. In addition, to finance the war the government marketed huge bond issues to the public and passed an Internal Revenue Act which imposed a large array of federal taxes for the first time, including a progressive income tax.[7]

McPherson proceeds to equate this outpouring of legislation under Lincoln with the "First Hundred Days" of Franklin D. Roosevelt, and he quotes from three other historians that the 1861–62 period was a watershed in the development of American capitalism. According to McPherson,

> This astonishing blitz of laws, most of them passed within the span of less than one year, did more to reshape the relation of the government to the economy than any comparable effort except perhaps the first hundred days of the New Deal. This Civil War legislation, in the words of one historian, created a "blueprint for modern America." It helped promote what another scholar termed "the last capitalist revolution" whereby the Civil War destroyed the "older social structure of plantation slavery" and installed "competitive democratic capitalism" in unchallenged domination of the American economy and polity. That this capitalism itself became a form of entrenched conservatism exploiting labor and resisting change a generation or two later does not nullify the revolutionary meaning of its triumph over the slave South and plantation agriculture in the 1860s. And as a former Whig who had favored these measures to promote banking, transportation, and industry as a means of bringing a higher standard of living to all Americans, and who believed that the abolition of slave labor would enhance the dignity and value of free labor, Abraham Lincoln was one of the principal architects of this capitalist revolution.[8]

While McPherson gives noticeable credit to the Republican Party for this policy agenda, it is his summary judgment that Lincoln was "one of the principal architects" of this revolution. To support his grand conclusion about capitalistic innovation under Lincoln, McPherson cites works by Leonard P. Curry, Barrington Moore Jr., and Gabor S. Boritt.[9] However, the Boritt volume is really a philosophical study of Lincoln's economic views, not an analysis of his legislative leadership, and Curry, though he actually gives details of selected legislative enactments, denies that Lincoln had much to do with what Congress achieved. Unfortunately, Curry also does not systematically analyze Lincoln's role in the agenda-setting process or his legislative strategy and tactics. Yet, in ending his essay, McPherson concludes that "it was his [Lincoln's] own superb leadership, strategy, and sense of timing as president, commander in chief, and head of the Republican party that determined the pace of the revolution and ensured its success," and, thus, he joins Charles Beard and Mary Beard in declaring that "Lincoln was not a conservative statesman but a revolutionary statesman."[10]

The debate among historians about Lincoln's role in the transformation of the American economic system, in other words, poses questions that are directly relevant to assessing Lincoln's place in political history and whether he was a pivotal figure in the development of our political and economic regime and a precursor to modern progressive government, including a strong presidency. Given the Beards' status among Progressive historians, McPherson seems to be making the claim noted in chapter 3 that Lincoln is a precursor to the Progressive defense of unlimited government. To address the political side of Lincoln, three approaches from political science offer rich theoretical perspectives from which to judge the "domestic" (nonmilitary) Lincoln.

First, from the perspective of the modern presidency literature, Lincoln, by coming before Franklin D. Roosevelt in time, would be regarded as a "premodern" president who would have limited impact as a presidential leader. Second, from the perspective of the public policy literature, as defined by the work of Theodore J. Lowi, we would anticipate that Lincoln in his executive position would have a passive role because the nineteenth century was characterized as an era of Congress-centered policy making. Third, from the perspective of electoral theory, however, Lincoln could have had a decisive impact on both the policy-making process and legislation because 1860 elevated the Republican Party as the dominant political party in America.

We will consider how Beard and Beard, Curry, Boritt, and Moore depict Lincoln's economic policy on three different matters: the role of economics in the formation of the Republican Party, the types of economic legislation considered by Congress during the Civil War, and, finally, Lincoln's role in the passage of this legislation. Analysis of these historians will constitute the beginning of an appraisal of McPherson's revolutionary claim that Abraham Lincoln was instrumental in ushering in a new economic era in American history. But first a more detailed discussion of McPherson's extraordinary claim is in order.

The McPherson Revolution Thesis

Given the perspectives with which to evaluate the revolutionary thesis, it worth taking some time to describe that theory more. McPherson sees a dramatic shift in economic policy during the Civil War, as well as the breaking of the Jacksonian political stranglehold on the national government. The secession of the Southern states allowed the passage of legislation creating a national banking system, a protectionist tariff, and homestead legislation that had long been blocked by the Jacksonian Democrats.[11]

McPherson notes that, in 1861, the Constitution had been in operation for seventy-two years. For forty-nine of those years, the president had been a Southerner and a slaveholder. After the Civil War, it was one hundred years before another Southerner, Lyndon Johnson, won the White House.[12] Twenty-three of the thirty-six Speakers of the House had been Southerners before the Civil War, while for half a century following the war there were no Southern Speakers. Before the Civil War the South always had a majority on the Supreme Court, but in the following half century only five of twenty-six justices appointed to the court were Southerners.[13] Much of this reduction of Southern power can be attributed to the dominance of a largely Northern Republican Party, especially in winning the presidency and control of the Senate, until Franklin Roosevelt and the New Deal realignment.

McPherson argues that the war can be seen as the "second American Revolution" in three different ways, with Lincoln playing "a crucial role in defining the outcome of the revolution in each of the three respects." First, it may be reasonable to define Lincoln's defense of the Union and the Declaration of Independence as revolutionary, as "secession was a counterrevolution to forestall the revolutionary threat to slavery posed by the government Lincoln headed." Second, Lincoln abolished slavery, a revolutionary act in McPherson's view. These two "revolutionary" acts are not relevant here, although discussion in previous chapters makes clear that regarding slavery and union Lincoln saw himself as simply fulfilling the founding rather than innovating. Yet, in addition to these "revolutionary" acts, the Civil War is revolutionary because, McPherson says, "it altered the direction of American development." McPherson agrees with Charles Beard and Mary Beard in saying that the war instigated a massive shift in the arrangement of classes, the distribution of wealth, and setting the nation inexorably on the course of industrialism. The Republican Party, true to its Hamiltonian and Whig roots, became the instrument of the capitalist class, seeking to use government power to advance its own cause. The Republicans did so by advocating and then passing legislation "to protect industry, a centralized and regulated banking system, investment subsidies and land grants to high-risk but socially beneficial transportation enterprises, . . . government support of education," and a homestead act to promote westward expansion. The Jacksonian Democrats, frustrating the attempts of the old Whig Party to advance the economic nationalist cause, had opposed all of these items. But as we have seen, McPherson notes that the Civil War Congresses passed a bevy of nationalist bills.[14]

McPherson cites Charles Beard as the prime source for his claim that the Civil War was a "second American revolution." He also refers to Leonard Curry, Barrington Moore, and Gabor Boritt for the importance of domestic legislation and Lincoln's crucial role in it. To assess McPherson's claim that Lincoln spearheaded a domestic program of "revolutionary" proportions, we must first look to McPherson's own sources for this claim and consider whether their evidence warrants his conclusion that the Civil War was revolutionary in regard to economic policy. This analysis will show that McPherson's own sources do not provide the evidence that would support his thesis.

McPherson's Historians and the Republican Party

The ascendancy to power of the Republican Party following the 1860 election necessitates investigating the origins of this new political party. What were the factors that led to its rise in the 1850s? What was the makeup of the political Republican coalition? Finally, what was the role of Abraham Lincoln in the rise of the Republican Party?

Charles Beard and Mary Beard seem a bit confused about the nature and cause of the rise of the Republican Party. They argue that the Kansas-Nebraska Act of 1854 caused the partisan realignment of the 1850s. The Kansas-Nebraska Act undermined the Missouri Compromise of 1820 and led to a coalition among "northern Whigs persuaded that their old party was moribund, Democrats weary of planting dominance, and free-soilers eager to exclude slavery from the territories." In 1856, the Beards further state, the Republican Party put economic questions on the backburner to coalesce around opposition to slavery.[15]

Yet, in almost the same breath, the Beards argue that the Civil War was not a war over slavery or the Union. The war "at bottom . . . was a social war . . . making vast changes in the arrangement of the classes, in the accumulation and distribution of wealth, in the course of industrial development, and in the Constitution inherited from the fathers."[16] They contend that because abolition, as opposed to mere antislavery, was not politically successful before the Civil War, it follows that slavery was not an important cause of the war and that the Republican Party was a coalition of "capitalists, laborers and farmers of the North and West [seeking to drive] from power in the national government the planting aristocracy of the South."[17]

According to the Beards, the Republicans' 1860 campaign was not based on fighting the South or protecting the Union; "indeed, the new party embraced a large number of people interested primarily in the protective tariffs, free homesteads, and related matters; practical people who thought the less said about slavery the better."[18] Presumably the party nominee, Abraham Lincoln, agreed to this campaign strategy of accentuating economics over slavery. It is not clear why the Kansas-Nebraska Act would cause these economic nationalists to form a new party, since they already had the Whig Party dedicated to economic nationalism. Still, the Beards are convinced that battlefield deaths and heroics were simply "means to ends." The "supreme outcome" of the war was the overthrow of the Southern planting aristocracy and its replacement with "northern capitalists and free farmers."[19] Beard and Beard never mention Lincoln or any other politician as playing a crucial role in this capitalist revolution. According to their rigid class interpretation, the rise of the Republican Party was more a creation of businessmen than politicians.

Barrington Moore, while agreeing that economics was important to the sectional conflict of the mid-nineteenth century, assigns to slavery a much larger role in the burgeoning Republican coalition. Moore sees the Civil War as the "violent dividing point between the agrarian and industrial epochs in American history." The "real issue" between the South and North was that while Southern plantation owners may have been capitalists, they were not Northern bourgeoisie. Slavery was a crucial difference between the feudal-style capitalism of the South and the bourgeois capitalism of the North. Moore states that the Beards mistake the indifference to slavery on the part of a majority of Americans to mean that slavery was unimportant.[20]

While Charles Beard and Mary Beard feel slavery was of little importance to the rise of the Republican Party and Moore thinks it had coequal status with economics, Gabor Boritt argues that slavery was of primary importance to the Republican Party. Like the Beards, Boritt portrays the Kansas-Nebraska Act as central to the rise of the Republican Party but, in contrast to the Beards, remains consistent on this theme. For Lincoln, says Boritt, Kansas-Nebraska showed that as proslavery forces became more "aggressive," economic questions become less important. Whig economic reforms made little sense in the absence of free labor. In addition, the bond between the former Whigs and former Democrats who formed the new party was an antislavery one, not an economic one. After Kansas-Nebraska, slavery became the key question, and Lincoln felt that there was little use in discussing economics when slavery was the crucial issue. Leading up to the presidential nomination in 1860, Lincoln counseled silence on economic matters because they would distract from the antislavery coalition, although he privately assured people of his own Whiggish economics.[21] In Boritt's estimation, then, while nonslave domestic policy was important to Lincoln, it was of less importance to him and to the GOP than slavery.[22] Boritt also mentions Lincoln as a leader of the nascent party and describes him as an "important local leader" in Illinois. Boritt seems to agree with Moore that there is symmetry in the Republican opposition to slavery and its general support for Whig economics, although Boritt gives slavery a somewhat larger role in that equation. Like Moore, Boritt suggests that political entrepreneurship was important to the rise of the party, mentioning Lincoln by name.

While Leonard Curry's treatment is of the Civil War Congresses but not the birth of the Republican Party, his discussion of the factions within the U.S. Senate during the Civil War Congresses tells us something about the nature of the Republican Party. Curry describes three factions in the Senate: the radicals, the moderates, and the conservatives. The radicals, mostly from New England, defended a position of no compromise with the South. To them, the war was a chance to "reshape the American Union and change the structure of Southern society and politics." The moderates, who were mostly former Whigs, supported a limited reshaping of Southern society. While the radicals saw the war as an excuse to act outside the Constitution, the moderates valued working within the existing constitutional framework.[23] Conservatives, former Whigs and Know-Nothings, many of whom would one day become Democrats, saw no reason to remake Southern society and fought the war only to save the Union. There were no "extra-constitutional" powers for the legislature or the executive.

While Curry identifies these groups on a continuum based on prosecution of the war, their views of the Constitution are instructive. As one moves from the radicals to the conservatives, one perceives an ever-decreasing tolerance for government activism in remaking society. The radicals were ready to use federal power to reshape the South, so they may have been more eager to advocate government policies to promote industrialism and economic growth. With a limited view of constitutional power, the conservatives may have been less sanguine about the use of the government to promote economic growth. The moderates, naturally, fell in the middle. This suggests that it may be difficult to identify a definitive "Republican" position on government activism either in defeating slavery or in advancing industrialism.

The four sources McPherson references display contradictions. Each has different views regarding the role economics played for Republicans. Beard and Beard believe that economics was at the center of the Republican coalition, while the other three historians suggest there was a mixture of economic and antislavery sentiments. Boritt proposes that economics was reduced in importance to the antislavery message in the 1860 election. Important to McPherson's argument, however, none of these authors places Lincoln at the center of national Republican Party thought or organization, although Boritt suggests he was an important local leader. This certainly does not suggest Lincoln as a central figure in a revolution.

McPherson's Historians and Public Policy

Whether or not economics was central to Republicanism, the party did produce important domestic legislation during the Civil War. We now move to consider exactly what kinds of domestic policies were passed during the Civil War. On this issue there seems to be more agreement among the historians McPherson cites.

In the Beards' view, "all that two generations of Federalists and Whigs had tried to get was won within four short years, and more besides." Beard and Beard list higher tariffs, the national banking system, the Pacific railway legislation, the Homestead Act, and freer immigration as the Federalist/Whig policies passed by the Republicans. As noted, the Beards see these policies as at the center of the conflict of the Civil War. The withdrawal of the South from the Union, coupled with armed conflict, gave Congress reason and capability to raise revenues by increasing tariffs. But these tariffs, the Beards say, were written to benefit industry, not to raise revenue. The National Bank Act extended federal authority over local banking associations and allowed for federal control over private bank notes.[24] Beard and Beard describe the Bank Act as a kind of regulatory policy, using government power to control the banking segment of the economy.

Barrington Moore sees some of the same forces at play. He too notes the advocacy of tariffs by Northern industrialists to protect their industries, the seeking of "aid in setting up a transportation network" of railroads, and the promotion of a central banking system. These Northern industrialists wanted to do business "without bothering about state and regional frontiers." Radical Republicans such as Thaddeus Stevens worked as go-betweens for the railroad and iron and steel industries. A "fundamental issue" was "whether the machinery of the federal government should be used to support one society or another."[25] In Moore's view, the Republican Party was not shy about using governmental power to support its brand of industrial capitalism. Governmental power should be used to promote some segments of the economy over others, Moore concludes.

Boritt concentrates on Lincoln's economic vision. He shows that economics had long been of great concern for Lincoln and perhaps formed the core of his thought. The Whiggish economic nationalism was so important to Lincoln that he refused to support the Free-Soil Party in 1848 and blamed abandonment of Whig economics by Henry Clay and Daniel Webster for the party's demise.[26] As president, Lincoln had a Treasury secretary, Salmon P. Chase, who, by the time Chase left office, could be described as a "good Hamiltonian, and a Western progressive of the Lincoln Stamp on everything from a tariff to a national bank."[27] This suggests an administrative-wide commitment to using government to promote economic nationalism.

Curry takes note of the passage of domestic legislation that had long been bottled up by Democrats. Homestead legislation, for example, had been on the congressional agenda for fifteen years, only to be killed by Democrats in Congress or vetoed by Democratic presidents. The Republican Party put passage of a homestead act as a plank in its 1860 platform and then translated that plank into law.[28]

Curry also maintains that it was highly unlikely that private capital could have laid a railroad across the Great Plains. The size of the task was beyond private means, yet a railroad was necessary for economic development in the interior. The passage of railroad legislation "made it feasible for one-quarter of the continental United States to be occupied."[29] This was no mean feat.

The Civil War Congresses also passed revenue bills that affected almost all the wealth or "earning capacity" of the nation, and this brought almost every citizen in touch with the federal government. They passed an income tax, the first in the nation's history, and recognized that "purely financial operations" were playing a greater role in the American economy and that a great proportion of the "nation's wealth now existed in the form of liquid and rapidly revolving capital." The government could access this money by use of an income tax rather than relying on tariffs and duties.[30]

One can sense from the analyses of these historians that the government extended its grip over the American economy and citizenry during the Civil War. Through banking regulation, taxation, land policy, and internal improvement legislation such as that involving railroads, the amount of space isolated from federal involvement shrank to a significant extent. The Land-Grant College Act, passed by the Thirty-Seventh Congress, began the federal government's involvement in education. In Curry's view, the domestic legislation of the Lincoln presidency signified movement from a government that sought to benefit all to a government for powerful groups of individuals and corporations. Whether this rise in government power could be considered "revolutionary" is another question, but McPherson is correct that it represented a significant activity by the federal government and that something novel in the way of public policy occurred during the Civil War. The question remains as to how important Lincoln was to this augmentation of power. Was Lincoln "one of the principal architects" of this groundbreaking legislation?

McPherson's Historians on Lincoln's Presidential Leadership

While Charles and Mary Beard and Barrington Moore, respectively, call the Civil War a "second American Revolution" and the "last capitalist revolution," they have virtually nothing to say about Lincoln's role in the passage of the key domestic legislation that would seem to underpin this revolution. Moore is absolutely silent on the question, while the Beards simply note that Lincoln was a minority president with a less than unified party.[31] Thus, for information on Lincoln's role in the passage of domestic legislation, we must focus on Boritt and Curry for any evidence.

In his two chapters on Lincoln's presidency, Boritt argues the Whig view was one of presidential deference to Congress. In this view, the president should allow Congress a free hand in passing legislation, with his only role in the legislative process to sign bills, because the Whigs frowned on the use of the veto for policy reasons. That practice was inaugurated by the despised Andrew Jackson concerning the Whig-backed Bank of the United States. Boritt notes the outsized discussion of the veto in the 1848 Whig platform.

Boritt depicts Lincoln as a strong war president but one who "in his relationship with Congress and his cabinet . . . remained reserved." Lincoln, while running for the presidency, said that he desired "the legislation of the country to rest with Congress . . . undisturbed by the veto except in very special clear cases." After becoming president, he noted that his "political education" inclined him against any influence over Congress. As a minority president with no executive experience, it may have been best for him to defer to his cabinet and to Congress. Boritt declares that apart from annual messages, Lincoln rarely attempted to influence the economic work of Congress.[32]

Most of the key domestic legislation passed Congress with little overt leadership from Lincoln, says Boritt. He was not much involved in the shift from external taxes—tariffs and duties, for example—to internal taxes, namely the income tax. While Congress did pass tariffs that were "unbelievably high," they needed no prompting from Lincoln. They simply passed one increase after another, and Lincoln signed them. He did no work on passage of the Homestead Act, although when he advised amending the bill to give soldiers special benefits, Congress took his advice. Boritt concludes that Lincoln did not direct a nationalist revolution, but he did not oppose it as others had.[33]

Curry agrees with Boritt's claims of Lincoln's presidential passivity in domestic legislation. He also points to Lincoln's minority election. As a president of a new party, and as a compromise candidate who ran behind the congressional ticket, lacked executive experience, and was out of favor with congressional leaders like Thaddeus Stevens, Charles Sumner, and Benjamin Wade, Lincoln had little pull with Congress. As Curry puts it, few presidents have been subjected to such brutal criticism from both opponents and party "friends." Curry claims that most all legislative activity had a congressional initiative. In fact, Congress worked to undermine presidential power, accelerating "the trend toward congressional dominance" that would characterize the second half of the nineteenth century.[34]

Curry barely mentions Lincoln throughout his book. Lincoln's role in forming the "blueprint for modern America" was negligible. With the Beards and Moore silent on the issue of Lincoln's leadership on domestic matters, and both Boritt and Curry downplaying Lincoln's activity on this matter, there does not seem to be much support for McPherson's "principal architect" thesis among the historians he references.

It is still unclear whether Lincoln challenged the Whig assumption that he brought to the office, that of presidential deference to Congress. In addition, historians cannot seem to agree on the nature of the Republican coalition. Was it an antislavery coalition, or was it a coalition of economic interests? Maybe it was both. What was Lincoln's role in developing the Republican Party, both ideologically and organizationally? There is some evidence that he was at least a local leader. We must also ask what effect the 1860 realignment had on the legislative activity in the Thirty-Seventh and Thirty-Eighth Congresses. None of the references cited by McPherson seriously consider Lincoln's role in the Republican realignment. Lincoln and his relations with Congress must be assessed in light of realignment, which McPherson and the other historians do not do.

McPherson's references address public policy questions, but for the most part they characterize policy innovation as a change in the size of government rather than a change in kinds of policy. They do not consider the way certain types of public policy types affect the nature of presidential and congressional relations. Political science may allow us to view with additional perspectives the phenomena surrounding the domestic Lincoln. By addressing the confluence of presidential power, realigning parties, and changing public policy types, we can gain deeper insight into the domestic Lincoln.

Understanding Lincoln: Three Political Science Perspectives

To build upon and distinguish from the historical studies, we can use various perspectives coming from political science that allow us to address Lincoln's domestic presidency. Political science can help us with the three central issues: the role of the president in our political order, specifically in the legislative process; the way in which differing policy types affect presidential and congressional relations; and the effects of realignment on public policy.

The first perspective is that of the "modern presidency" thesis, or what Richard J. Ellis calls "the progressive presidency," hearkening back to Woodrow Wilson and those influenced by Wilson who advocated for a president-centered government. "Only aggressive and skilled presidential leadership, progressives argued, could make this anachronistic eighteenth-century system work in the modern world," Ellis stated. "What was needed, in short, was a 'modern presidency' for a modern world."[35] Fred Greenstein argues that Franklin D. Roosevelt set a new paradigm for presidential activity that sharply deviates from the "traditional presidency." Previous to Roosevelt there had been small shifts in power from president to president, but with Roosevelt there was a "general increase in the size and impact of American government," and "the presidency began to undergo not a shift but rather a metamorphosis."[36]

Greenstein posits four characteristics of the modern presidency. First, the president is not just interested in the activities of Congress; he also initiates and leads legislative action. Second, the modern presidency has evolved from the traditional limits on unilateral powers to "direct policy making through executive orders and other actions not formally ratified by Congress." Third, the modern presidency has seen a grand expansion in White House staff and bureaucracy. Last, the modern president attracts far more attention from the public than chief executives previously had. Every president now is a "hero president" like Washington, as the public holds the executive responsible for all things, good or bad. Legislative leadership is a crucial component of the modern presidency, according to Greenstein, who points to Roosevelt's "First Hundred Days" of 1933 as evidence of the new power of the modern presidency over the legislative process.[37]

The foremost work of modern presidency scholarship by Richard Neustadt argues that the constitutional powers of the presidency are inadequate to the tasks that the chief executive faces in the post-FDR era. The president is central to our system, the "focal point of politics and policy," whereas in the past he was essentially a mere clerk who simply did the bidding of a dominant Congress. Only a crisis, such as a war, might have elevated the president to equal footing with the legislature. While the "traditional" chief executive deferred to Congress, for the modern president it is "common law" to pursue his own legislative program and to personally campaign, even in congressional races.[38]

In Neustadt's view, ultimately "presidential power is the power to persuade."[39] Everything the president "says and does . . . becomes significant to everyone's appraisals regardless of the claims of his officialdom."[40] Constant scrutiny of him by the public and by Washington players means that the president must constantly be aware of how others perceive his actions. Perception of presidential leadership matters more than the legal powers of his office.

Franklin D. Roosevelt is Neustadt's model of how a modern president should act. "Any President who valued personal power would start his term with vivid demonstrations of tenacity and skill in every sphere. . . . This is no more than Franklin Roosevelt did in his first term. It is the ideal formula for others." Roosevelt was always the first to know things, unlike the amateurish Eisenhower, who was always the last to know. Roosevelt's mark of distinction was his love of power. It was Roosevelt who first recognized that the key to presidential power is personal power. As Neustadt puts it, "Roosevelt was a politician seeking personal power," in contrast to Eisenhower, who was a war hero merely seeking national unity. Neustadt writes, "Competitive personalities mixed with competing jurisdictions was Roosevelt's formula for putting pressure on himself, for making his subordinates push up to him the choices they could not make for themselves."[41]

The Greenstein and Neustadt views of the "modern" presidency dominate the field. While skeptical about the chances for the president's success, George Edwards claims that "our political system virtually compels the president to attempt to lead Congress."[42] Likewise, Jon Bond and Richard Fleisher write, "The modern president has no choice but to enter the legislative arena."[43] In their view, "since FDR, presidents have been judged more by their success as legislative leaders than by executive ability. And all postwar presidents live 'in the shadow' of the benchmark set by FDR's legislative success." Harold Barger writes, "FDR changed the power ratio between Congress and the White House, publicly taking it upon himself to act as the leader of Congress at a time of deepening crisis in the nation. More than any other president, FDR established the model of the powerful legislative presidency on which the public's expectations still are anchored."[44] Eric A. Posner and Adrian Vermeule call the Roosevelt administration a "watershed" that regularized the ensuing powerful presidencies.[45] "Roosevelt built the post-war presidency" notes Jeremi Suri, while warning that "he was the last to tame it."[46] These scholars all contend that FDR's is a departure from a "traditional" or constitutional presidency. Particularly Roosevelt's legislative leadership set a new precedent for executive activity that represents a sharp break from the past.

There are those who dispute this modern presidency thesis. They argue that it misreads the Constitution and rests on a misunderstanding of the presidency in the political regime. For example, David K. Nichols maintains that the modern/premodern distinction is false. Rather, "we find 'modern' Presidents throughout our history, because the essential elements of the modern Presidency, including the President's role as a popular leader, are a logical outgrowth of decisions made at the Constitutional Convention and embodied in the Constitution." Nichols does not deny that the office has developed across time, "but that does not alter the fact that most developments can be traced to the forces set in motion by the structure of the Constitution in general and of Article II in particular."[47]

Another who questions the modern presidency model is Jeffrey Tulis. Alexander Hamilton, as the main exponent of presidential power in the *Federalist Papers*, Tulis points out, favored a president with less prerogative than a monarch but more than any state governor could claim. As a strong executive is "indispensable to *any* government," a way must be found to make a powerful executive compatible with republican government.[48] Thus the framers constructed a presidency that has power to rival Congress. Article II, Section 1, of the Constitution gives all executive power to the president. This grant of power is open-ended, unlike the grant of legislative power to Congress in Article I, Section 1, which limits Congress to powers "herein granted." While legislative power is limited to powers written in the Constitution, the president is granted "the executive Power" without any caveat. The presidency also has "unity, independence from the legislature, and re-eligibility," at least until the Twenty-Second Amendment. In *Federalist* No. 70, Hamilton asserts that unity and independence make the president a powerful force of his own in our constitutional order. When Neustadt says that the president has certain advantages in leadership because "no one else sits where he sits," this is simply another way of articulating the unity and independence of the executive.[49]

Tulis, in a disagreement with Nichols, hastens to add that Hamilton did not support, nor does the Constitution, "popular leadership," defined as "the routine appeal 'over the head' of Congress in support of executive initiatives." The framers feared that there were "no institutional means to prevent the *routinization* of popular appeals short of a general prescription." However, while "popular leadership was proscribed, statesmanship was not." The Constitution encourages the president to "initiate, plan, and direct" as well as withstand public opinion.[50] Nichols and Tulis agree, though, that the constitutional presidency is already strong; thus the modern presidency is the realization of latent power, not a deviation from its founding.

Where Neustadt saw public opinion—the president's "prestige"—as an indirect factor undergirding his leadership, Samuel Kernell argues that the causal relationship today is more direct. This strategy Kernell calls "going public." The founder of the modern presidency, Franklin D. Roosevelt, may have more in common with Abraham Lincoln than with Barack Obama or Donald Trump in respect to going public. FDR generally engaged in elite-to-elite bargaining rather than directly addressed the public on behalf of his agenda. Attempts to influence Congress typically occurred behind the scenes rather than in plain daylight.[51] A model of a "going public" strategy is actually John F. Kennedy's, representing a repudiation of FDR's behind-the-scenes bargaining.

> Each feature [of Kennedy's "going public" style] violates some ground rule of institutional pluralism . . . which its predecessor, the FDR system, had founded. . . . From the perspective of institutionalized pluralism, the live telecast of news conferences is the most objectionable of all. Its antithetical nature was summed up [by Ted Sorenson, who said] that the forum was intended more to inform the public than the press.[52]

Not only was FDR more a traditional bargaining president, but even his celebrated First Hundred Days legislative achievements have been called into question by research. The significant enactments of the Roosevelt First Hundred Days of 1933 were driven by the exigencies of the Great Depression, crisis conditions that were uniquely traumatic to the nation.[53]

So if Lincoln is a model for the modern presidency as a revolutionary figure, a series of questions arises. Did Lincoln exercise "personal" leadership over Congress, as in the Neustadt model, or did he operate indirectly through other members of his administration? Did he penetrate the legislative process by lobbying individual members of Congress, as did Roosevelt? Was Lincoln's legislative leadership limited to agenda setting, through the annual address and special messages, or did it extend throughout later stages of the lawmaking process? Is there any evidence that Lincoln attempted a "going public" strategy to shape the legislative process, or did he primarily operate in the bargaining mode? What was Lincoln's vision of the presidency as part of our constitutional order? What kind of presidential statesman was Lincoln?

The second political science perspective is that of the relationship between public policy and presidential power. Let us call this the public policy perspective. Theodore J. Lowi suggests that a vital variable to understanding presidential power lies in public policy. The government, especially in the present day, assumes many responsibilities. When assessing Lincoln's strength as a legislative leader, a consideration of public policy is in order. If some types of policy lend themselves to presidential dominance—are modern presidents powerful because of the nature of the office or simply due to a shift in the kinds of public policy that dominate?—then we need to know whether they were part of the domestic agenda during the Civil War era.

It was Woodrow Wilson who noted that in the nineteenth century, "the predominant and controlling force, the center and source of all motive and all regulative power, is Congress." While the Constitution may have set up coequal branches, experience had shown that Congress reigned supreme. Wilson points to the committee system of Congress as the source of this power. The efficiency of the committee system allows Congress to work on many bills at one time and pass legislation in an orderly and productive manner. The president watches from the sidelines as Congress does the heavy lifting of governing. For the president, "most of the time it is mere administration and mere obedience to the directions from the masters of policy, the Standing Committee." The president is little more than an "exalted" businessman.[54]

It is not difficult to see that in modern times the president plays a much stronger role in the policy process than Wilson claimed for his time. In fact the president now seems essential to the creation and implementation of public policy. As the committee system still exists, one must look to other factors to explain this supposed change in the balance of power between the branches.

Lowi argues that the type of policy at stake determines the political relationship among key policy makers, so that for every type of policy there is likely a distinct type of political relationship.[55] We need to define "policies in terms of their impact or expected impact on society." Lowi categorizes policy as distributive, regulatory, and redistributive, each developing "its own characteristics, political structure, political process, elites, and group relations."[56]

Lowi describes the nineteenth century as dominated by distributive policy. The policy of that time had to do with "rivers and harbors . . . defense procurement and research and development; labor, business, and agricultural 'clientele' services; and the traditional tariff." In this type of policy, governmental goods are "distributed" to client groups in the populace. Distributive policy may be used as a kind of patronage, given to people or areas that support the party in power. It also has the characteristic of being a non-zero-sum bargaining game, because funding a new harbor in Norfolk, Virginia, does not mean the government cannot also fund a new post office in Sandusky, Ohio. Distributive policy is thus characterized by relationships of "mutual non-interference." Each group seeking the benefit looks out for its own interest. For this reason the making of distributive policy is dominated by logrolling. As Lowi puts it, "The 'pork-barrel' is a container for unrelated items." Public lands legislation for rural areas and protective tariffs designed for urban industry pass hand in hand. The people who broker the logrolling deals tend to be committee chairmen within Congress, as they have the most power in deciding who gets what in these relationships.[57] Because distributive policy creates little conflict, what disputes do arise are resolved at the lowest level of the policy process, namely the congressional committee, through a "you support my project and I'll support yours" bargain. Randall Ripley and Grace Franklin agree with Lowi that controlling any policy type has to do with the level of conflict. Distributive policy takes the form of the famous "iron triangle" with committees or subcommittees, bureaus, and clientele groups working at this less visible level of decision making to reach agreement.[58]

Regulatory policy differs from distributive policy in that "the impact of regulatory decisions is clearly one of directly raising costs and/or reducing or expanding alternatives of private individuals."[59] Further, regulatory policy cannot be disaggregated; it always affects specific sectors of the economy. The same can be said for redistributive policy, which affects whole social classes. "The aim [of redistributive policy] is not use of property," as in regulatory policy, "but property itself, not equal treatment but equal possession, not behavior but being."[60]

Unlike distributive policy, regulatory and redistributive policies create adversarial coalitions of common rather than uncommon interests. If distributive policy is characterized by "win-win" relationships, regulatory and redistributive policies have winners and losers. Some people bear direct cost of a regulation, but most do not. Some people receive redistributive benefits; some do not. Since these policies tend to be zero-sum games, there is an element of "us against them" involved. "Since coalitions form around shared interests, the coalitions will shift as the interests change or as conflicts of interest emerge," Lowi points out. A majority-sized coalition of shared interests on one issue may not be appropriate for some other issue.[61] While distributive policy is usually decided at the committee level, debates over economic regulation cannot be contained within committees and spill onto the floors of Congress and also implicate the president, who takes sides in the conflict.

Lowi argues that disputes over redistributive policy usually occur within the executive branch as different agencies react to particular "peak associations," agitating for or against redistribution. Congress is left to ratify agreements largely made within the executive branch.[62] As Ripley and Franklin put it, "The executive branch—particularly at the presidential level—is an important actor in redistributive policy formulation and implementation." The friction between "less-privileged economic and racial groups" and the "more-privileged" almost always involves major conflict that cannot be settled at the subgovernment level.[63]

With the hindsight of history, Lowi and Ripley and Franklin are able to note how the shift in policy carries with it the shift in power arrangements. Distribution was "almost the exclusive type of national domestic policy from 1789 until virtually 1890."[64] Lowi argues that the kinds of policy demanded by industrialization of the late nineteenth century and by the Great Depression necessitated new powers for the executive. What followed were greater expectations of the branch's head, the president, to deliver the goods.[65] The rise of centralized industry necessitated antitrust and labor regulations. The Great Depression made redistribution of wealth a logical step to alleviate the worst of the Depression's effects. Ripley and Franklin find regulatory policy developing in the late nineteenth century and becoming increasingly complex.

The discussion of policy theory relating to Lincoln's domestic leadership encourages us to ask what kinds of public policy Lincoln and the Thirty-Seventh and Thirty-Eighth Congresses considered. Were they distributive, as Wilson, Lowi, and Ripley and Franklin suggest? Or were there some policies that could be defined in part or in whole as regulatory?[66] If distributive policy was indeed the dominant type, did Lincoln play a passive role, as these authors assert? If there were regulatory policies, did Lincoln spearhead their passage?

The third and final political science perspective is that of party realignment theory. Any study of Lincoln and his importance to American political history must consider the birth of the Republican Party and the massive electoral shifts that coincided with that birth. Lincoln's ascendancy to power did not occur in a political vacuum. The 1850s saw a radical shift in the partisan allegiance within the American electorate. This shift in allegiance led to the rise of the Republican Party, the death of the Whig Party, and finally the replacement of the Democratic Party as the dominant party in American politics. Republicans would dominate presidential politics with only brief exceptions (Grover Cleveland and Woodrow Wilson) until Franklin D. Roosevelt and his Democratic New Deal coalition rose to power in the 1930s.

A consideration of the role Lincoln played in the realignment of the 1850s, culminating in Lincoln's election in 1860, is in order. Most political scientists would agree that there have been four major party realignments in American history, usually attached to the "critical elections" of 1828, 1860, 1896, and 1932. This first critical election, that of 1828, marked the ascendancy of Andrew Jackson to the presidency and the birth of a truly partisan era. Jacksonian Democrats became the dominant party, regularly defeating the Whig Party at the polls until the 1850s. The 1850s saw the weakening of the Whig coalition and the siphoning off of Democratic voters in the North by the newly born Republican Party. This new party gained in popularity until it became the victorious party, if not exactly a majority party, in 1860. The post–Civil War Republican Party solidified its power over time. The 1896 election marked a dramatic shift in the partisan makeup, as the Republicans, under William McKinley, became the party of industrialization and business, and the Democrats, led by William Jennings Bryan, fought a losing battle in defense of agricultural America. The Republican coalition of businessmen and urban laborers held sway until the Crash of 1929 and the ascendancy of Franklin D. Roosevelt to power. Roosevelt engineered a coalition of reformers, farmers, and lower- and middle-class laborers that dominated the political scene for at least forty years.

The chief concern here is the question of whether realignments occur as a "bottom-up" phenomenon or as a "top-down" phenomenon. Do realignments start with mass political behavior, the shifting of allegiances from one party to another? In the case of the 1850s, this would refer to a mass exit of Whigs and some Democrats to the new Republican Party. The bottom-up view would suggest that "grassroots" activity creates new cleavages within the electorate and drives political elites to adopt new positions or suffer electoral death. If this view holds true, then Lincoln and the leaders of the Republican Party in its nascent days were simply responding to shifts within the electorate. Perhaps they did so artfully and to the great benefit of their party and themselves, but still the "real action" was occurring in the minds and hearts of the public. A second view, the "top-down" view, suggests that change is initiated at elite levels of politics, only to take hold later in the electorate. Presidential leadership would seem crucial to this theory. In this view the response (or lack thereof) by elites to new conditions drives a partisan realignment.

Some realignment theorists posit that realignments are typically "bottom-up" phenomena.[67] In his seminal article "A Theory of Critical Elections," V. O. Key considers the shifts of partisan allegiance of voters in New England surrounding the elections of 1896 and 1932. Key announces, "Perhaps the basic differentiating characteristic of democratic orders consists in the expression of effective choice by the mass of the people in elections."[68] This is never truer than in realigning elections, when a mass segment of the voting population becomes so frustrated with the current partisan regime that it throws off old party ties to cast its lot with an alternative party with a wholly alternative vision.

Key believes that "central to our concept of critical elections is a realignment in the electorate both sharp and durable."[69] To illustrate this contention, Key investigates changes in the electorate in New England surrounding the 1896, 1928, and 1932 elections, but more to the point, while Key seeks to evaluate these critical elections he does not look to leadership by the nominal party leaders (William McKinley, Al Smith, or FDR) but rather to shifting behavior at the mass level.

The same grassroots perspective holds true for Angus Campbell, Philip Converse, Warren Miller, and Donald Stokes. For these authors, party loyalty in the electorate is the key: "No element of the political lives of Americans is more impressive than their party loyalties."[70] Thus it takes extraordinary events for voters to move with permanence to a new party.

A rare occurrence is a realigning election.[71] Realignments are shifts in both directions by the electorate, usually along sectional or class lines. Which party gains more from these shifts depends upon the "relative size of the groups affected and the solidarity with which their membership moves." It may be more accurate to speak of realigning eras. For example, the New Deal realignment was not complete in 1933 but was solidified after FDR's successful first term.

Lincoln, like McKinley and FDR, did not "ride in on a wave of great personal popularity," as he was not a distinguished war hero or "possessed any extraordinary personal appeal at the time he first took office." The distinguishing characteristic of realigning elections is a "great national crisis, leading to a conflict regarding governmental policies and the association of the two major parties with relatively contrasting programs for its solutions."[72] Thus, Campbell and his associates downplay the role of leadership in favor of broad mass level shifts in partisanship.

Walter Dean Burnham provides another analysis of realignment. Burnham says critical elections "may well be defined as the chief tension management device" for the "peculiar" American political system. Burnham lays out four criteria that differentiate "critical" elections from "normal" elections. First, a critical election consists of an "intense disruption" in previous voting patterns. Significant minorities shift allegiance from one party to another. Second, critical elections are high-turnout affairs. Third, Burnham claims that critical elections are not random occurrences; instead, there is a "uniform periodicity" to the phenomenon. Burnham notes that critical elections seem to occur roughly every thirty years (1800, 1832, 1860, 1896, 1932, and 1968).[73] Finally, and most important for our purposes, critical elections cause shifts in public policy. This shift in policy "arise[s] from emergent tensions in society which, not adequately controlled by the organization or outputs of party politics as usual, escalate to a flash point." Note that the new policy paradigm "arises" from the people, not from elites. Burnham continues to say that the new policies have "profound after effects on the roles played by constitutional elites."[74] The behavior of voters causes elites to react, not the reverse. While elites will set the policy in particular, the masses drive policy agenda in general.

Because early realignment theorists represented some of the most respected names in the field of political behavior, it is not a surprise that their vision dominates the literature on realignment. Still, there is some scholarship that calls into question the rather limited role that elite behavior plays in discussions of realignment. While it would be foolhardy to suggest that realignment is an either/or phenomenon—either mass driven or elite driven—there is reason to believe that elite leadership plays a larger role in the realignment process than the traditional literature would acknowledge.

Stuart Elaine MacDonald and George Rabinowitz argue that change is always going on in the political system and, moreover, change is visible to elites before it becomes incorporated into the "mass party system." New issues are introduced by elites. "Mass publics are slow to understand and react to" new issues, except for some social issues. The two parties must take opposing viewpoints *before* partisan support can change.[75] How exactly does this happen?

There are four steps according to MacDonald and Rabinowitz. First, a new issue is introduced by elites. Second, the new issue causes change in the congressional ideological coalition or in the dialogue between presidential candidates. Third, if the issue has changed ideological coalitions in Congress, that change becomes visible in presidential dialogue, assuming it has not already. Finally, the new ideological cleavage of elites becomes embedded in the mass party system.[76]

The presidency seems to play an important role in this process. Congressional debate is not enough to stimulate change in mass partisanship; it must occur at the presidential level. Even if the new cleavage is present in presidential dialogue, it may take time to take effect at the mass level. The local party apparatus will be slow to catch up and might blur distinctions on the issue. Thus, a new issue needs to sustain vitality over the course of time.[77] Like traditional realignment scholars, Rabinowitz and MacDonald feel that the phenomenon must be *durable* to be called a realignment.

Focusing explicitly on the president, Steven Skowronek argues that an essential characteristic of the presidency is its capacity to "transform" American politics. The presidency is an office that "routinely jolts order and routine elsewhere, one whose normal activities and operations alter system boundaries and recast political boundaries." This transformative characteristic of the presidency is not unstructured. The chief executive must act within a constitutional order, which includes two other branches and which gives him only certain formal powers. But the president does affect the order of the regime in three ways.[78] His office is "order shattering" in that he may "take charge of independent powers" and "exercise them in his own right." He is "order affirming" in that his independent actions must still be justified on constitutional grounds. Finally, the role is "order creating" insofar as each president tries to leave a legacy, either political or institutional, which stands the test of time.

Each president acts within two different contexts, which Skowronek defines in terms of "political time" and "secular time."[79] Political time refers to the specific ideological era in which the president serves. Thus, he will be limited by the view of government power and role of the president that dominates the nation at his time in history. Secular time refers to the evolution of the powers of the presidency and the institutionalization of those powers across the history of the office.

The propensity toward "order shattering" and "order creating" of the presidency will incline the chief executive to react against the dominant governing ideology of his day as he seeks to leave his own unique imprint on history. His goal is also to leave his own mark upon the office for all his successors to use as precedent. Some presidents "have found new ways to order the politics of the republic and release the power of government," writes Skowronek. He includes Jefferson, Jackson, Lincoln, Franklin D. Roosevelt, and Reagan in this group.[80]

There is a cyclical nature to American politics, as a president will either oppose the current governing commitments or support them. Four kinds of politics emerge, depending on the state of the dominant regime (vulnerable or resilient) and the president's stance toward that regime (opposed or affiliated).

Our concern is with the "politics of reconstruction," as this is essentially the concept of realignment. Politics of reconstruction arises in opposition to a vulnerable regime. Skowronek identifies four reconstructive presidents: Jefferson, Jackson, Lincoln, and FDR. In this kind of politics there emerges a consensus in both the Congress and the presidency that there is a deep flaw in the current regime. Like Rabinowitz and MacDonald, Skowronek believes that this realization comes first in Congress and the presidency. Skowronek argues that chief executives are great party builders. The president appeals to the opposition movement to create a new partisan order and forms a coalition to support his new order. The United States is a democracy, after all, so the president must rally the masses to support his reformist agenda. Skowronek argues that only when the other side is completely defeated is a new regime solidified. This may take a battle in the courts, as in the New Deal, or a literal battle, as in the case of the Civil War.[81]

Reconstructing presidents, while they are party builders, are not always responsible to parties because they have a penchant for independent action. What we have is a "presidentially driven sequence of change encompassing the generation and degeneration of coalitional systems or party regimes." Thus, Skowronek concludes, "The politics of leadership forms an essential counterpoint to shifts within the electorate in the explanation of political change. Presidents are the critical agents of interpreting the meaning of elections and translating electoral opportunities into new forms of politics."[82]

Skowronek defines Lincoln as a "reconstructing" president. One might not think that Lincoln would achieve such a status, Skowronek argues, considering the circumstances of his election. Lincoln seemed little more than an inconsequential party regular as he entered the White House. The patronage party system and the strength of Congress limited Lincoln. Skowronek describes his reconstructive presidency as the most "institution-bound" reconstruction up to that point.[83]

Lincoln was skilled at manipulating the political machine and dispensing patronage, argues Skowronek. Further, Lincoln's oratorical abilities helped him shape a Republican Party devoid of charismatic leadership. Lincoln lacked the reputation of a Jefferson or a Jackson. As a leader of a new party he could not fall back on his "party's historical identity," as could Polk or Pierce. But through his speeches, such as his debates with Stephen Douglas in 1858, Lincoln helped shape his own party. The very circumstances of Southern secession and the Civil War lent themselves to both the "order shattering" and "order creating" qualities of the presidency. Lincoln was able to paint a picture of a Democratic conspiracy that had so corrupted the regime that only a "frontal assault" upon the Democratic status quo was legitimate. Lincoln is thus an order-shattering president with "order affirming pretensions." Lincoln claimed to be simply protecting the Constitution while at the same time arguing that such protection requires radical change, such as freeing the slaves and destroying the Southern economic and social system.[84]

Lincoln was fortunate that the Southerners played right into his hands. Southern secession was itself an order-shattering act. The Confederacy and the Civil War gave Lincoln the legal grounding and the public support, at least in the North, to "fashion the Republican party's latent revolutionary ambitions."[85]

In 1864 Lincoln ran under the title of the Union Party.[86] This name shift suggests that Lincoln wanted to be a party builder in the tradition of Jefferson and Jackson.[87] While Jackson was able to shape his party in his own image, and later FDR was forced to abandon party as a mode of reconstruction, Lincoln held a middle ground of strongly molding his party's form while being subject to a strong party system. Still, it is Lincoln who was the driving force behind the new political order. Like the "bottom-up" theorists, Skowronek and Rabinowitz and MacDonald see interplay between the electorate and elite leadership, but these "top-down" theorists argue that the changes that occur in our politics start with those elites as they guide the electorate to accept radical changes.

This discussion suggests three questions to be addressed by our later examination of the Republican realignment. First, we must look at the prehistory of the Republican Party. What caused the demise of the Whig Party and the rise of the Republicans? Another question is whether the realignment was a "bottom-up" or "top-down" phenomenon. What leaders were influential in the rise of the Republicans, and was Lincoln one of them? Next, we must ask whether domestic policy motivated this realignment. Was it issues, ideology, events, or some combination of the three? Was the realignment of the 1850s driven by economics, or was slavery the overwhelming issue that caused seismic shifts in partisan ties? Rabinowitz and MacDonald say issues pushed by elites drive realignments. Finally, we must ask whether the Republican agenda of the late 1850s depended largely on Lincoln, or whether the early history of the Republican Party gave an indication of the issues that would finally bring the party to power. Thus we should keep the realignment era of the late 1850s in mind as we investigate the activities of the Thirty-Seventh and Thirty-Eighth Congresses. So the discussion now turns toward the realignment of the 1850s and Lincoln's role in ushering in a new partisan era. Following that discussion we will move to a consideration of domestic policy in the Lincoln administration to assess the presidential power and public policy aspects of the "revolutionary thesis."

5

★ ★ ★ ★ ★

Whigs and Lincoln:
A Realignment Reconsidered

To understand Lincoln's presidential statesmanship, one must first grasp the political trends that swept Lincoln into office. Lincoln obviously did not operate in a political vacuum. He lived and participated in a political world and belonged to a Republican Party that stood for particular things. One of the more remarkable aspects to the rise of Lincoln is the disappearance of a major party, the Whigs, and its replacement by another major party. This is heretofore the only time in American history that such a change in party arrangements has occurred.

This chapter represents an investigation of the extent to which non-slavery issues had a part in the emergence of the Republican Party and whether Lincoln played a major role as an elite in forming a new party based on those ideas. The discussion begins with a brief overview of the Free-Soil Party. The short life of this minor party represents the first indication of weakness in the Whig coalition. The chapter proceeds to consider the death of the Whig Party and the issues surrounding that demise. I go on to explore the relative importance of slavery and economic issues in the ascendancy of the Republican Party. The chapter concludes with an assessment of the role of political elites in the formation of the new party, with an emphasis on Lincoln.

In an age with a much stronger party system than we observe today, voters went to the polls in 1860 voting not just for a man but for a party. We must take into account what the Republican Party stood for and ask how central to the Republican Party appeal were the issues that would become the domestic agenda of the Civil War Congresses. When members of the electorate voted for Republicans, did they think they were voting for an antislavery party, an economic nationalist party, or both? To what extent can it be said that the electorate endorsed the ensuing "domestic" legislation of the Civil War Congresses? One aspect of the revolutionary thesis is that Lincoln spearheaded an electoral realignment based on economic issues and this realignment gave Lincoln the political power to introduce revolutionary economic legislation during the Civil War.

When contemplating the realignment of the 1850s, one must also ponder the origin of the change in party fortunes. Was there a transformation in public opinion that caused voters to abandon the Whig Party and spontaneously form a new Republican Party, or was it political leaders who foresaw the weakness of the Whig Party as an opportunity for a new party to emerge? Perhaps political elites ascertained the new conflicts of the 1850s earlier than the electorate and then led the people to a new party that better spoke to the emerging issues of the day. The query, then, is whether Lincoln was one of those elites.

Free Soil, Free Labor, Free Men

We have discussed the rise of the Whig Party and Lincoln's connection to it previously while articulating Lincoln's economic vision. So let us here simply summarize that narrative. The Whig Party arose from the so-called National Republicans, who split with the Jacksonian wing of the Democratic Party over the Jacksonian resistance to government action promoting economic growth and the perception by some that Jackson was abusing presidential power. So the basic foundation of the party was support for economic nationalism and opposition to the populist presidency. Eventually Henry Clay's "American System" would form the core of the Whig economic vision. We have seen how the Whig faith in the "right to rise" was one of the main factors drawing Lincoln to the party. Lincoln supported the economic dynamism represented by the Whigs and condemned the feudal capitalism of the slaveholding South. But changing times, particularly the emergence of slavery as the central national political issue, and the Whigs' failure to respond to these changes ultimately doomed the party.

How is it then that this unique event in American political history, the replacement of one major party with another, took place? To understand this phenomenon we have to leave for a moment a direct discussion of Lincoln and look at the partisan trends of Lincoln's time. It is the contention of James Sundquist that the origins of the Republican Party can be traced as far back as 1831, when William Lloyd Garrison founded the abolitionist newspaper the *Liberator.*[1] Perhaps this is something of an exaggeration, but certainly the origins of the Republican Party originate before its actual creation in 1854. Some argue that the Free-Soil movement and party of the late 1840s served as an indication of the instability of the party system.[2] By the mid-1840s, prominent politicians, many of them Whigs, like Salmon Chase of Ohio, had become dissatisfied with the current party structure and were looking for a party with stronger antislavery principles. In Chase's opinion the Whigs were destined for permanent minority status, so if he was going to be in the minority, he might as well do so in a party that more faithfully expressed his free-soil inclinations.[3] Chase would go on to become one of the most effective organizers of the new party as it worked toward fielding candidates for the 1848 election.[4]

The basis of the Free-Soil Party was opposition to the extension of slavery into the territories. This became an issue as early as 1844 as the nation debated the annexation of Texas into the Union. Some of the more sober antislavery men recognized that an antislavery party could not win with a radical abolitionist platform. The earlier discussion of political prudence noted that Lincoln was one of these sober men. The contention was that the antislavery movement needed to be more politically savvy than the more radical elements had been. Free-Soil leaders sought to broaden the appeal of the defunct Liberty Party, which had run in 1844 as a strong abolitionist party.[5] Thus Chase and other leaders formed a party around non-extension rather than around direct action against slavery. This free-soil ideology of the party mirrors that of the forthcoming Republican Party. In addition to keeping the West free from slavery, Free-Soilers believed in homestead legislation to promote diverse employment. A free West settled by small farmers would promote the respectability of labor so undermined by the quasi-aristocratic plantation system of the South.[6]

In 1848 the Free-Soil Party nominated former president Martin Van Buren as its presidential candidate. Its platform called for "no interference by Congress with Slavery within the limits of any State" but maintained strongly, "It is the duty of the federal government to relieve itself from all responsibility for the existence or continuance of slavery wherever that government possesses constitutional power to legislate on that subject."[7] The party's rejection of the extension of slavery, while allowing it to continue in states where it already existed, was unequivocal. The party also took stands in favor of river and harbor improvements, calling them "objects of national concern," and promoted "reasonable portions of public lands" free of charge to homesteaders.[8] In these later respects the Free-Soil Party out-Whigged the Whig Party, which had long been the champion of such positive uses of national power to encourage economic growth. In 1848 the Whig Party could do little but advocate the election of Zachary Taylor on the grounds that he was a good man and was not a Democrat.[9] Apparently this was good enough, as Taylor won the election over Democrat Lewis Cass of Michigan, with Van Buren finishing a distant third.

The Free-Soil Party would have its successes, but the nation had not yet the reason to abandon the existing party system. The Compromise of 1850 represented an attempt by the two major parties to settle the regional dispute over slavery. To a certain extent they were successful as the candidate for president promoted by the Free-Soil Party (or, as adherents were by then known, the Free Democrats), John Hale, performed even more poorly than had Van Buren. Still, while the Free-Soil Party might have died, the free-soil idea had not. It only needed a better opportunity to come to the fore. First it needed to see the demise of the wounded animal that was the Whig Party.

The death of the Whig Party is somewhat stunning when one considers how swiftly and surely the demise came. In the election cycle of 1846–47, the Whig Party elected 57 percent of the members of the House. In 1848, 71 percent of the governors elected were Whigs. Yet by the early 1850s, the party could win barely a third of House seats. In the Thirty-Third Congress, which passed the Kansas-Nebraska Act, Whigs made up only 35.5 percent of the Senate. By 1856, the party that had won the White House eight years before had ceased to exist.[10] The death of the Whigs is important for this project because we must see what the Whigs were *not* doing before we can appreciate what the Republicans did.

In the late 1840s, there arose a breed of political animal known as the Conscience Whig. These Northern Whigs struggled to move the party toward a more unequivocal stand against slavery. The party should at least oppose slavery's expansion into the western territories, these Whigs believed. In states such as Massachusetts and Ohio, the split among Whigs regarding slavery was so deep in the late 1840s that the two-party system of each state teetered precariously. Recognizing the growing fissures in the party, the Whigs attempted to use the Compromise of 1850, constructed as a last act by the great Whig founder Henry Clay, to come to some resolution of the party's slavery problem. This attempted conciliation seems only to have hastened the death of the party. Provisions for settling the slave question by popular sovereignty in the Utah and New Mexico Territories opened the West to slavery, anathema to Free-Soil-leaning Whigs. Further, the compromise contained a strong fugitive slave provision that many Northern Whigs could not swallow. Despite outlawing the slave trade in the District of Columbia and admitting California as a free state, many Northern Whigs found the compromise antithetical to their free-soil sensibilities.

While attempting to bring unity to the party, the compromise only furthered the split between the Northern and Southern Whigs. Northern Whigs voted overwhelmingly in both the House and the Senate against the popular sovereignty and fugitive slave items in the act.[11] The party was dealt another blow in 1852 when a relatively minor political actor, Democrat Franklin Pierce, beat its presidential candidate, General Winfield Scott, quite soundly. The Whig platform once again did little more than encourage the electorate to vote Whig because Whigs were not Democrats. The party remained silent about traditional Whig issues such as the national bank and use of public lands while advocating a protectionist trade policy and internal improvements.[12] But the platform also contained a plank pledging the party's support for the fugitive slave provision of the 1850 compromise. It was just this kind of sellout to the Southern wing of the party, known as the Cotton Whigs, which caused Northern Whigs to leave the party. John Sherman, onetime Whig and future Republican senator and cabinet member, looked upon the 1852 election as the beginning of the end for the Whig Party.[13]

If the Compromise of 1850 and the weak showing by Scott in the 1852 election showed the feebleness of the Whig Party, the support of Southern Whigs for the Kansas-Nebraska Act doomed it. For men like John Sherman, this was the last straw that caused him to bolt the party for an emerging Republican Party.[14] Kansas-Nebraska, which opened up even more of the West to popular sovereignty and explicitly repealed the Missouri Compromise of 1820, caused free-soil Democrat Henry Wilson of Massachusetts to contemplate forming a new antislavery party with Northern Whigs. The country was in need of "one great Republican party" that would unite all antislavery forces.[15] In Maine, William Pitt Fessenden was one of those Whigs who left the party to join with anti-Nebraska Democrats, gaining election to the U.S. Senate in 1854. By 1855, most Whigs in Maine were Republicans.[16]

The Whig Party was simply not internally strong enough to withstand all of these blows. After leaving Congress in 1849, Abraham Lincoln noted that the new Taylor administration did not use its patronage power to build up the Whig Party. Taylor left Democratic Party members in government jobs while refusing to reward the most loyal of the Whig faithful, like Lincoln himself.[17] Consequently, the party could not depend upon the loyalty of its members when the going got tough. It would not be long after the Kansas-Nebraska issue took over the national debate that

Northern Whigs left for a new party while Cotton Whigs such as Julian Benjamin of Louisiana and Robert Toombs of Georgia would become leaders of the Democratic Party in the Senate.[18] While the Democrats had the support of some Northern men, such as Presidents Pierce of New Hampshire and Buchanan of Pennsylvania, Cotton Whigs increasingly were at odds with their Northern leaders.

So why exactly did the Whig Party die? Was it because their founders, Daniel Webster and Henry Clay, had died, leaving the party leaderless? Was it the slavery issue? Was it the rise of such parties as the Republicans and Know-Nothings? Michael Holt points out that other parties, the Democrats especially, have faced similar threats yet still survived.[19] Holt notes that attempts by the Whigs to blur the distinction between itself and the Democrats met with mixed results. In the 1852 election, both parties accepted the 1850 compromise, but the Whigs still held one view of slavery in the North and another in the South. Also in 1852, the Whigs made a half-hearted attempt to woo Catholics and immigrants, but these constituencies were not buying it; meanwhile, the party succeeded only in irking its significant prohibitionist and nativist elements. Finally, with the glut of gold coming from California gold strikes, there was plenty of money in private hands, leaving the positive state long advocated by the Whigs seemingly unnecessary.[20]

The circumstances of the times made it far easier to supplant a major party than it would be today. Unlike today, there was no government control of election ballots, so there was no hurdle for Republicans and Know-Nothings to jump over to get on the ballot. Also, because of the importance of local and state races, the new parties had an opportunity to create a new party dynamic that was as deep as it was wide. Issues such as prohibition and public support for Catholic schools were local issues.[21] Also, as the U.S. Senate was then elected by state legislatures, these state races took on national importance.[22] In modern times, third-party movements tend to start at the presidential level and not create the grassroots organization necessary to form an enduring party. They tend to be episodic and personality-driven parties. The George Wallace and Ross Perot phenomena provide perfect examples of the tendency for modern third parties to form for a short time around a compelling personality, but they lack any ability to transfer the allegiance from the personality to the party. Republicans, having every electoral and institutional incentive to build a party state by state, did not fall into this trap.

The Whigs died because key elements of the electorate, led by prominent politicians, had both cause and ability to start new parties. The cause was largely a disagreement over slavery, not disagreements over economic matters, although perhaps the party had done itself a disservice by almost ceasing to speak to economics. The task now is to see what issues the Republican Party exploited to take the Whig Party's place as the second major party in America.

Slavery and the Birth of the Republican Party

Andrew Crandall does not exaggerate when he writes, "The controversy over slavery in the United States was the source of far-reaching political events."[23] A sharp ideological and sectional division ultimately resulted from the slavery issue and its juxtaposition against American ideals. Whether it was Northern abolitionists and Free-Soilers using the Declaration of Independence to attack slavery or Southern apologists trying to explain the Declaration away, by the 1850s the nation found itself at loggerheads over a problem of deep complexity. How the political parties responded to the growing split in the electorate over slavery would determine their very survival and perhaps the survival of the Union.

The rise of the Liberty Party in 1844 and the Free-Soil Party in 1848 foreshadowed the coming conflict over slavery. Issues such as the tariff and national banking policy had supporters and detractors on both sides of the Mason-Dixon Line. In hindsight it becomes apparent that only slavery split the nation in two. In 1848 the Democrats responded to this new issue with an early version of popular sovereignty, while the Whigs and Zachary Taylor responded by ignoring the issue.[24] Free-Soil men such as Salmon Chase, on the other hand, saw combating slavery as the primary concern. Economic issues were irrelevant as long as slavery existed. There was no more direct affront to the free-labor principle than the ability to hold another person's labor in bondage.[25]

At the turn of the decade, new concerns began to creep into American politics. Anti-Catholicism and temperance movements began to take root. With the Compromise of 1850 and the Kansas-Nebraska Act of 1854, slavery went in a few short years from being a side issue to the dominant subject. Free-Soil went from fringe to mainstream. New issues meant new political movements. These movements founded new parties, namely the Republican and Know-Nothing Parties, rather than attaching to old ones. While the Whigs had made the mistake of seeming like "me-too" Democrats, white Southerners, Catholics, and immigrants saw the Democratic Party as their defense against new hostile political movements.[26]

Those who would go on to form the Republican Party found slavery to be the impetus to form new political alliances. In his first speech as a congressman, Thaddeus Stevens of Pennsylvania in 1850 proclaimed his belief in the non-extension of slavery in the West.[27] John Sherman likewise recalled that early in his political career he had two "definite ideas in respect to . . . public policy": protectionism and fighting against the extension of slavery.[28] Once of William Pitt Fessenden's first utterances in 1854 as a new senator from Maine was to decry the evils of slavery,[29] and Henry Wilson of Massachusetts noted that every defense of slavery by the South only fueled the ranks of the antislavery movement.[30]

Few events contributed to the birth of the Republican Party more than the Kansas-Nebraska Act. Many, if not most, Americans thought that the slavery question had been settled by the twin compromises of 1820 and 1850. The 1820 measure had brought the slave state of Missouri and the free state of Maine into the Union. It also drew a line at 36° 30' latitude, above which slavery would not be allowed.[31] The 1850 act was needed, as new territory had been acquired to the west. As described above, this new compromise allowed for popular sovereignty in two new territories and the admission of California as a free state. While the 1850 measure had angered many Free-Soilers and likeminded Whigs and Democrats, the Kansas-Nebraska Act sent them to form a new political party based on opposing the Nebraska bill.

Introduced by Illinois Democratic senator Stephen Douglas early in 1854, the Kansas-Nebraska Act intended to set up the terms by which the states of Kansas and Nebraska would become organized out of the Nebraska Territory. Douglas suggested that the principle of popular sovereignty should guide how the new states would deal with slavery. In other words, the federal government would not dictate the new states' slave laws but instead leave the matter to them to settle as they saw fit. This was problematic, however, as the area in question was covered by the Missouri Compromise and obviously north of the 36° 30' line. Thus, Douglas included a provision repealing the sacred compromise.

To folks dedicated to the non-extension of slavery, this was anathema. In their view, the repeal of the Missouri Compromise opened the entire West to slavery. It also established a principle that the federal government had no power over slavery in the federal territories and could not set any conditions on the admission of new states. One must remember that as merely a territory, Nebraska had no sovereignty of its own. The federal government had complete authority, at least until the Kansas-Nebraska Act organized territorial governments. To many Northern Whigs, Northern Democrats, and Free-Soilers, the Kansas-Nebraska Act seemed like an attempt by the South to extend slavery all over the West and thus strengthen the slave power's weakening hold on the national government. Douglas was the tool of the South, as he needed Southern support to gain the Democratic presidential nomination in 1856.[32]

Horace Greeley traced the beginnings of the Republican Party to Kansas-Nebraska, noting that it roused latent antislavery feelings in the North.[33] Historians Coy Cross and Andrew Crandall agree that the Republican Party was created to fight against the extension of slavery.[34] In the words of Hans Trefousse, biographer of Radical Republicans Thaddeus Stevens and Benjamin Wade, the Nebraska bill "destroyed the Whigs, weakened the Democrats, and gave rise to the emergence of new organizations, of which the Republican party . . . proved the most lasting."[35]

Republican John Sherman of Ohio pronounced that if moderate Whigs and Democrats had held firm to the 1850 compromise, all would have been well, as there were not enough people on the extremes of the issue to constitute a majority. But some Democrats, namely Stephen Douglas, made a fatal error by reneging on the old compromises.[36] This drastic move by Douglas caused most people to admit "that the slavery question [was] now of paramount importance."[37]

The losses were not only on the Whig side.[38] Democratic representative Galusha Grow predicted that the Nebraska bill would destroy the Democratic Party in the North. He worked to convince his fellow Pennsylvanian Democrats that their party was now controlled by the Southern slave power, and he left to join the Republicans.[39] Democratic senator Hannibal Hamlin of Maine, who would become Abraham Lincoln's running mate in 1860, eventually resigned as chairman of the Senate Committee on Commerce and quit the party over the repeal of the Missouri Compromise. Being a free-soil-minded Democrat, he saw the pro-slave agitation in his party as dooming his career. If he was ever to gain reelection, he would have to do so as a Republican.[40] Hamlin learned how radical his party had become when he was called to the White House to meet with Democratic president Franklin Pierce. Pierce asked for Hamlin's support for the Nebraska bill, which Hamlin refused. Pierce pushed him. What if support were to become a measure of party loyalty? Hamlin still refused and became one of four Democrats to vote against the measure in the Senate. He knew his days in the Democratic Party were over.[41]

State after state organized new parties based upon opposition to slavery. In Maine, Hamlin and Lot Morrill held a meeting in Augusta to form a new party based upon support for the old compromises.[42] New York saw a split in the Whig Party, with William Seward carrying the anti-Nebraska forces into the Republican Party, while Millard Fillmore brought the more conservative Whigs into the Know-Nothing Party.[43] Pennsylvanians organized a new party based upon the dual principles of no more slave states and combating Franklin Pierce as a tool of the slave power.[44] In Ohio, all members of Congress who had voted for

Kansas-Nebraska lost in their next election, turned out by a fusion of anti-Nebraska Democrats and Free-Soilers.[45] Schuyler Colfax told the anti-Nebraska forces of Indiana that they should, "without renouncing any of their political principles[,] . . . unite their forces with honest men of all parties . . . and fearlessly strike a manly, earnest, telling blow in favor of freedom."[46] In Iowa, a new party quickly and smoothly formed around opposition to Kansas-Nebraska.[47]

The Thirty-Fourth Congress, the first elected after Kansas-Nebraska had passed, contained an "unusual proportion" of members new to politics, a sign of the shakeup of parties caused by the act.[48] That same Congress elected, by a plurality, Nathaniel Banks of Massachusetts as Speaker of the House. Banks opposed the Kansas-Nebraska Act. While still relatively unorganized and needing the support of Know-Nothings to get Banks elected, Republicans had accomplished a great deal in a very short time. At the beginning of 1854 the party had not existed. By the end of 1855 it had elected a Speaker of the House. In 1857 Stephen Douglas broke with his fellow Democrats over phony electioneering in Kansas by pro-slave forces, leaving the Democratic Party divided and weak. The Republican Party could smell blood in the water. All it needed was the right appeal to push it to majority party status. But while slavery had given rise to the party and given it its first successes, it would take more to win the presidency.

Economic Issues and the Birth of the Republican Party

There is no doubt that the opposition to slavery formed the cornerstone of the Republican message. But there are a host of other issues, some of which would become part of the domestic agenda of the Civil War Congresses and helped put the party over the top electorally.

Some argue that ethno-cultural issues such as nativism and temperance were as central as any to the death of the Whigs and rise of the Republicans.[49] Yet these issues had their own standard-bearer in the Know-Nothing Party. It is true that this party was very strong in the North, stronger than Republicans in some places. Some Republican leaders, such as Henry Wilson and Schuyler Colfax, were also members of the "secret society" of Know-Nothings.[50] While some major leaders, such as Salmon Chase, were happy to work with the nativist party if it suited their ends, others such as Charles Sumner, William Seward, and Abraham Lincoln opposed the nativist movement to one degree or another. Indeed, Seward may have cost himself the presidential nomination in 1860 by being too strongly allied with anti-nativist sentiments. But here nativist influence, such as it was, more denied the nomination to

Seward than gave it to non-nativist (and privately anti-nativist) Lincoln. The Know-Nothing Party most served the Republicans as a bridge for former conservative Whigs into the Republican Party.[51]

The economic issues that would spur the domestic agenda of the Civil War years were far more central to the Republicans than nativism and temperance. The connection of economics to Free-Soil politics was clear in the 1848 Free-Soil platform, which promoted the improvement of rivers and harbors and land grants for Western settlers and was also pro-tariff.[52] This was in stark contrast to the Democratic Party platform of 1848, which proclaimed that "the Federal Government is one of limited powers" that had no rightful power to "carry on a general system of internal improvements." The Democratic platform also denounced any protective tariff that would "foster one branch of industry to the detriment of another."[53] The early Republican Party, though, was more cautious when it came to economics and the use of government power. Being an amalgam of various types of politics united only by an opposition to slavery, the party had an interest in keeping the discussion of economics to a minimum. Most early state platforms dealt only with slavery and avoided these economic differences.[54] Indeed, many of the most radical Republicans felt that economics was much debated because the subject was "sectionally innocuous" and obscured the real issue of slavery.[55]

The driving force of the early Republican Party was overwhelmingly antislavery sentiment, and since the party wanted to differentiate itself from the Whig Party, this could best be done on slavery grounds, not economics.[56] William Pitt Fessenden was convinced that all other disagreements should be set aside in the fight against slavery.[57] In Pennsylvania the party ignored such hot-button issues as immigration, the tariff, and homestead legislation to keep intraparty clashes to a minimum.[58]

This was still the strategy during the 1856 election. The party platform did include economic planks, but only those "that were safe vote getters in the North"; this meant advocating a Pacific railroad and internal improvements.[59] Primarily it was an anti-Nebraska platform. But in the aftermath of John C. Frémont's defeat, the party recognized that it could not win as a single-issue party. It needed to have some appeal in border states such as Maryland, Kentucky, and Missouri. Also, the Democrats had craftily run Pennsylvanian James Buchanan, ensuring themselves of the hefty Electoral College prize that was his home state. Republicans knew that if they were to compete for this electorally significant state, they would have to push harder for a tariff. This was a crucial issue for steel-producing Pennsylvanians, as they sought protection against foreign competition. Advocating a high tariff would not only gain the party votes but also secure the financial backing of pro-protection industrialists.[60] The Republicans could also help themselves in the West with economic issues. The untamed West was naturally more in favor of internal improvement projects supported by the federal government than was the already developed East. Also, Westerners favored strong banking legislation, as they did not have the advanced state banking systems of the East. Homestead legislation held out the promise of development for the relatively poor West.[61]

Between the 1856 and 1860 elections, the Republicans worked hard to exploit economic issues. They were helped tremendously by a severe economic downturn in 1857, which allowed them to attack the Buchanan administration for failing to act on many of the economic ideas now springing forth from Republicans. State party platforms in 1859 and 1860 capitalized on the recession by promoting economic issues far more than in 1855–56. In Pennsylvania, Thaddeus Stevens attacked Buchanan for opposing a needed tariff hike, thus hurting the economy and particularly the workingman.[62]

Republicans began exploiting Southern opposition to homestead legislation. On this issue, the South was in a bind. Southerners were in need of Western political support, but they were afraid that homestead legislation would cause the migration of antislavery Northerners and European immigrants to the new Western states.[63] Pennsylvanian Galusha Grow worked tirelessly for homestead legislation in the House of Representatives. When he finally got a bill passed in the Thirty-Sixth Congress, only one Northerner opposed the bill and only one Southerner voted for it. Western Democrats began to worry that Southern Democratic opposition to homestead legislation had doomed the party in the West.[64] The Republicans were fully aware of this. They passed the bill knowing Buchanan would veto it, ever the captive of Southern interests. But they also knew that it would embarrass the Democratic Party in the eyes of Westerners.[65] In the Thirty-Sixth Congress, Republicans gave the greatest support of all political factions to such legislation as the Homestead Act, a land-grant college bill, the Morrill Tariff, a railroad bill, and a rivers and harbors improvement bill. Pro-Buchanan Democrats opposed all of these bills, and Buchanan vetoed the Homestead Act and the land-grant college bill.[66]

By 1860 the Republicans had learned their lesson well: the 1860 platform promoted homestead legislation, a tariff, and a Pacific railroad.[67] The platform demanded "the passage by Congress of the complete and satisfactory homestead measure which has already passed the House." Tariff rates, proclaimed the Republicans, needed to be raised to the level that would "encourage the development of the industrial interests of the whole country." Finally, the platform stated, "a railroad to the Pacific

Ocean is imperatively demanded by the interest of the whole country."
Thus the government "ought to render immediate and efficient aid in
its construction."[68] It did not hurt that the Republicans nominated Abe
"Rail-Splitter" Lincoln, tied to the railroad by myth and in reality by
the extensive legal work he had done for railroad interests in Illinois.
As Allen Nevins describes it, there were four key aspects to the 1860
Republican campaign. First, opposition to slavery in the territories was
crucial. Second, Republicans painted the Democrats as corrupt. Next,
Republicans avoided discussing anti-immigrant legislation. Last, they
supported the tariff, agricultural colleges, homestead legislation, the railroad, and internal improvements. They tailored the economic message
to the audience, pushing tariffs in Pennsylvania while promoting the
homestead bill in the West.

The transformation in the party can be expressed by the shift of
Salmon Chase on the issue of protectionism. Many former Democrats
who turned Republican modified their opposition to the tariff when
they recognized the importance of winning Pennsylvania.[69] Chase was
no exception. In 1855 he wrote, "I believe in free trade and would gladly
see all the world adopt its principles."[70] By 1860, prospective presidential
nominee Chase had figured out that opposition to the tariff was not such
a wise political position in the Republican Party. When rumors circulated
that he was a free trader, he put out the word that duties for the "encouragement of our home industry" were his idea of sound public policy. He
even tried to get John Sherman to go to Pennsylvania to convince its
residents that Chase was a protectionist.[71]

With no public opinion polls available, it is impossible to say whether
the Republican Party's newfound interest in economic issues turned the
1860 election in its favor. After all, its presidential candidate received only
39 percent of the vote. But, on the other hand, Lincoln won the states of
Pennsylvania, Indiana, Illinois, and California, all of which had gone to
Buchanan in 1856. In these moderate states, where Whiggism and Know-
Nothingism had been strong, it was essential for the party to move beyond
the image of a single-issue party and broaden its appeal. No doubt the
protectionism of the party helped win Pennsylvania, while its advocacy of
homestead legislation was certainly popular in the new states of Oregon
and Minnesota, both of which it won. Both Oregon and California stood
to benefit greatly from a Pacific railroad. All Midwestern and Western
states had a stake in agricultural colleges and internal improvements.
Perhaps it could be said that while economics was not the basis of the
Republican Party's birth, it did play a necessary role by cementing the
electoral realignment that culminated in the victory of 1860.

Leadership and the Republican Realignment

That economics seems crucial to the ultimate electoral success of the Republican Party is relevant in that it shows that Republicans could claim something of a mandate for the innovative public policies they passed into law in the Civil War Congresses. The presence of Lincoln was key, as some of these measures, namely the Homestead Act and Land-Grant College Act, had been vetoed by his predecessor, Democrat James Buchanan. Of more immediate importance is assessing the degree to which Lincoln, like a modern president might be, was a leader in forming the new Republican Party.

Certainly there were giants among the founders of the Republican Party. As early as 1854 William Seward saw the West and the Kansas-Nebraska Act as an opportunity to create a party unified in the way his Whig Party was not.[72] And Eric Foner argues that "no one did more to formulate an anti-slavery program in political terms than Salmon Chase of Ohio." The *New York Tribune* declared that Chase had made antislavery "the inspiration of a great political party,"[73] and Chase himself smugly claimed in 1860 that neither Seward nor Lincoln nor Missouri's Edward Bates had done a tenth for the party as he had.[74] It was in 1854 that Chase and other Democrats in Congress (Charles Sumner and Joshua Giddings were two) authored *Appeal of the Independent Democrats*, a widely read pamphlet urging Democrats to oppose Stephen Douglas and the Nebraska bill.

While Chase and Seward have as good a claim as any for national leadership in inspiring the party, the actual work was done on a state-by-state basis. In Maine, after the passage of the Nebraska bill, William Fessenden immediately set out to establish a sectional antislavery party in the North. By autumn such a party had been loosely formed around a non-extension plank.[75] Benjamin Wade of Ohio and Senators Hale and James Bell from New Hampshire ventured to Maine to help in the party's formation,[76] and Representative Anson Morrill of Maine worked with Whigs and Know-Nothing leaders to create a workable party organization.[77] In New York, Seward gave major speeches in 1855 and 1856 that attempted to place the Nebraska issue in a larger context. In speeches in Albany and Buffalo in 1855 he "offered the most important statement . . . of the Republican party's purposes and goals."[78] In Pennsylvania, leading Democrat David Wilmot of the famous Wilmot Proviso abandoned the party,[79] and Thaddeus Stevens took the lead in signing a declaration asking that all antislavery men join a new Republican Party to fight the slave power.[80] In Ohio, Chase organized all sorts of antislavery groups into one movement, and by the summer of 1855 an unnamed party had been established.[81] An Iowa meeting of "lawyers, farmer, newspaper editors . . . leading non-extentionist Whigs [and] Know Nothing chieftains" resulted in the formation of a new party.[82] In state after state, leading men took the initiative in exploiting the Nebraska issue, seizing the moment to form a new antislavery party. While it is difficult to lead people where they do not already want to go, people also need organization. These politically savvy men coalesced a latent antislavery feeling into a major party apparatus.

In this effort they had the support of the nightly news anchors, political pundits, and bloggers of the day: the newspapermen. The influence of Horace Greeley and the *New York Tribune* was enormous, as this paper was one of the few with a truly national readership.[83] John Medill, owner of the *Chicago Tribune*, was a backer of Salmon Chase and the Republican cause,[84] and the *Tribune*, along with the *St. Louis Democrat*—a Republican paper despite its name—were instrumental in stoking the fires over the Kansas-Nebraska issue.[85] Early Republicans knew that formation of newspapers was important, as they were needed for spreading propaganda and changing opinion.[86]

The party leaders also recognized that having men of stature in Washington to set the agenda was crucial. William Seward, Henry Wilson, Lyman Trumbull, and others went to Washington in 1855 to provide anti-Nebraska forces with the national leadership they so needed.[87] It was the national stature of Chase, Giddings, and Sumner that made the *Appeal of the Independent Democrats* so influential. The break of national leaders from the Democratic Party had far more import than a purely localized split. Members of Congress pushed the anti-Nebraska agenda to keep it in the public eye.

In early 1856 the major figures in the party, spurred on by Chase, organized a meeting in Pittsburgh to create a national Republican organization. This was clearly necessary if the party was to run a credible candidate for president later that year. State organizations had to be brought together to form a coherent strategy. At that meeting a national committee was formed with Frank Blair of Maryland as the chairman. This national committee planned to coordinate the local organizations that, in turn, would register with the national organization. This way, when the national party made decisions or put out literature, it could efficiently spread word across the nation through its network of local organizations.[88] According to Andrew Crandall, "From the time of the convention forward, the progress of the party was pretty largely usurped by the newcomers and managed from Washington."[89]

The Republican Party was formed state by state by the leading men of each state. It can be said the creation of the Republican Party required both an issue and men equal to the task of forming a new party. It had the issue in the Kansas-Nebraska Act. This piece of legislation shocked Northerners, most of whom were antislavery and assumed that the West would remain free from slavery; Kansas-Nebraska proved them wrong. As for leadership, it was ably supplied by men such as Horace Greeley, Salmon Chase, William Seward, Nathaniel Banks, and a number of others who broke from their old parties to set a new course in American politics. Perhaps doing so was mere expediency; Whigs like Seward probably saw that their party was dying anyway, and ambitious Democrats like Chase and Sumner recognized that they could never get ahead in the Democratic Party.[90]

Assessing Lincoln on this matter is a difficult task. On the one hand, Lincoln was the first Republican president. On the other hand, he was relatively late in joining the party. Although quite a political operative in his own right, Lincoln's greatest gift to the party seems to have been his ability to articulate better than any leading man of the time precisely why opposition to the extension of slavery was important enough to split from old alliances and form new ones.

Perhaps the first bit of national attention that came Lincoln's way was his one term in Congress from 1847 to 1849. At this time Lincoln already saw the slave issue splitting the Whig Party apart. The Wilmot Proviso, which attempted to keep lands gained in the Mexican War free from slavery, caused tension between Northern Whigs, like Lincoln, and their Southern compatriots. Lincoln seemed to think that the party needed new issues, with opposition to the aggressive use of presidential power being one of them.[91] Lincoln also gained some notoriety at the Whig national convention of 1848, where he was something of a novelty as the lone Whig representative from Illinois.[92]

At that time and previously, as a member of the Illinois General Assembly, Lincoln was a major organizer for the Whig Party in Illinois. In 1852 he stumped for Winfield Scott, although his speeches sounded more like criticisms of Franklin Pierce than recommendations for Scott.[93] In one speech in Springfield he used his time attacking his constant rival Stephen Douglas.[94] A dedicated Whig, Lincoln refused to join the Republican Party when it formed in Illinois in 1854, and he did not attend its convention held in October of that year.[95] The men who organized at the convention named Lincoln to the state central committee anyway.[96] Even in his speeches that fall opposing Douglas and fighting for a non-extension slave policy, Lincoln continued to call himself an "old whig."[97] In the elections that autumn, the anti-Nebraska/Douglas forces in Illinois were an assortment of different parties: some were Republicans, some Whigs, and some simply anti-Nebraska Democrats. Lincoln campaigned for the Whig ticket.[98]

It was not until 1856, a full two years after the Republican Party took shape, that Lincoln finally took the plunge. Early that year he wrote to Republican representative Owen Lovejoy that he was not against a fusion party of antislavery forces, although he was not overtly for it either.[99] But that May he signed a letter with leading men of his home Sangamon County to call for a Republican county convention. At that convention Lincoln gave the "keynote" address.[100] Once a Republican he campaigned heartily for John C. Frémont. He even received some consideration for the vice presidential slot. In the fall of 1856 he traveled all over Illinois, particularly the southern half, and made a campaign trip to Kalamazoo, Michigan.[101] He wrote letters to his old Whig friends attempting to persuade them to support the Republican ticket over Millard Fillmore and the Know-Nothings.[102]

After the loss of Frémont to Buchanan, Lincoln turned all of his energy toward defeating Stephen Douglas and the principle of popular sovereignty. These battles, famously rising to a climax in the Lincoln-Douglas debates of the 1858 Illinois senatorial contest, were exclusively over the subject of slavery. It was the debates with Douglas that propelled Lincoln to national stature; their formal debates were published and distributed nationwide. Lincoln traveled extensively, repeating and refining his arguments. The fall of 1859 found him in Ohio, Indiana, Wisconsin, Iowa, and Kansas espousing his non-extension philosophy. His Indiana and Wisconsin remarks included a defense of free labor principles, although he did not explicitly defend policies like homestead or railroad legislation so connected to that philosophy.[103] Early in 1860 he ventured to the East Coast, delivering his celebrated remarks at Cooper Union in New York City and also visiting Rhode Island, New Hampshire, and Connecticut.[104]

The conclusion by Eric Foner that Lincoln was chosen as the 1860 nominee because he was not a national figure and thus not controversial seems to be incorrect.[105] While Lincoln was not as prominent as Seward or Chase, he was known well enough by leading Republicans across the nation. Even in 1856 he was popular enough to get votes for the vice presidential nomination. By 1860, unlike Seward, he had not taken strong public stances against nativism, and unlike Chase, he had not alienated many party leaders with his arrogance and ambition. Lincoln demonstrated that contrary to the modern bias toward activity and amorphous "change" as the hallmarks of a statesman, sometimes what a statesman does not do is just as important as what he actually does.

Also, over the two years leading up to the nomination, no one had been as articulate as Lincoln in explaining the free labor/antislavery agenda. In doing so he had forced his nemesis, Stephen Douglas, to take positions that would alienate Douglas from Southern Democrats. This made Douglas electorally unviable and forced the Democrats to split into pro-Douglas and anti-Douglas factions, paving the way for Lincoln to win with just under 40 percent of the popular vote.

Thus, the extent that Lincoln was a national figure was not based on issues such as homestead legislation, railroad legislation, banking legislation, and the other legislation that would be enacted during his administration. The economic issues seem to have been more important to congressional Republicans who needed to differentiate themselves from Democrats. But Lincoln did help shape the party's language regarding slavery, eloquently arguing for the place of morality in the politics of slavery.

It seems fair to conclude that economics played a significant part in the realignment of the 1850s. While economic questions did not create the fissure in the electorate that would lead to a seismic shift in partisan alignment, economics seems nonetheless to have been essential to Republican success in the critical election of 1860. One could say that the Republican Party arose because of slavery, but it was economic issues that put it "over the top." Without doubt the institution of slavery was the driving force behind the political conflict of the age. Charles Beard and Mary Beard are wrong in their view that the Republican Party was formed by men "who thought the less said about slavery the better."[106] There was symmetry between Republican opposition to slavery and the promotion of government activism for economic development. Both slavery and agrarian economics were opposed to the "right to rise." The evidence seems to indicate that while opposition to slavery alone could have helped Republicans supplant the Whigs, slavery alone would not have catapulted them into a majority party. The Whig position of fence straddling was not tenable. If an actual realignment requires a sustained shift in partisan alignment, it seems doubtful that Republicans would have experienced prolonged success based on slavery alone.

By the end of the decade, the Republicans had learned to exploit the Southern Democrats on economic questions. Economic ties between the North and West were growing. Republicans cemented these ties by forcing Southerners and the Democrat Buchanan to oppose homestead legislation of great interest to the West. The South opposed homestead legislation in order to keep the relatively antislavery West, consisting of small farms rather than large, slave-dependent plantations as in the South, unpopulated and perennially weak. Both on slavery and on economic issues, the South appears to have been on its way to political isolation. Defending an agrarian/slave society in the face of an oncoming industrialization definitely put the South against the prevailing economic winds. On economic issues as well as slavery, the South and the Democratic Party, which supported its institutions, were fighting a losing battle against progress.

At the same time, it does not seem that Lincoln can be given much credit for leading the party on economic issues. Lincoln was certainly as dedicated to Whig economics as anybody. However, during a speech at a Republican banquet in late 1856 Lincoln said, "Let past differences, as nothing be; and with steady eye on the real issue, let us reinaugurate the good old 'central ideas' of the Republic."[107] It seems quite clear that the "real issue" Lincoln had in mind was slavery. He wanted past differences on other matters put aside in order to focus on slavery. There is no evidence that he opposed the new emphasis by Republicans on economic issues during the 1860 election. Yet, it does not seem Lincoln was especially forceful in pushing these issues to the forefront. While Leonard Curry suggested that the contending wings of the Republican Party differed on the role of government, at least through the 1860 election the party was united on basic principles and policies. It is possible that once in power they disagreed on how best to put their beliefs into law. It is reasonable to conclude that the Republican Party was the inheritor of the Whig economic vision, although this vision was subsumed by slavery, especially during the party's formative years. Many Whigs were so committed to these principles that they were reluctant to leave the party for the upstart Republicans. Lincoln can be counted in this number. As the party nominee in 1860, Lincoln certainly would have been aware of the importance placed on tariffs in the key state of Pennsylvania and the appeal of homestead legislation in the West. These policies were in harmony with Lincoln's own views, and he would support these and other economic nationalist legislation as president.

Still, the evidence does not suggest Lincoln as a revolutionary political leader. Lincoln's path into Republicanism was cautious and pragmatic. The idea that Lincoln was at the tip of a revolutionary spear would be to suggest that Whig economics that had been articulated for the previous three decades had suddenly become "revolutionary" and also that Lincoln was at the forefront of the advancement of this economic revolution. What is more likely is that it was precisely because Lincoln did not appear revolutionary and hyper-ambitious, in contrast to Seward and Chase, that he was the consensus candidate of the Republicans in 1860. Lincoln's approach to the political party was similar to Jeffrey Tulis's assessment of Lincoln's presidential rhetoric: sometimes less is more. Tulis argues that it was Lincoln's cautious use of rhetoric that made his words so effectual. Because he did not make promises he could not keep or speak before all information was gathered, Lincoln avoided having to backtrack on his word or having events shift in ways to make him look weak. This is similar to Lincoln's approach to his rise in the party. He did cultivate party leaders and was willing to play the good soldier. But he took positions on inessential items only after it was clear the party had consensus. The idea of Lincoln as a revolutionary party leader simply does not hold up to scrutiny.

6

★ ★ ★ ★ ★

The Domestic Lincoln and
Congressional Government

The previous chapter led to the conclusion that Lincoln did not exhibit presidential party building or revolutionary leadership in the rise of the Republican Party. We now turn to the two other perspectives in political science mentioned earlier to help with our evaluation of the Lincoln presidency, namely those of public policy and the theory of the modern presidency.

Conventional wisdom says that, while Lincoln may have been aggressive in conducting the Civil War, he was unwilling to push important domestic legislation through Congress. This would conform to Lincoln's own Whig political values that included presidential deference to Congress. Gabor Boritt argues that Lincoln's "political education" inclined him against any influence, direct or indirect, over Congress.[1] David Herbert Donald calls Lincoln a "Whig in the White House," noting that Lincoln never addressed Congress in person.[2]

The Republican Congress was often in need of strong leadership, and the party had difficulty holding to a coherent agenda. Historian Burton Hendrick observed, "The so-called party comprised several groups, under chieftains personally hostile and full of jealousy and rivalry."[3] While members found some agreement on tariffs, the party was more split over such issues as government subsidies of a Pacific railroad, use of public lands for colleges and universities, and the introduction of paper currency to complement hard specie.[4] Further, with Thaddeus Stevens as chair of the House Ways and Means Committee and thus the de facto party floor leader, "the Republicans had a man who demanded loyalty from his colleagues . . . but was himself a model of insubordination."[5] Members of Congress were not necessarily open to presidential influence. Given "their belief in congressional prerogatives . . . the possibility of accepting presidential initiatives unquestioningly probably never occurred to them."[6]

But other evidence suggests that Lincoln may have exerted some influence over Congress. At a minimum, as a Westerner and a former Whig he could be counted on not to veto such policies as homestead legislation, high tariffs, and internal improvements. There are examples of direct administration influence on Congress. For instance, Lincoln met with Galusha Grow, Speaker of the House in the Thirty-Seventh Congress, "several times each week."[7] It was well known that Lincoln's Treasury secretary, Salmon Chase, had a close relationship with Thaddeus Stevens.[8] Lincoln's presidential secretaries John Hay and John Nicolay wrote that Lincoln "sometimes made suggestions of financial measures . . . and when the Secretary [of the Treasury] needed his powerful assistance with Congress he always gave it ungrudgingly." During "frequent and informal conferences at the Executive Mansion he exerted all his powers of influence and persuasion to assist the Secretary in obtaining what legislation was needed."[9]

Chase has been described by Gabor Boritt as "a good Hamiltonian, and a Western progressive of the Lincoln stamp in everything from a tariff to a national bank."[10] The earlier discussion of Chase's political genealogy should cause us to doubt the description of him as Hamiltonian. Still, by the time he became secretary of the Treasury he was more amiable to strong government than he had been in the past. He also was one of the few cabinet members with whom Senate members were content.[11] One key senator, Finance Committee chairman William Fessenden, had close contact with Chase and was "reluctant to oppose" him.[12] Coincidently, Fessenden would replace Chase as secretary of the Treasury.

These general statements suggest that Lincoln and his administration were not hermetically sealed off from Congress on domestic matters. This chapter will analyze the passage of key domestic legislation of the Thirty-Seventh Congress to highlight any Lincoln administration influence over the passage of that legislation. James McPherson points to the following pieces of legislation as forming the foundation of the "second American Revolution": tariff legislation, a homestead act, the Land-Grant College Act, the Pacific Railroad Act, the creation of an income tax, and the National Banking and Legal Tender Acts.[13] This chapter studies this legislation with the exception of the tariff (the famous "Morrill Tariff" became law on March 2, 1861, two days before Lincoln became president), which will be considered only as part of the internal revenue act of 1862, and explores whether the administration attempted to influence Congress on the nonwar legislation that made its way through Congress during those tumultuous times. On the whole, the evidence will suggest little in the way of presidential leadership in the manner of modern presidents.

Land Legislation

In one of his few policy statements between his election and inauguration, on February 12, 1861, in Cincinnati, Lincoln said that he favored improving the conditions of man and ameliorating the position of the poor. He stated that the Homestead Act would help accomplish both ends.[14] Homestead legislation had been a crucial component of the Republican platform of 1860, as it attracted Westerners into the Republican fold. Homestead proposals had been enacted in previous Congresses, only to see them vetoed by Democratic presidents, most recently by Buchanan in the summer of 1860.[15] With a Westerner like Lincoln in the White House, victory seemed inevitable.

In reality, it was not so simple. Republicans themselves were split over the legislation despite the fact that the 1860 Republican platform demanded "the passage by Congress of the complete and satisfactory homestead measure which has already passed the House."[16] As debate on the bill began in the winter of 1861, among the leaders of the opposition was Republican Justin Morrill of Vermont, who was sponsor of the land-grant college proposal. Morrill feared that homestead legislation would expropriate land he needed for his college bill. Morrill's view was also that the Homestead Act represented a giveaway of land much needed to buttress the nation's credit. His college bill, he argued, would actually increase the value of the land.[17] Republican George Julian of Indiana countered by saying the Western lands no longer brought any revenue to the government. The government should let people improve the land, he maintained, to make money and expand the tax base. Julian stated that if the lands were "cut up into small farms, to be tilled by their occupants, who will build villages, school houses, and churches . . . and organize civil communities in the wilderness," the whole country "will share in the blessing and benefits" of public lands.[18] This sentiment was echoed by Speaker Grow, who stepped down from the chair to state that the "real wealth" of the nation was not in "the sums of money paid into the Treasury, but in its flocks, its herds, and cultivated fields, and above all in the comfort of its laboring classes; not in its mass of wealth, but its diffusion."[19]

The Homestead Act was finally signed into law May 20, 1862 (An Act to Secure Homesteads to Actual Settlers on the Public Domain). Besides

Lincoln's remark in early 1861 regarding the concept of a homestead bill, there does not seem to have been much administration agitation for such legislation. The congressional debate barely even mentioned the executive branch, only once citing an Interior Department report proving Representative Julian's point that public lands had ceased yielding revenue to the government.[20] In the end, the Homestead Act was relatively uncontroversial. The bill first passed the House, 107–16, and the Senate, 33–7.[21] After a conference committee ironed out some differences, both chambers passed the final version of the bill without a recorded vote.[22]

The proposal for land grants for colleges and universities provided each state with 30,000 acres of public land for each representative and senator. In Western states with large tracts of federally owned land, the state would select actual parcels of land. Other states would receive scrip, which they could sell. The proceeds from the sale of land scrip would then be invested in a fund to pay "the endowment, support, and maintenance of at least one college" in each state.[23]

Like homestead legislation, Buchanan had vetoed a previous land-grant college act. But unlike the homestead proposal, the 1860 Republican platform did not endorse any land-grant college schemes. Still, the act had broad support among Republicans. The only opposition came from Western state congressmen concerned about Eastern states acting as absentee owners of land within their own states. This was the only objection to the bill as it worked its way through the Senate.[24] After passing the Senate, it was approved by the House with virtually no debate. In fact the bill was so well known, because of its study in the previous Congress, that it did not even go to committee for consideration.[25] As with the Homestead Act, the Land-Grant College Act (or Morrill Act, as it is sometimes called) had such overwhelming support that the administration needed to provide no pressure for passage. The bill passed the House, 90–25, and the Senate, 32–7.[26]

The same cannot be said for the Pacific railroad bill. While support for the bill was localized in Western states, the opposition heeded no section. Despite the fact that the Republican platform of 1860 and both the Douglas and Breckenridge Democratic platforms supported a Pacific railroad, there was significant opposition to the new railway. The Republican platform called for the federal government to give "immediate and efficient aid in [the] construction [of a Pacific railroad]."[27] The Douglas Democratic platform supported "such Constitutional Government aid as will insure the construction of a Railroad to the Pacific coast," while the Breckenridge wing called for the passage of a bill to aid "at the earliest practicable moment" the railroad from the Mississippi to the Pacific Ocean.[28]

Debated from January to June 1862, the major justification for the railroad legislation was on military grounds. This rationale allowed for executive influence, since military affairs are indisputably under executive jurisdiction. In the House, Republican James Campbell of California cited a report from Secretary of War Edwin Stanton stipulating that troops and supplies could be moved much more efficiently using railways rather than waterways or overland methods. Secretary of War Gideon Welles reported, Campbell also said, that defending the West Coast would be much easier if a railroad were in place.[29] The Welles report caused Campbell to conclude,

> The only way to secure economy, celerity of movement, and certainty is to employ steam. This new element of power has been brought into requisition in all departments of life. To dispense with it now would be to return to the dark ages. Government will derive the benefit from introducing it wherever it can be done, in the military, postal, and other operations of the nation. During the existing rebellion we have been enabled, by means of steamboats and railroads, to concentrate more decisive action on any given point in three months, than otherwise could have been done within one year; and this, too, at one fourth the cost.[30]

Another California Republican, Aaron Sargent, mentioned that the "minister at the Court of St. James," Charles Adams, reported that trade and military needs required a Pacific railroad connecting coasts. Adams argued,

> Our export trade is seriously threatened and can only be preserved by a railway system proportioned to the magnitude of our territory and its natural resources, by which everything that the industry of the country can produce can have its market. The union of the Pacific and sea-board states by an iron road never appeared so clearly a national necessity as it has since the recent threatened rupture with England. *The first and inevitable result of a war with any great naval Power would be the loss of our California possessions.* Whatever may have been the traditional policy of the Government heretofore, some easy, sure, and rapid communication between the Atlantic and the Pacific is now a subject of such a direct national concern that the Government must charge itself with the execution of it without much delay.[31]

Sargent noted that President Lincoln, in a message to the Senate, had passed along a report from the State Department regarding the advanced state of the French railway system.[32]

Sargent also appealed for accountability to the people. Noting that all party platforms endorsed the bill, Sargent stated that a party must keep its "pledges to the people" and not discard promises made before an election.[33] Justin Morrill opposed the bill, stating that he would rather forgo a party plank rather than "knock out my brains" against it. Republican Samuel Fessenden of Maine—William Pitt Fessenden's brother—rejoined, "I think . . . passing this bill is the only way to keep the brains in the Republican party."[34]

Senator Lyman Trumbull typified the opposition to the plan. While some thought the act was merely a payoff to railway interests, Trumbull's argument was constitutional.[35] His contention was that federal government had power to build railroads through territories but not through states.[36] He also disputed the military nature of the bill. Perhaps, if this was a case of military necessity, the federal government could build across states, but there was no necessity. Trumbull pointed out that by the time the railroad was completed, the Civil War would almost certainly be over (and he was correct).[37] Trumbull offered a poison pill amendment changing the eastern terminus of the railroad so as to render Eastern lines unprofitable, but the amendment failed.[38] The railroad bill passed the Senate, 35–5, and the House, 104–21.[39] The large vote difference belies the extent of opposition.

Unlike the Homestead Act and the Land-Grant College Act, no Pacific railroad legislation had ever passed Congress before—not surprising, with such large financial interests affected by this huge undertaking. Perhaps it is not coincidental that the Lincoln administration, and even Lincoln himself to some extent, acted as advocates for the measure. It was advantageous that there was some military connection to justify administrative involvement in the legislative process, though it cannot be said that the administration "lobbied" Congress on the bill. However, the administration did put information in the hands of known supporters.

The significance of these land and transportation policies cannot be overestimated. The Homestead Act and Pacific Railroad Act in particular helped make the West hospitable to settlement: the Homestead Act gave financial incentive for settling the West, and the railroad connected the West to the rest of the country. The railroad also aided in turning a large and dispersed country into one nation, much as Alexander Hamilton and Henry Clay had imagined. If Hamilton and Clay had not anticipated this use of federal authority to promote national unity, one might be tempted to call it revolutionary. Still, there is no evidence regarding these pieces of legislation that Lincoln was intimately involved in their passage; in fact, any action by the executive branch is hard to find excepting the railroad bill. One cannot say, as James McPherson does, that Lincoln was the "principal architect" of these important laws.

Banking and Currency Regulations

According to Lincoln's secretary John Hay, bank legislation was one is-sue that Lincoln and Salmon Chase talked about frequently: "He had generally delegated to [Chase] exclusive control of those matters falling within purview of his department. This matter he had shared in, to some extent."[40] Richard J. Ellis indicates that the banking legislation was one matter in which Lincoln dismissed his usual "Whiggish decorum" of noninterference with Congress.[41] There can be no doubt, on both the Legal Tender Act of 1862 and the National Bank Act of 1863, that Salmon Chase and Congress worked hand in hand. Chase himself believed that one principle of the Republican Party should be a national bank system with the federal government furnishing the bank notes,[42] and the bud-getary stresses caused by war spurred the executive branch to propose legislation to help bring greater order to the nation's financial system and greater power to the federal government to pay for war activities.

On January 23, 1862, Republican John Alley of Massachusetts stated on the floor of Congress three things needed to buttress the economy. First, he felt that the government needed to issue $100 million in Trea-sury notes. Second, a tax of $150 million needed to be levied. And third, the government should "provide a uniform currency, by adopting the recommendation in the report of the Secretary of the Treasury."[43] Over the next month Congress spent much of its time debating a bill to allow the issue of Treasury notes to be used as legal tender for all debts, public and private. These notes would become the famous "greenback" and constitute the introduction of paper money into the American economy.

One of the key players in the House supporting passage of the Legal Tender Act was Republican Elbridge Spaulding of New York, who was considered the finance expert on the Ways and Means Committee. Like many members of Congress, Spaulding used Chase's annual report to Congress as the basis for his support of the bill. In his initial speech on the House floor regarding the bill, Spaulding cited liberally from Chase's report, using Chase's own numbers on the financial condition of the gov-ernment.[44] He remarked that Chase had two plans to reinforce the nation's finances: "first, the issue of demand Treasury notes; and second, a national currency secured by a pledge of United States stocks, to be issued by banks and associations, with proper regulation for their redemption by the banks themselves."[45] In this report Chase maintained, "It is too clear to be reasonably disputed that Congress, under its constitutional powers to lay taxes, to regulate commerce, and to regulate the value of coin, pos-sesses ample authority to control the credit circulation which enters so largely into the transactions of commerce, and affects in so many ways the value of coin."[46] Chase went on to make the case for a sound currency and the dangers of uncertainty in the value of money. He then proceeded to present his plan for the easy circulation of a stable currency:

> Two plans for effecting this object are suggested. The first contemplates the gradual withdrawal from circulation of the notes of private corporations, and for the issue, in their stead, of United States notes, payable in coin on demand, in amounts sufficient for the useful ends of a representative currency. The second, contemplates the preparation and delivery, to institutions and associations, of notes prepared for circulation under national direction, and to be secured as to prompt convertibility into coin by the pledge of United States bonds and other needful regulations.[47]

Chase claimed, "In this plan the people, in their ordinary business, would find the advantages of uniformity in currency; of uniformity in security; of effectual safeguard . . . against depreciation; and protection from losses in discounts and exchange." Chase continued to say, "A further important advantage to the people may be reasonably expected in the increased security of the Union, springing from the common interest in its preservation, created by the distribution of its stocks to associations throughout the country."[48]

Spaulding also mentioned that he had solicited Attorney General Edward Bates's opinion on the constitutionality of the bill. Not surprisingly, Bates had reported back positively on Congress's power to issue paper money. Bates wrote to Spaulding, "Certainly the Constitution contains no direct prohibition [of a national currency], and I think it contains no inferential prohibition that can be fairly drawn from its express terms. The first article of the Constitution, section eight, grants to Congress specifically a great mass of powers." In regard to the "necessary and proper" clause of Article I, Section 8, Bates drew on Joseph Story's *Commentaries*, writing,

> If the word *necessary* were used in the strict rigorous sense, it would be an extraordinary departure from the usual course of the human mind, as exhibited in solemn instruments, to add another word, the only possible effect of which is to qualify the strict and rigorous meaning, and to present clearly the idea of a choice of means in the course of legislation. If no means are to be resorted to but such as are *indispensably* necessary, there can be neither sense or utility in adding the word "*proper*" for the *indispensable necessity* would shut out from view all consideration of the propriety of means.[49]

Bates concludes by presenting Alexander Hamilton's argument from *Federalist* No. 23:

> The authorities essential to the common defense are these: to raise armies; to build and equip fleets; to prescribe rules for the government of both; to direct their operations; to provide for their support. These powers ought to exist *without limitation,* because it is impossible to foresee or to define the extent and variety of national exigencies, and the correspondent extent and variety of the means which may be necessary to satisfy them.[50]

On January 29, Republican Roscoe Conkling of New York inquired on the floor of the House into Chase's constitutional opinion of the matter, which Spaulding asked for. Chase replied to Spaulding and Congress in general that, in his opinion, the war required the extreme measure of paper money. He was supportive of congressional efforts to put his requests into law.[51]

Both opponents and supporters of the currency measure referenced Chase during the discussion of the bill. Currency supporter John Bingham, Republican from Ohio, citing the Chase annual report against the likes of New York Republican F. A. Conkling (Roscoe Conkling's brother) and Justin Morrill, argued that some "persons and institutions" were refusing Treasury notes. Making the notes legal tender for all debts would solve that problem.[52] On the other hand, Union Party member William Sheffield of Rhode Island referred to the legal tender bill as a "financial scheme presented to this House by the Secretary of the Treasury."[53] Republican Valentine Horton of Ohio insisted that though he respected the knowledge of the Treasury secretary, he did not think Chase had made a strong enough case for the necessity of introducing paper money: "I know perfectly well that the Secretary of Treasury thinks that it is necessary, and I have the utmost confidence in his ability and zeal. I think he is mistaken. At any rate, whether he is mistaken or not, he has not furnished the *proof* of the correctness of his opinion."[54]

President Lincoln did not go unmentioned in the congressional debate on this matter. Republican Frederick Pike of Maine quoted from Lincoln's July 4, 1861, message to Congress to defend as necessary for the defense of the government the extreme measure of introducing a paper currency. Pike stated,

> Upon the consideration of every financial measure there might well present itself anew the same question fitly put by President Lincoln in his message to Congress in July. "Is it better to

assume powers, the exercise of which shall violate a portion of the Constitution, rather than allow the whole to be destroyed?" And the country came to the paradoxical conclusion that it was his duty, as president, to violate the Constitution to preserve it.[55]

The implication of his statement is, of course, that under ordinary circumstances this legislation would be unconstitutional. Given the dire straits that the country faced, however, the passage of the legal tender bill was as important as the controversial military measures Lincoln had made the previous year.

The Senate debate included more references to Chase, often mentioning his opinion as gospel. Senator John Sherman stated that Chase's annual report had a significant effect on his thinking.[56] Senator John Hale opposed one particular amendment but said, "As the committee on finance and the Secretary of the Treasury seem to insist upon it, I will not make a noise about it."[57] Sherman opposed a separate amendment, but he said, "I do not pretend now to call for a division [on the amendment] because the Secretary of the Treasury earnestly desires this."[58] On an amendment concerning different types of bonds to be issued by the Treasury, Sherman and Finance Committee chairman William Fessenden politely argued over Chase's position. Fessenden maintained that Sherman had Chase's general opinion correct, but the secretary had indicated support for a particular amendment that differed with that general position. Fessenden said that "on matters of detail . . . I am much more inclined to trust the judgment of the Secretary of the Treasury than my own."[59]

There was also some question as to what kind of notation would appear on the back of the proposed legal tender notes. Fessenden noted that "in an interview with the Secretary of Treasury this morning," the secretary indicated that Congress should not act on the matter, leaving Chase with discretion.[60] Finally, Fessenden proposed an amendment allowing the Treasury to issue certificates of deposit for not less than $500 for 5 percent per annum. James McDougall of California spoke up and said that he wanted to offer an amendment making $100 the minimum deposit. "I was at the Treasury Department this morning," he stated, "and the Secretary himself said . . . the amendment would be a just and wise one." Fessenden acquiesced: "I accept the modification if the Secretary amends it."[61] In every single one of these matters, the position of Secretary Chase won the day.

McDougall's mention of his early morning trip to the secretary of the Treasury indicates that there was some behind-the-scenes politicking done by Chase. On the floor of the Senate, John Sherman indicated that Chase was involved in "private intercourse" with members on important matters.[62] Chase's own diary indicates that giving dinners for congressmen was not untypical. His entry for January 8, 1862, states that he "gave the usual dinner to committees of finance of the Houses." Senators present were William Fessenden, Sherman, Republican Timothy Howe of Wisconsin, Republican James Simmons of Rhode Island, and Democrat James Pearce of Maryland. House members were Stevens, Morrill, Spaulding, Horton, Republican Samuel Hooper of Massachusetts, Union Party member Horace Maynard of Tennessee, and Republican John Stratton of New Jersey.[63] Eventually the legal tender bill passed the Senate, 30–7, and the House, 97–22.[64]

As Congress in early 1863 debated the bill to create a national banking system to complement the national currency, Chase had much the same influence as he did on the currency initiative. The matter of a national bank system, however, drew some direct involvement from President Lincoln. In his annual message of December 3, 1862, Lincoln advocated the "organization of bank associations, under a general act of Congress." The creation of these banks would augment the issuing of paper money, as the national banks would be furnished "circulating notes, on the security of the United States bonds deposited in the treasury." These national banks could control the issuing of paper money and thus keep inflation in check.[65] In a subsequent letter to Congress in January 1863, Lincoln digressed from the point of the letter to make these same arguments in favor of a national bank association.[66]

These efforts by Lincoln were not lost on Congress during the debate on a national bank system in early 1863. Elbridge Spaulding noted how the president had advocated such a measure in his annual address in 1862, where Lincoln had stated,

> I know of [no way of guaranteeing a stable currency] which promises so certain results, and is, at the same time, so unobjectionable, as the organization of banking associations, under a general act of Congress, well guarded in its provisions. To such associations the government might furnish circulating notes, on the security of the United States bonds deposited in the treasury. These notes, prepared under the supervision of the proper officers, being uniform in appearance and security, and convertible always into coin, would at once protect labor against the evils of a vicious currency, and facilitate commerce by cheap and safe exchanges.[67]

Lincoln also took advantage of his signing a bill providing for immediate payment of the military to lobby for the National Bank Act. He argued that "Congress has power to regulate the currency of the country," and it was important to do just that so as to keep inflation down. "To that end, a uniform currency . . . is almost, if not quite indispensable." Further, "Such currency can be furnished by banking associations, organized under a general act of Congress." The secretary of the Treasury made the same argument in his annual report. In fact, Spaulding referred to the bill as the "national bank bill proposed by the Secretary of the Treasury."[68] Republican Reuben Fenton of New York called it "substantially the scheme of the Secretary of the Treasury," and he supported the bill because Chase considered action necessary.[69]

In the Senate, John Sherman once again drew heavily from Chase to defend the bank act. He mentioned liberally Chase's support of such a bill in the secretary's annual reports of 1861 and 1862, which Sherman used to rebut his opponents.[70] After Charles Sumner noticed that the amount of Treasury notes circulated under the act had been changed, Sherman said that after "consultation" with Chase, both the secretary and Sherman thought the change should be made.[71] Sherman even quoted the *London Times*, saying "the bill promoted by Mr. Chase" would provide order to a confused system where so many different banks could issue their own notes.[72]

Sherman's constant defense of Chase and the administration eventually offended some turf-conscious senators. Republican Jacob Collamer of Vermont castigated Sherman for insinuating that senators should support the bank bill simply because the administration desired it:

> We are told in the Senate that the whole cabinet are in [the bill's] favor. . . . It is not many years since a man would have been called to order for using an expression of that kind in the Senate. . . . Legislation is to be left to the House of Representatives and the Senate; it is the exercise of their judgment, not the authority of others, which is to give currency and support to measures.

Collamer asserted that any implication that the administration might exert influence on congressional deliberation suggested "subserviency" on the part of the Senate. Collamer pointed out that, unlike Great Britain, the United States did not have ministers of the government sit in on the legislature.[73]

Sherman responded to this criticism by saying that he merely wanted to point out that the secretary of the Treasury, the cabinet, and "a great body of the people" supported the bill. If Collamer was able to cite opinions of people who thought the bill would bring ruin upon local banks, than Sherman could cite "the opinions of grave and honorable men who are charged with the responsibilities of administering the Executive Departments of the Government." Sherman assured Collamer that this was not done to "influence our feeling" but simply to show that these men "gave this bill their hearty approbation."[74] Of course one can hardly believe that Sherman mentioned the strong support of the administration only to put that support on record. Chase's annual report and Lincoln's annual address were public documents. Common sense dictates that Sherman hoped appeals to executive authority would sway votes, but the conventions of his time required him to deny that. This itself is notable in that one can hardly imagine any contemporary United States senator taking offense at the involvement of the president or a cabinet official in the debate over important legislation.

As the vote on final passage neared in the Senate, an anticipated close vote had the administration lobbying specific senators in an attempt to sway their votes. Chase had discussed the act with Senator Benjamin Wade, and "a good many callers" from Congress convinced him that there "seems an increasing disposition to favoring the bill for banking."[75] Secretary Chase also brought pressure upon Republican Henry Anthony of Rhode Island to vote for the measure. Anthony exclaimed that "he believed it to be his duty to vote for the bill, although it would be the end of his political career."[76] Chase, Interior Secretary John Usher, and Lincoln's personal secretary William Stoddard lobbied Timothy Howe and Republican Jacob Howard of Michigan, both of whom switched votes based upon this pressure.[77] This proved crucial as the bill barely passed the Senate by a scant 23 to 21 margin. The bill passed the House by a similarly slim margin of 78 to 64.[78]

The National Bank Act provides the clearest example of widespread administrative influence on the legislative process. Chase's statement that he perceived an "increasing disposition" toward the act suggests that he was counting votes. It is clear that the administration was not averse to twisting arms when the vote became extremely close in the Senate. In announcing his support for the bill in two messages to Congress, President Lincoln put his stamp of approval on it. The enactment of a national banking system was one of the most modern of the Lincoln administration's efforts.

With all of this activity on the Legal Tender Act and the National Bank Act, it is surprising that an analysis of the congressional debate on the revenue measures of 1861 and the Internal Revenue Act of 1862 show little administrative involvement. Senator James Simmons did make some adjustments to his tariff proposal in July 1861 upon the request of the secretary of the Treasury.[79] Later Chase sent a letter to Finance Committee chairman William Fessenden asking for a joint resolution exempting from new tariff duties goods that were already in the warehouse when the duties became operative.[80] This resolution did end up passing.[81] Also, Thaddeus Stevens raised a point of order against Representative William Richardson of Illinois for commenting on the conduct of the administration in appropriating money. The Speaker did not sustain Stevens on this parliamentary matter.[82] By and large the references to Chase and the administration are perfunctory remarks regarding facts and figures.[83] The revenue measures of the special congressional session of 1861 included the creation of the first income tax in the history of the nation. But still, this seems to have been largely a congressional initiative. Perhaps the task of raising revenue was considered ordinary business that Congress could do on its own, while innovations such as a national currency and national banking system required more administrative involvement.

The Lincoln administration had its most profound influence on economic measures, but it also influenced the content of other legislation and attempted to sway the votes of congressmen. Yet on other bills—the Homestead Act, the Land-Grant College Act, the Pacific Railroad Act, and the Revenue Acts of 1861 and 1862—the administration was on the outside looking in. Gabor Boritt argues that Lincoln did not direct a nationalist revolution but simply did not oppose it as previous presidents had. On the land, transportation, and revenue acts, this characterization appears true. However, the administration was active in promoting the legislation that had the most direct effect on the economy: the Legal Tender Act and National Bank Act.

It cannot be denied that the lesser enactments were significant in their own right. The Homestead Act promoted settlement of the West, and the Pacific Railroad Act helped make the West prosperous. The Land-Grant College Act aided in democratizing higher education. The Revenue Acts, although subsequently amended or partially repealed, did set a precedent for the future. But they were all part of the prototypical distributionist public policy of the nineteenth century. The Legal Tender Act and the National Bank Act, however, altered the relationship between the national government and the nation's monetary system. The Legal Tender Act and the following acts taxing rival currency out of existence made national Treasury notes the only currency of the nation, eventually supplanting specie as the medium of economic activity. This represented a huge increase in the government's power to regulate currency. The bank system supplemented the Legal Tender Act of the previous year by increasing the nation's power over the nation's banking system. The importance of these two pieces of legislation cannot be overestimated. As economic historians Lance E. Davis, Jonathan R. T. Hughes, and Duncan M. McDougall write,

> Most important of the [economic] events of the [Civil War] pe-
> riod was the passage of the National Banking Act in 1863. . . . As
> a result [of this act], for the first time the economy could boast
> of a national currency . . . national bank notes redeemable at
> par by *any* national bank instead of the thousands of different
> notes previously circulated. More important, the act established
> a national banking system with all the member banks required
> to maintain minimum standards.[84]

Similarly, William Greenleaf says of the Legal Tender Act that it was a "turning point in American monetary history."[85] These may be legitimately viewed as regulatory policies of the type that would become commonplace in the late nineteenth and early twentieth centuries.

In this policy sense, Lincoln may have been "revolutionary." Yet the methods Lincoln used were less revolutionary. In his study of presidential rhetoric, Jeffrey Tulis says Lincoln typified the "old way," which held that the president must not comment publicly on a matter upon which Congress had not reached an outcome. Lincoln seldom spoke on public policy, not wishing to take a position that would hem him in. He also preferred the written form of communication with Congress over public speeches. This is true of the matters considered here. Lincoln's policy pronouncements were strategically placed in veto messages, messages to Congress, annual messages, and the like. Further, most of Lincoln's activity was behind the scenes and through proxies. On the surface Lincoln was respecting the time-honored divisions between Congress and the presidency. He did not engage in any going-public strategy that openly publicized his role in the policy process. Indeed, Lincoln was criticized in *Harper's Weekly* for being too deferential to Congress and not being "a great orator."[86] One calculation has Lincoln speaking publicly fewer than one hundred times in his four years as president.[87] Richard J. Ellis is left to conclude, "Lincoln was largely content to leave economic policy in Chase's capable hands."[88]

The McPherson thesis claims events of the Civil War warrant being called a second American Revolution. This revolution consisted, in part, of various momentous pieces of legislation that laid the groundwork for a tectonic shift in the American regime. McPherson writes, "It was [Lincoln's] own superb leadership, strategy, and sense of timing as president, commander in chief, and head of the Republican party that determined the pace of the revolution and ensured its success."[89] The significance of this claim lies in the assertion that Lincoln was not only central to the war effort and to combating the evil of slavery but also indispensable to the passage of historic pieces of domestic public policy. These policy enactments were quite distinct from the war effort.

Were McPherson's claim true, historians and political scientists alike would have to change the way in which they envision not only Lincoln but also the presidency itself. To judge the validity of the McPherson thesis, we have turned to three political science perspectives: those of public policy, realignment, and presidential leadership. Regarding public policy, the evidence seems to indicate that the Lincoln administration acted differently on regulatory policy than on distributive policy. The administration was largely passive in regard to such distributive policies as the Homestead Act, the Land-Grant College Act, and the Pacific Railroad Act. To the contrary, the Legal Tender Act and National Bank Act gained significant attention from the administration and from Lincoln himself. Lincoln's own reticence to engage in the domestic policy-making process only makes his activity on these two bills all the more remarkable.

Toward a More Modest Presidency

The analysis of the realignment of the late 1850s suggests that while slavery was the seed that gave rise to the Republican Party, it seems that economics put the party "over the top" electorally. The election of 1856 had shown the Republicans that as long as they had nothing but an antislavery position to offer voters, the party would be doomed to second-class status; it would be seen as a one-issue sectional party. However, it is difficult to say that Abraham Lincoln led the charge to amend the young party's vision more toward economics. Virtually all of Lincoln's post–Kansas-Nebraska Act speeches were on the subject of slavery. As developed in chapter 3, there can be no doubt of Lincoln's dedication to economic nationalism. While the defense of Whig economic programs was the focus of his public life in the 1840s, it was Lincoln's opinion in the 1850s that the particulars of Whig economics meant little if free labor itself was overwhelmed by slavocracy. Lincoln's primary contribution to the Republican Party was in eloquently articulating the defense of free labor and the evils of slavery and, in the 1860 election, simply being a Westerner. Even if the realignment of the 1850s was a "top-down" realignment, Lincoln does not seem to be one of the leaders advocating an economic program. As president, Lincoln was the head of the Republicans, but the evidence does not support McPherson's suggestion that Lincoln helped form the economic agenda of the burgeoning party.

In regard to the presidency itself, analysis suggests a mixed record on the part of Lincoln as a legislative leader. Lincoln's aides, and sometimes Lincoln himself, insinuated themselves into the legislative process, particularly regarding the Legal Tender Act and the National Bank Act. But the evidence does not seem to support McPherson's claim that President Lincoln "determined the pace of the revolution." It is fair to say that Lincoln's participation and actions in the legislative process were few and judicious. On two celebrated pieces of legislation, the Homestead Act and the Land-Grant College Act, the administration was virtually silent. In addition, to the extent to which Lincoln did attempt to influence legislation, he worked primarily through intermediaries, particularly Salmon Chase. In this sense Lincoln acted more like George Washington than a modern president.

The working relationship between Lincoln and Chase is similar to that of Washington and his secretary of the Treasury, Alexander Hamilton.[90] Washington, as a "patrician" president, deemed it un-presidential to dirty himself in the muddy political waters of the legislative process. But economic nationalism and executive involvement in the passage of a nationalist agenda were manifested in the earliest stages of the republic. Washington's Farewell Address, similar to Henry Clay's American System, defended the notion that all regions of the country could be united by commerce. A commercial republic "directed by an indissoluble community" would eventually form "one nation." Washington used Alexander Hamilton as a liaison to Congress. Hamilton used Treasury officials to lobby Congress and would sometimes sit in the gallery during debate. Despite the fact that no party system yet existed, in the First Congress Hamilton led what might be called a proto-party that was the germ of the Federalist Party.

These descriptions of Hamilton's activities bear remarkable similarity to Chase's as he was used by Lincoln. Despite being an active war president, common practice necessitated that Lincoln operate mostly through intermediaries. Chase's reports to Congress served as a baseline for congressional action on currency and banking policy. Like Hamilton, it was Chase who did the individual lobbying of congressmen.

There were some "modern" aspects to Lincoln's legislative leadership. First, in his messages to Congress, Lincoln took public stands on issues that were before Congress. And, like modern presidents, Lincoln made use of his personal staff, personal secretaries Stoddard, Nicolay, and Hay. These men were loyal to Lincoln himself, not to some bureaucracy, as is often the case with cabinet secretaries. For example, Stoddard vigorously lobbied for the banking act on behalf of the administration.

Of course the administration used those with more formal positions: Chase, Attorney General Bates, the ambassador to Great Britain Charles Francis Adams, and others. Finally, as in modern times the suggestions of Chase often made themselves directly into law. The executive branch was directly affecting the content of legislation and manipulating the votes of congressmen.

But there are significant deviations from modern practices that should cause us to question McPherson's "principal architect" claims and help us place Lincoln in presidential history. First of all, unlike in the modern presidency, Lincoln was a bargaining president, meaning to the extent he and his administration attempted to influence legislation, it was in private negotiations with Congress, not through a "going public" strategy. Lincoln avoided public speeches that tried to sway the audience to favor this or that version of current legislation. In fact, Lincoln seldom spoke in public, and when he did it was almost always about war policy. As opposed to modern times, Lincoln had no institutionalized coordination between the administration and Congress. The truth about the modern presidency thesis is that the strong presidency has more institutional support than it once had. The Executive Office of the President and the enormous White House staff have regularized the president's legislative and political operations in ways Lincoln could not have imagined. Whatever legislative leadership the Lincoln administration showed was ad hoc and episodic. There was nothing approaching the normalized contacts between congressional leaders and the president that are routine for the modern president. The modern chief executive is considered derisory if he is not leading Congress. One can barely imagine a significant candidate for president running on a platform of deference to Congress.

Lincoln picked and chose his battles. In addition to the Whig economic nationalism, he believed in the Whig view of the presidency. Yet Lincoln can be seen as a confluence of both modern and premodern characteristics. In many ways he revealed the potential of the presidency. His enlarging of presidential powers in light of national crisis has been well documented. In suspending habeas corpus and raising troops and spending money out of the Treasury without congressional approval, Lincoln executed unilateral powers of a breathtaking scope. Even on the domestic side, Lincoln, in limited instances, showed the willingness to use his administration to promote particular public policies. The two policies where his administrative influence is the clearest, banking and currency legislation, were the two most far reaching and most controversial. Even with large majorities in Congress, administrative influence was needed to pass such contentious pieces of legislation. Lincoln thus was more active in certain areas than the orthodox nineteenth-century president, but the custom of his time did affect the manner in which Lincoln led Congress. Jeremi Suri claims too much when he argues that "Lincoln might be the best analogue for [Franklin] Roosevelt" and that Lincoln's presidency "anticipated Roosevelt's."[91]

The different kinds of policy considered in the Thirty-Seventh Congress brought on a different brand of leadership by Lincoln. Presidency scholars see distinctions between the modern and premodern presidents, yet what they perceive may be largely a change in public policy. The modern presidency may be simply the routinization and institutionalization of powers that are inherent in the office.[92] Industrialism and postindustrialism necessitate regulatory and redistributive policies that lend themselves to presidential leadership. And the modern president has institutional support for his entrees into the legislative process. Alexander Hamilton perceived that economic nationalism and a strong presidency went hand in hand. Lincoln never made the connection. His activity on the banking and currency acts should instruct us as to the linkage of policy and politics and to the inherent potential of the presidency, but in regard to Lincoln these represent more the exceptions than the rule. Lincoln found himself holding contradictory positions. He favored economic nationalism but not the executive guidance perhaps necessary to make such policies a reality. In all senses, Lincoln was a Whig in the White House.

That "Whig in the White House" appellation speaks to the central theme of this work, namely the necessity of democracy to live within limits. While the Whig theory of the presidency may have been an overreaction to the presidency of Andrew Jackson, it serves as a powerful antidote to today's obsession with a presidency-centered government. Americans seem to be perplexed as to why they are consistently disappointed in their president, why the performance rarely matches the promise. At least since the presidency of Lyndon Johnson, the occupants of the executive office have been of different parties and temperaments but share the common attribute of underperforming expectations, with Ronald Reagan perhaps being the lone exception. The modern presidency carries with it certain pathologies that could be avoided or mitigated if the example of Abraham Lincoln were more closely followed.

First, the modern presidency is what Theodore Lowi calls a "personal presidency," defined by Lowi as "an office of tremendous personal power drawn from the people . . . and based on a new democratic theory that the presidency with all his powers is the necessary condition for governing a large, democratic nation."[93] The American people expect the president to personify their government, to singlehandedly solve all of the nation's problems, and to give meaning to our national existence. Lowi asserts that "the national government also embedded itself in the expectations of the American people. Psychologists would probably call this process an important aspect of political socialization, wherein the government actually became part of citizens' perspectives and their calculation of life chances."[94] With the rise of "big government," which is expected to do all and be all, and with that unlimited government personified in the president, the challenges of the office are more than any individual could possibly bear. David Nichols, in his study of the modern presidency, argues,

> The problem of contemporary American politics is not that we expect too much of the president but that we expect too much of the government. As the most visible symbol of the national government, the president is bound to suffer from disappointed expectations regarding the performance of the government as a whole. But we will not solve this problem by placing limits on the office of the Presidency. The solution will come only through reexamination of the ends of government.[95]

Jeremi Suri concludes, "The modern president is constantly beaten down by demands, large and small. His work is never done. He is alone in his struggle to fight off those who want a piece of him. Every hour brings another demand, another obligation, another crisis."[96]

The framers, while creating a strong presidency, balked at such a personal office. Central to their concerns regarding free government was the fear of the demagogue. If granting absolute power to a legislature was bad, and the framers thought it was, so much the worse if absolutism is located in a particular individual. Famously in *Federalist* No. 1, Hamilton warns against the flatterer, the spokesman for "the people." Hamilton cautions

> that a dangerous ambition more often lurks behind the specious mask of zeal for the rights of the people than under the forbidden appearance of zeal for the firmness and efficiency of government. History will teach us that the former has been found a much more certain road to the introduction of despotism than the latter, and that of those men who have overturned the liberties of republics, the greatest number have begun their career by paying an obsequious court to the people; commencing demagogues, and ending tyrants.[97]

It is the rare person who will be given this sort of power who will not abuse it. And, as Hamilton suggests, the danger is not that the demagogue will appear as a caricature of the Hitlerian despot but will with some legitimacy speak in the name of the people, flattering their prejudices and exploiting their fears. One need not think hard to see shades of Donald Trump in these words. Trump sets up dichotomies between "the people" and "elites," encouraging antipathy against the latter. His appeal is not to something grand or aristocratic or, as Hamilton notes, to efficiency in government. His appeal is precisely to the people. Thus the contemporary anxiety over the rising populism of modern politics, typified by Trump.[98]

James Ceaser notes that minimizing the harmful effects of ambition was one of the fundamental goals of premodern presidential politics. As the process of presidential selection has become more plebiscitary— that is, as attempts have been made to make presidential selection more representative (in a crude sense) and more responsible to the people in an undifferentiated mass—the use of the "popular arts" of demagoguery have become more common.[99] As one scholar puts it, "The distance between the voters and the president is a republican remedy against the influence of image and charisma, a remedy that we today have decided to do without. We complain about the manipulation of voters, but we forget that the right we insist on—to have voters make the final choice—makes manipulation easier."[100]

Why is this problematic? Perhaps an anecdote will suffice for explanation. In 2010, it will be recalled, a British Petroleum oil pipeline in the Gulf of Mexico ruptured as a consequence of an explosion on the Deepwater Horizon oil rig. This massive oil spill caused an environmental catastrophe. President Barack Obama, not wishing to repeat the perceived mistakes of George W. Bush in the wake of Hurricane Katrina, rushed to the Louisiana coast in a show of concern. But what precisely did the American people expect President Obama to do? Not being the superhero Aquaman, it was not as if Obama was going to swim to the bottom of the Gulf and patch up the massive leak in the oil line. Obama's job, apparently, was to stand on the beach and get his picture taken while looking concerned. This is the illusion of action. Like King Cnut's inability to affect the tides, President Obama was essentially powerless to influence the situation. To the extent action was needed, it was the technical action of professionals with expertise, which President Obama lacked. This is not meant as a criticism of Mr. Obama, who was merely doing what was expected of him, but illustrates the disproportion between what the public expects of its presidents and what they can actually accomplish. Perhaps one reason why modern Americans are consistently disappointed in their chief executives is that they ask more than those presidents can deliver.

Ceaser connects the lack of restraint on the part of candidates and the people to the second pathology of the modern presidency, that of the permanent campaign. Both Ceaser and Lowi note that the decline in relevance of the modern political party, largely caused by reforms of our electoral system (namely the rise of primary elections) and campaign finance law (creating candidate-centered campaigns and strengthening interest groups at the expense of parties), has left presidents electorally unaccountable to anyone but the people at large. It is difficult to imagine in our day, for example, a sitting president being denied his party's nomination for a second term, but this was not uncommon in the nineteenth century (for example Millard Fillmore, Franklin Pierce, and James Buchanan suffered this ignoble fate in the decade immediately preceding Lincoln's presidency). A strong party system would have prevented Donald Trump's capture of the Republican nomination in 2016 and his ultimate ascension to the presidency. Trump is a nominal Republican who has done little to support the party and campaigned expressly against the party leadership.[101] The plebiscitary system allowed Trump to direct his campaign straight to the people and win the Republican nomination for the presidency, despite barely being a Republican.[102]

The party-centered system that elected Lincoln had its own problems, such as corruption, but it also advanced certain goods. Parties tended to endorse those who expanded the party's electoral coalition. Those politicians who showed skill in forming coalitions, convincing those with superficial differences that they had deeper similarities, were promoted. Those who were divisive or failed to add to the alliance could be easily dismissed. A coalition-based system encouraged moderation. Also, it attached the skills that led to electoral success, such as coalition building, to actual governance. In many ways the art of legislation is the art of compromise. In the party-centered system, electoral skills and governing skills overlapped.

In our day of candidate-centered elections, politicians are encouraged to make extreme appeals. This is true for various reasons. First, with the weakening of party through various electoral reforms, candidates are more reliant on interest groups for money and organizations. Interest groups do not have the concern with building broad-based coalitions that parties do. Interest groups by definition tend to be more narrow and extreme in their focus. Thus, so is our politics. Also, politicians are more uneasy about reelection, even when reelection rates of incumbents are quite high. But because politicians are personally responsible for their own reelection, they spend an inordinate amount of time on election activity, distracting them from the actual task of legislation.[103] Finally, the lack of party discipline allows political amateurs, such as Donald Trump, to gain power based on personality or charisma while possessing little of the knowledge or talent necessary to actually perform their role competently. In a healthy political system, legislators who spent their career simply positioning themselves for reelection would give way to those who actually did the task of legislating.

Our selection system, Ceaser notes, has led to a prolonged presidential cycle—now typically two years—so that there is rarely a time when presidents and presidential aspirants are not angling for a potential run at the high office.[104] This influences how presidents govern. Presidents now spend a disproportionate amount of time fund-raising for election and typically have their travel schedule dictated not by the needs of the country but by their reelection needs, for example avoiding states that have little to offer the president electorally.[105] This is true of presidential aspirants as well, usually state governors or U.S. senators, who now who have every incentive to govern based on how their actions may influence their presidential ambitions rather than focusing on the "grunt work" of governing. An example of this is former Louisiana governor Bobby Jindal, who left his state's budget in shambles after promoting deep tax cuts he thought would position him well for a 2016 run for the Republican nomination for president. He was wrong and left his state holding the bag.[106]

Such a mindset adds to the pathology of the permanent campaign and lends itself to divisiveness and an inability to actually govern. Campaign rhetoric thrives on the making of distinctions: why this candidate is better (or worse) than that candidate. But governing succeeds due to compromise and moderation. If elected officials never leave campaign mode, then the ability to actually govern is severely hampered. All actions are taken merely for the consumption of the public, thus making the presidency more a public relations office than a governing office. One can think of the many congressional committee hearings wherein the atmosphere is more of a circus or show-trial than a serious effort to write legislation. It is not an accident that reality television star Donald Trump thrives in a system in which party loyalty and a record of accomplishments mean little while the ability to orchestrate spectacle and media pseudo-events can elevate the most amateur candidate to high office.

This is the cost of a "going public" strategy as identified by Samuel Kernell. Such a strategy, partaking more of electoral than governing rhetoric, makes all presidential actions public in a plebiscitary sense. Candidates and presidents are tempted to overpromise so as to get the greatest amount of attention and to package their proposals as a cure-all for our ills. One observes this in consumer advertising. Rarely is a product promoted as being "good enough." Rather, products are always "new and improved," "maximum strength," or "now with 20% more!" Whether it is President George W. Bush promising to create democracy halfway around the world in places that have never known stable democracy or candidate Barack Obama pledging to increase spending on education, the environment, health care, and infrastructure without raising taxes on the middle class yet still balance the budget, presidents continually raise expectations either beyond what can be realistically expected (as in the Bush example) or even in violence to basic arithmetic (as with Obama). One might think of Trump's claim that the United States could build a wall on its southern border (credible) and get the Mexicans to pay for it (incredible). The features that many Americans say they hate most about politics—that is, both the divisive character of our politics and the tendency of politicians to make promises left unfulfilled—are directly tied to the rise of the permanent campaign that is endemic to the modern presidency.

This leads us to the third and final pathology of the modern "personal" presidency, that of the perpetual crisis. Crisis rhetoric, it has been argued, is definitional for the modern presidency.[107] "Such are the president's channels of mass communication," writes Lowi, "that he must simplify and dramatize his appeals, whether the communication deals with foreign policy, domestic policy, or something else again. Almost every initiative is given a public relations name. Every initiative has to be 'new and improved.' Every initiative has to be a response to 'threats to the national interest.'"[108] As Harvey Mansfield puts it, "A strong executive may well be regarded as having a disconcerting taste for the sensational, so eagerly does he seize upon an accident of politics to magnify it for his own use. He may even create accidents; he is a master of what [Richard] Neustadt calls 'initiatives,' which are motions toward something new—designs for him, surprises to others." Thus, says Mansfield, the modern strong executive differs from that envisioned by the founders, who believed that "steady administration" would impress the people more than "sensational examples."[109] Within living memory of many Americans today are declarations of war, not against any actual invading army but against poverty, inflation, crime, illiteracy, and drugs. Even the "war on terror" is more of a war on a concept than a war against any actual enemy, its very fluidity of definition allowing for maximized presidential power. We have had a health care crisis, a global warming crisis, a spending crisis, an energy crisis, an immigration crisis, and so on. All of these "wars" on each "crisis" is used to justify greater executive power.

Mansfield correctly notes that the executive by nature, with the position's energy and dispatch, as noted in *Federalist* No. 70, is designed to act with great vigor in times of emergency.[110] Also, it should go without saying that sometimes when a president declares a thing a "crisis," it really is a crisis. Often Lincoln is regarded as instituting the "crisis presidency" in that he argued that due to the exigencies of the Civil War, he gained power that he normally would not have as president. The Civil War, to point out the obvious, was an actual crisis, and Lincoln was operating under the president's commander-in-chief role, where the president is most powerful. But we have seen that outside of that war-commander realm, Lincoln behaved much more like the typical nineteenth-century president.

The founders anticipated that in the normal course of things, Congress would drive American policy. The regularization of crisis thus distorts the constitutional order by making the initiation of measures a presidential task rather than that of Congress. To be sure, Publius in the *Federalist Papers* concerned himself with limiting the scope of congressional power, but this was precisely because it was assumed that the legislature is the strongest branch in a democracy. "The legislative department is everywhere extending the sphere of its activity and drawing all power into its impetuous vortex," writes Madison in *Federalist* No. 48.[111] Still, it is worth noting that the checks on this power are largely negative. The president has the veto. The judiciary has the power to nullify acts of the legislature that exceed its constitutional powers. Even within the legislature, Madison is at pains to explain that the purpose of the Senate is to slow down the legislature so its actions are deliberative rather than passionate. At some length in *Federalist* No. 62, Madison argues that the Senate brings stability to the legislature by limiting the amount of legislation passing Congress. Madison warns against the evils of numerous and mutable legislation:

> It poisons the blessing of liberty itself. It will be of little avail to the people, that the laws are made by men of their own choice, if the laws be so voluminous that they cannot be read, or so incoherent that they cannot be understood; if they be repealed or revised before they are promulgated, or undergo such incessant changes that no man, who knows what the law is to-day, can guess what it will be to-morrow. Law is defined to be a rule of action; but how can that be a rule, which is little known, and less fixed?[112]

The problem of democratic government, according to the founders, was not that the government would be too slow to act but that it would act too quickly, too impetuously, violating the rights of minorities. This was the *normal* course of things. Crisis government, as the term suggests, should exist only in extremis.

Lincoln shows us a better way. Even in response to a genuine crisis, Lincoln attempted to limit his power within the confines of the Constitution, albeit pushing at the edges in regard to prosecuting war. In those parts of the government that were not in crisis mode, Lincoln was largely deferential to Congress. He rarely spoke in public, and when he did speak on public policy it was usually directly to Congress in the form of written communication, as in his annual messages. As we have seen in detail above, when Lincoln did involve himself or his administration in the creation of "domestic" policy, such involvement was limited and behind the scenes. He did not wish to make any move that might suggest that the power of initiating the regular legislation of government lay anywhere but with Congress. Lincoln never claimed an electoral mandate or that his power came from "the people." Rather, he regularly couched his actions in the legal powers of the office. By limiting the expectations he had for himself as president, he also limited the expectations the people had of the office.

Conclusion

This book has argued that Lincoln attempted to reinvigorate a tired democracy by inciting a love for natural rights and a respect for the dignity of free labor. In doing so he exemplified the prudence and moderation that is the best of democratic statesmanship. When he thought power had a rightful legal backing, he was in strong favor of its use, whether in developing the nation's economic infrastructure or in fighting a civil war. When he thought power was not granted, even in the case of just causes such as the emancipation of slaves, he bowed to the legal limits placed upon government and upon himself as that government's chief executive. Rather than advancing his own ambitions by stoking the fears and prejudices of the people or by making promises unlikely to be kept, he sought to focus the attention of the people on what was practically and legally possible. It was in this appeal to the best in a democratic people that Lincoln sought to revitalize a democracy that was losing sight of its highest aspirations and giving in to the temptations of self-interest and the demagoguery of lesser statesmen.

Lincoln's example is one that is pertinent to our day. If Lincoln worried about a weary democracy a mere four score and seven years after the nation's founding, how much more so should we, now nearly 250 years removed from that founding, concern ourselves with an enervated democracy? The centralization of power in the presidency, the confusion of politics with entertainment, and a growing gap between what the people demand from government and the government's ability to meet those demands—a gap encouraged by overly ambitious politicians who continue to make promises they know cannot possibly be fulfilled—have given rise to an anger that is not healthy for a democratic people.

I write in the second year of Donald Trump's presidency. There is much angst about the rise of Trump as a force in American politics. The fact that a significant minority of the electorate is enthused by Trump is not a sign of a healthy demos. This is not to say that the Trump phenomenon does not have some justice behind it. To put it simply, and thus somewhat crudely, the globalized economy has created winners and losers in America. While it can be argued with some fairness that globalization has been a net plus for the nation, winners in this system seem to ignore the fact that there are tens of millions of Americans for whom globalization just does not work.[1] It is a pathology of our governing elite that they seem to listen only to the winners in the globalization game while ignoring or having active contempt for the game's losers. Note Hillary Clinton's infamous denunciation of the "irredeemable" "deplorables" who had the temerity to back Trump over her. But the anger that explains a good portion of the rise of Trump does not change the fact that Trump himself succeeds based mostly on his talents as an entertainer and by stoking the anxieties and resentments that economic dislocation has naturally produced. As noted in the discussion of prudence and moderation, anger can be a spur to justice; we call that righteous anger. For President Trump, who as a candidate said, "I will gladly accept the mantle of anger," anger is often an end in itself.[2] This is more the characteristic of the demagogue than that of a statesman. Trump's presidency so far shows the marks of an immoderate, imprudent man. Too ready to take offense at all criticisms and consistently engaging in overblown and vituperative rhetoric, Trump creates controversy when there should be none and in the process distracts from his own agenda. He is governed by his passions, often broadcast to the world via Twitter, too worried about how he appears to the public and indifferent to actual governance. Lincoln wrote during the war, "I shall do nothing in malice. What I deal with is too vast for malicious dealing."[3] How far is this from Donald Trump, for whom the gratuitous insult is a regular rhetorical trope, who feels the need to respond to any criticism with deep invective? Seldom have we seen a nationally prominent politician with less magnanimity. More than ever we need Lincoln's example of wise, prudential, moderate statesmanship.

The claim of some, especially those coming out of a more progressive historical tradition, is that Lincoln had to refound the republic to save it, to inaugurate a "second American Revolution." But the evidence gathered herein indicates Lincoln was not a revolutionary statesman of any sort. Lincoln's defense of the founding, his political moderation, his scrupulous adherence to the law, and his limited view of the presidency all testify to his nonrevolutionary credentials. But what was Lincoln, then, if not revolutionary? One need only look at what Lincoln defended to arrive at the answer to that question: Lincoln was a liberal statesman. He defended individual rights and the rule of law that protects those rights. He believed in equality and the need for government by consent. There is nothing here that could not be defended by the typical American founder. Lincoln was a liberal in that he defended the liberal principles of the founding. Natural individual rights, rule of law, equality, and consent all make up Lincoln's liberalism. Granted, there are more progressive and conservative interpretations of these liberal principles, but there is no doubt Lincoln was dedicated to those principles.

The idea of Lincoln as liberal statesman is drawn directly from historian James Randall. Randall argues that the "men who opposed Lincoln were 'radical' in the sense of being drastic or violent, not in the sense of being liberal. To combat such men was in truth a mark of liberalism." Lincoln, as has been shown, was defending liberal thought and liberal institutions against those who would overthrow them with violence. He did this in a moderate, dare one say conservative, way. As Randall puts it, "Liberalism is associated with democracy, and democracy requires moderation. It is among the enemies of democracy, as we know by bitter experience in our day, that we find violence." "Lincoln," Randall continues, "believed in planting, cultivating, and harvesting, not in uprooting and destroying."[4] Lincoln saw that the proposition "all men are created equal" needed cultivation to become a reality. The presence of slavery and the ultimate violent defense of that institution thwarted progress toward making the proposition an actuality. Lincoln's antislavery principles, support for women's suffrage, and cool attitude toward nativism put him squarely on the side of the progress of equality and against some of the prevailing views of his day.[5] For Lincoln, all progress had to harmonize with founding principles. As Joseph Fornieri ably puts it, "Progress in this sense is not a matter of historical inevitably that supersedes the principles of the founding, but of prudent deliberation that recurs to fixed principles and extends them under new circumstances in a manner that accords with their inner logic and dictates."[6] One can use a concept sometimes found in Christian ecclesiology, namely that change occurs within a "hermeneutic of continuity." This is the application of timeless truths to new situations. Change is possible, but it is not the result of mere innovation. All change must occur respecting certain foundational doctrines that precede and serve as limits to innovation.

Richard Brookhiser, in a work that explicitly ties Lincoln to the American founding, writes, "Lincoln's most important allies in these efforts were the founding fathers. They were dead. . . . But Lincoln called them back to life for his purposes. Their principles, he maintained, were his; his solutions were theirs. He summoned the past to save the present."[7] So as a Christian might view Scripture and the early church as the source of continuity, Lincoln viewed the American founding. All change should be in continuity with fundamental principles.

The march toward equality could occur faster than prudence would dictate, as abolitionism indicated, and it could also be reversed, as the defenders of slavery evidenced. Yet Lincoln had faith in American political institutions and was confident that they were built upon solid ground. Thus, he opposed radical threats to them from any quarter. The metaphor of the statesman as a gardener who cultivates suggests care and ordered growth, not uprooting or tearing down. Order is both hard to create and perhaps more difficult to maintain over time. Randall says, "If in procedure he wanted to be sure of his ground, in the content and purpose of his program he wanted liberal causes to succeed. If his conservatism was a kind of brake or saving common sense, liberalism was its spark."[8] His desire for "sure ground" led him to oppose radical attacks on liberalism, such as those coming from the South, and radical plans for social reform, such as those coming from the extreme elements of the temperance movement or from abolitionists.

Lincoln separated himself from his opponents left and right by maintaining a sound respect for public opinion. He recognized that statesmanship in a democracy is less the assertion of will than the molding of public opinion. Both abolitionists and slaveholders were ready to simply separate from those with whom they disagreed. Abolitionists declared, "No union with slaveholders," and then in 1861 the South took them up on the offer. To the contrary, Lincoln both accepted the opinions of the public, even some of the unsavory ones, and attempted to lead opinion at the same time.

Lincoln's defense of natural rights against popular sovereignty was at the core of the Lincoln-Douglas debates of 1858 and formed the heart of Lincoln's political thought. He abhorred the indifference to slavery exemplified in the concept of popular sovereignty, as well as the assault on natural rights it represented. He argued that the conflict was between "the common right of humanity and . . . the divine right of kings."[9] The question was whether the nation would continue to honor natural rights, rights true for all time and for all people, or yield to the "might makes right" foundation of popular sovereignty. Stephen Douglas sought to change the opinion of the people against natural rights and toward tyranny of the majority. Douglas encouraged the people in an indifference to the moral wrongness of slavery and its incongruity with natural rights. To combat indifference to the natural rights outlined in the Declaration was the impetus behind Lincoln's political activity after the passage of the Kansas-Nebraska Act of 1854 had made popular sovereignty national policy. Lincoln believed a democratic regime must be tempered by veneration of natural rights and rule of law. The disrespect for law endangers all, Lincoln argued, as the law is "erected for the defense of liberty and property of individuals."[10] Let a people lose the law, and they lose their rights. Popular majorities must be limited by rule of law to avoid arbitrary assaults against natural rights.

Lincoln's defense of natural rights and the rule of law and his respect for public opinion showed the profound recognition that to be an advocate of democracy, one must be a moderate advocate. Democracy is not a good in itself, Lincoln believed. If it is, then popular sovereignty should rule. Democracy is good only as long as it serves to protect natural rights. Defense of constitutionalism and care for public opinion are the tools a statesman uses to protect natural rights from the abuses of the people.

Lincoln's moderate defense of liberalism led him to oppose both pro-slavery and abolitionist ideologues. Abolitionists, like those fervently in favor of temperance, were illiberal in the face of human failing and sought to eradicate it by any means necessary. This led to the fanaticism of people such as John Brown, people who could not see that justice must exist in a world of sin and any effort to obliterate sin runs up against human nature. Impatience with human failings can lead one to become frustrated with the compromise that is essential to democracy. Lincoln understood that democracy necessarily consists of half loaves. Very seldom does a majority form without some compromise being made. Any principle, even the principle of equality, can be taken to extremes, which are unhealthy for a liberal democratic polity. Lincoln's head was not with the theorists or utopians, seeking to remake the world based on some idea of justice divorced from human nature or caution. Lincoln understood that the primary political virtues are moderation and prudence, and in defense of liberalism he practiced both excellently.

★ ★ ★ ★ ★

Acknowledgments

Notes

Bibliography

Index

★ ★ ★ ★ ★

Acknowledgments

This book was a long time coming. Thus, there are many people to thank, and surely I will forget someone. My former professors James H. Read and the late Tom Engeman introduced me to the thought of Abraham Lincoln. Ray Tatalovich served as a mentor and a friend. Much of what I have accomplished in my career is due to Ray's influence. Northern State University supported this project with a research sabbatical and travel funds to conferences, where much of this work was originally presented. Robert Russell and the staff at Beulah Williams Library gave invaluable help, especially by providing office space during my sabbatical. This book could not have been written without that assistance. My colleagues Peter Ramey and Steven Usitalo read drafts of the manuscript and offered keen insight. Peter, along with Anthony Wachs and Father Tom Anderson, allowed me to bounce ideas off of them at our weekly book group gathering. Former student Jordan Abu Sirriya also read portions of the manuscript. For reasons we have both forgotten, Kelsey Luckhurst Stock wrote a paper in my American Political Thought course that inspired my connection of Lincoln to distributism. Tracy Vogel, good friend and ace photographer, snapped the author photo. Friend and scholar Jon Lauck helpfully suggested I approach Southern Illinois University Press about the book, and at SIU Press Sylvia Frank Rodrigue shepherded the book through what at times seemed an endless review process. Finally, my wife, Katy, and our children, Frederick, Bridget, George, and Lewis, put up with my many hours in the office instead of at home. And they simply put up with me, which is high praise indeed.

Notes

Introduction

1. Chesterton, *Everlasting Man*, 9–10.
2. Chesterton, 59.
3. Ferguson, *Land of Lincoln*, 115.
4. Thurow, *Abraham Lincoln and American Political Religion*, 42.
5. See Vodolazkin, "New Middle Ages," 31–36.
6. One can imagine artists in particular playing the role of "statesman" even though they have no formal role in the operation of the institution we call "the state." A Mark Twain may be a more able interpreter of his times than any politician. At various times Americans were more likely to find statesmen among U.S. senators than among presidents. One thinks of Henry Clay, Daniel Webster, and John C. Calhoun as obvious examples. One of the pathologies of our time is the almost total absence of statesmen in any realm. This is true in art, as that world has been overtaken by commercialism and by a crass nihilism. Among our political leaders, the fact that our politicians are largely given a professional education, typically in the law, has denied to them the kind of liberal education that is necessary for statesmanship. In order to be a statesman, one must have the eyes to see those fundamental commitments of a people, the historical temper to appreciate the spiral of time, and the eloquence to articulate fundamental principles to the people in a manner they understand. It is ironic that Lincoln, having far less formal education than any American politician today, possessed these qualities more than any contemporary politician.
7. Healy, *Cult of the Presidency*, 268.

1. Lincoln and the Political Virtues of Prudence and Moderation

1. Lincoln, *Collected Works*, 2:234.
2. Lincoln, 2:323. William Seward's public and decisive denunciation of the Know-Nothings may have cost him the Republican nomination for president in 1860, as the party did not want a candidate who might cost them crucial Know-Nothing votes. Lincoln, through his careful language, did not carry such baggage.
3. D. Wilson, *Lincoln's Sword*, 148
4. Jaffa, *Crisis of the House Divided*, 27.
5. Ethan Fishman, "Under the Circumstance: Abraham Lincoln and Classical Prudence," in Williams, Pederson, and Marsala, *Abraham Lincoln*, 3.
6. Fornieri, *Abraham Lincoln*, xi–xii.
7. Aristotle, *Nicomachean Ethics*, 152, 1140a25.
8. Aristotle, 168, 1143b26.
9. Aristotle, 153, 1140b7.
10. Aristotle, 23, 1099b30.
11. Aristotle, 36, 1104a15.
12. Aristotle, 70, 1115b18.
13. Aristotle, 50 1109a27.
14. Clor, *On Moderation*, 13.
15. Aristotle, *Politics*, 250–51, 1292a7.
16. Aristotle, 161, 1273b35.
17. Aristotle, 369, 1318b27.
18. Aristotle, 330, 1309b14.
19. Fornieri, *Abraham Lincoln*, 59.
20. Jaffa, *Crisis of the House Divided*, 190. For a further discussion of Lincoln and the tradition of prudence and moderation, see Allen Guelzo, "Prudence, Politics and the Proclamation," Heritage Foundation Online, August 17, 2007, https://www.heritage.org/political-process/report/prudence-politics-and-the-proclamation. Guelzo's discussion of prudence largely mirrors mine, but I find his argument that moderation is not a political virtue to be unconvincing.
21. Foote, *Civil War*, 2:883.
22. Holzer, *Lincoln at Cooper Union*, 144.
23. Striner, *Father Abraham*, 6.
24. Striner, 212.
25. DiLorenzo, *Real Lincoln*, 13, 14.
26. Bennett, *Forced into Glory*, 198, 201.
27. Lincoln, *Collected Works*, 1:109.
28. Mob violence was becoming more and more common in Lincoln's day. Donald Fehrenbacher writes, "Mob violence against abolitionists and free blacks, which had been increasing in the United States, reached its

peak during the summer of 1835, and the city of Washington contrib-
uted dramatically to the alarming trend." Fehrenbacher, *Slaveholding
Republic*, 74. In 1835 the *Richmond Whig* denounced "the present su-
premacy of the Mobocracy." Over fifty riots had taken place across the
United States in that year alone, sometimes with the encouragement of
President Jackson. Howe, *What Hath God Wrought*, 431, 437.

29. Lincoln, *Collected Works*, 1:109–10.
30. Lincoln, 1:110
31. Lincoln, 1:110.
32. Meier, "Drugs, Sex and Rock and Roll," 681–95.
33. Lincoln, *Collected Works*, 1:110–11.
34. Lincoln, 1:112.
35. Lincoln, 1:114.
36. Here as in many cases there is a similarity between Lincoln's cautious
    support of democracy and that of Alexis de Tocqueville. Tocqueville
    believed that the notion that there should be no limits on liberty is the
    "seed of tyranny." See Tocqueville, *Democracy in America*, 240 and 426
    (on "indefinite perfectibility") for two of many examples.
37. Jaffa, *Crisis of the House Divided*, 195.
38. Lincoln, *Collected Works*, 1:271.
39. Lincoln, 1:271–72.
40. Lincoln, 1:272, 273. Emphasis in the original.
41. Lincoln's views correspond with those of contemporary psychologist
    Jonathan Haidt. Haidt's research in *The Righteous Mind* suggests that
    morality starts as an emotional response, wired into our minds through
    centuries of evolution. Haidt tends to downplay, perhaps to a fault, the
    function of reason in coming to moral conclusions. In truth, morality
    is likely an interplay between reason (*logos*) and spiritedness (*thymos*).
42. Lincoln, *Collected Works*, 1:274.
43. Morel, *Lincoln's Sacred Effort*, 131.
44. Lincoln, *Collected Works*, 1:278.
45. Lincoln, 1:277.
46. Lincoln, 1:275.
47. Burlingame, *Abraham Lincoln*, 1:156, 159–60.
48. Lincoln, *Collected Works*, 1:74–76.
49. Lincoln, 1:347–48.
50. Lincoln, 2:255.
51. Lincoln, 2:255–56.
52. Lincoln, 2:255–56.
53. Fishman, "Under the Circumstance," 6.
54. Lincoln, *Collected Works*, 2:385.
55. Douglas used the term "Black Republican" fifty-nine times in their sev-
    en debates, twenty-nine times in the debate at Freeport, Illinois, alone.
56. Fehrenbacher, *Slaveholding Republic*, 287.

57. Lincoln, *Collected Works,* 3:9.

58. Lincoln, 2:491.

59. Burlingame, *Abraham Lincoln*, 1:465.

60. Lincoln, *Collected Works,* 3:16.

61. Lincoln, 3:17–18.

62. Lincoln, 3:276.

63. Lincoln, 3:304.

64. Lincoln, 4:5.

65. Lincoln, 2:385.

66. Lincoln, 2:465. Emphasis in original.

67. Lincoln, 3:27.

68. Quoted in Guelzo, *Abraham Lincoln*, 140.

69. Lincoln, *Collected Works,* 2:14.

70. Lincoln, 4:149–50.

71. Lind, *What Lincoln Believed*, 159.

72. Lincoln, *Collected Works,* 4:270.

73. See Lincoln, 5:222.

74. Lincoln, 5:387–89.

75. Lincoln, 6:28–31.

76. Lincoln, 6:428–29.

77. Lincoln, 8:332–33.

78. W. Miller, *President Lincoln*, 365.

79. Jaffa, *Crisis of the House Divided*, 370.

80. Clor, *On Moderation*, 15.

81. Jaffa, *Crisis of the House Divided*, 377.

82. Clor, *On Moderation*, 29.

83. W. Miller, *President Lincoln*, 318, 325.

84. O'Connor writes, "In the absence of this faith now, we govern by tenderness. It is a tenderness which, long since cut off from the person of Christ, is wrapped in theory. When tenderness is detached from the source of tenderness, its logical outcome is terror. It ends in forced labor camps and in the fumes of the gas chamber." See O'Connor, *Collected Works*, 830.

85. Morel, *Lincoln's Sacred Effort*, 2.

86. Cavanaugh, *Myth of Religious Violence*, 66.

87. For a compendium of Trump statements regarding Mexicans, see Katie Reilly, "Here Are All the Times Donald Trump Insulted Mexico," *Time*, August 31, 2016, http://time.com/4473972/donald-trump-mexico-meeting-insult/, or for this story regarding intemperate remarks by Republican representative Steve King, see Jennifer Steinhauer, "Steve King, Hurling Insults at Immigrants, Is Rebuked by His Party," *New York Times*, March 13, 2017, https://www.nytimes.com/2017/03/13/us/politics/steve-king-babies-civilization.html.

88. Examples are boundless, but here is one from Nancy Pelosi: Janice Timm, "Pelosi: Race Is Why GOP Is Blocking Immigration," MSNBC.com, March 10,

2014, http://www.msnbc.com/msnbc/pelosi-racism-stalling-immigration; and one from Bernie Sanders: Thomas Howell Jr., "Sanders: Trumps 'Racist' Immigration Moves Distract from Cabinet, Health Reform," *Washington Times*, February 12, 2017, https://www.washingtontimes .com/news/2017/feb/12/bernie-sanders-trumps-racist-immigration -moves-dis/. Democratic Senate leader Harry Reid tweeted in December 2015, "Racism has long been prevalent in Republican politics. Only difference now is that Trump is saying out loud what other Rs merely suggest." Sophia Tesfaye, "'Racism Has Long Been Prevalent in Republican Politics': Harry Reid Blasts GOP for Fomenting Trump's Xenophobic Campaign," *Salon*, December 8, 2015, https://www.salon .com/2015/12/08/racism_has_long_been_prevalent_in_republican _politics_harry_reid_blasts_the_gop_for_fomenting_trumps _xenophobic_campaign/.

2. Lincoln and the Defense of Natural Rights

1. See Postman, *Amusing Ourselves to Death*, 99–113, 125–41. For a contemporary account, see Sasse, *Them*, 75–104.
2. Lincoln, *Collected Works*, 2:225.
3. See, for example, *Federalist* No. 55: "Were the pictures which have been drawn by the political jealousy of some among us faithful likenesses of the human character, the inference would be, that there is not sufficient virtue among men for self-government; and that nothing less than the chains of despotism can restrain them from destroying and devouring one another." Rossiter, *Federalist Papers*, 343.
4. Rossiter, 282.
5. Lincoln, *Collected Works*, 4:240.
6. Lincoln, 3:534–35.
7. Lincoln, 3:376.
8. Lincoln, 3:375.
9. Lincoln, 3:296.
10. Lincoln, 2:406–7.
11. Lincoln, 2:499–500.
12. Lincoln, 3:328.
13. Lincoln, 2:405–6.
14. Lincoln, 1:260, 2:320.
15. Neely, *Fate of Liberty*, 25.
16. Lincoln, *Collected Works*, 2:3.
17. Lincoln, 2:20.
18. Guelzo, *Abraham Lincoln*, 188.
19. Both territories allowed slavery, although Congress acted during the Civil War to ban slavery in these two areas.
20. Quoted in Jaffa, *Crisis of the House Divided*, 22.
21. Peterson, *Lincoln in American Memory*, 308.

22. Foote, *Civil War*, 1:26–27.
23. Lincoln, *Collected Works*, 3:9.
24. Lincoln, 3:55–56.
25. Lincoln, 3:3.
26. Lincoln, 3:6.
27. Lincoln, 3:293.
28. Lincoln, 3:8–9.
29. Lincoln, 3:209.
30. Lincoln, 3:274.
31. Lincoln, 3:11–12.
32. Lincoln, 3:286.
33. Lincoln, 3:54.
34. Guelzo, *Abraham Lincoln*, 188.
35. Lincoln, *Collected Works*, 3:306–7.
36. Fornieri, *Abraham Lincoln*, 143. I should note that I believe Fornieri works too hard to reconcile Lincoln with Christianity. One must be cautious when discussing Lincoln's religious views, but suffice it to say that there is little evidence that Lincoln was a Christian in any orthodox sense of the word.
37. Lincoln, *Collected Works*, 3:220.
38. Lincoln, 3:302.
39. Lincoln, 3:530–35.
40. Lincoln, 3:523.
41. Lincoln, 3:537.
42. It is worth remembering that in Jefferson's original draft of the Declaration of Independence, King George III was excoriated for waging a "cruel war against human nature" for having introduced slavery into the American colonies.
43. Lincoln, *Collected Works*, 3:222.
44. Lincoln, 4:18.
45. Lincoln, 3:29.
46. Lincoln, 3:303.
47. See Tocqueville, *Democracy in America*, 407–10, 485–86.
48. Lincoln, *Collected Works*, 2:462.
49. Lincoln, 3:92.
50. Lincoln, 2:225.
51. Lincoln, 3:550.
52. Lincoln, 3:225–26.
53. Lincoln, 3:314–15.
54. Lincoln, 2:265–66.
55. Rossiter, *Federalist Papers*, 290. This is the source of the quotes in this paragraph and the next.
56. Lincoln, *Collected Works*, 3:466–67.
57. Lincoln, 2:222–23.

58. When interpreting these lectures, one must deal with a problem of documentation. Roy Basler, editor of Lincoln's *Collected Works*, separates Lincoln's ruminations on discoveries and inventions into two lectures, the first taking place on April 6, 1858, and the second on February 11, 1859. Contemporary consensus is that the lectures were actually one presentation, offered on multiple occasions. See E. Miller, "Democratic Statecraft and Technological Advance," 488; Emerson, *Lincoln the Inventor*, 37–50; and Winger, *Lincoln, Religion, and Romantic Cultural Politics*, 16.

59. D. Wilson, *Lincoln's Sword*, 40.

60. Brookhiser, *Founders' Son*, 140.

61. Fornieri, *Abraham Lincoln*, 47.

62. Lincoln, *Collected Works*, 2:437.

63. Lincoln, 2:437. Emphasis in the original.

64. Lincoln, 2:440. Emphasis in the original.

65. Lincoln, 2:440.

66. Lincoln, 2:439.

67. Lincoln, 2:441–42.

68. Winger, *Lincoln, Religion, and Romantic Cultural Politics*, 21.

69. Lincoln, *Collected Works*, 3:356.

70. Lincoln, 3:357. Emphasis in original. Lincoln is quoting the poem "Cato's Soliloquy" by Joseph Addison, which begins

    It must be so—Plato, thou reason'st well—
    Else whence this pleasing hope, this fond desire,
    This longing after immortality?

71. Lincoln, 3:357.

72. Lincoln, 3:357. Emphasis in original.

73. Lincoln, 3:356–57.

74. Lincoln, 3:357.

75. Lincoln, 3:357–58.

76. Lincoln, 3:358. Emphasis in original.

77. Lincoln, 3:358.

78. Lincoln, 3:358.

79. Lincoln, 3:358.

80. Lincoln, 3:359–60.

81. Lincoln, 3:360.

82. Lincoln, 3:361–62.

83. Lincoln, 3:362.

84. Lincoln, 3:362.

85. Lincoln, 3:362–63.

86. Lincoln, 3:363.

87. Lincoln, 3:362.

88. E. Miller, "Democratic Statecraft and Technological Advance," 505.

89. Winger, *Lincoln, Religion, and Romantic Cultural Politics*, 43.

90. Quoted in McPherson, *Battle Cry of Freedom*, 19–21.
91. See Postman, *Technopoly*.
92. Storing, *What the Anti-Federalists Were For*, 76.
93. Levin, *Great Debate*, 105.
94. Levin, 105.
95. Burke, *Reflections on the Revolution in France*, 194–95.
96. Quoted in Levin, *Great Debate*, 106–7.
97. Levin, 110.
98. Burke, *Reflections on the Revolution in France*, 151.
99. Kraynak, *Christian Faith*, 23.
100. Kraynak, 169.
101. MacIntyre, *After Virtue*, 6–35.
102. MacIntyre, 69.
103. MacIntyre, 69–71.
104. I have here tried to summarize roughly the second half of MacIntyre's book *After Virtue*. For a similar argument regarding habit and virtue, and one that is more accessible than MacIntyre's, see Matthew Crawford's 2015 work *The World beyond Your Head: Becoming an Individual in an Age of Distraction* (New York: Farrar, Straus and Giroux).
105. Lincoln, *Collected Works*, 4:169. The biblical reference is to Proverbs 25:11, "A word fitly spoken *is like* apples of gold in pictures of silver" (KJV).

3. Lincoln's Political Economy in the American Tradition

1. Chernow, *Alexander Hamilton*. For a historical discussion of American attitudes toward Hamilton, see Knott, *Alexander Hamilton and the Persistence of Myth*.
2. Lincoln, *Collected Works*, 3:375–76.
3. Lincoln, 2:249.
4. Randall, *Lincoln: The President*, 23.
5. Randall, 24.
6. Hofstadter, *American Political Tradition*, 102.
7. Wills, *Lincoln at Gettysburg*, 85.
8. Engeman, *Thomas Jefferson and the Politics of Nature*, 1–3.
9. Jaffa, *Crisis of the House Divided*, 70.
10. Knott, *Alexander Hamilton and the Persistence of Myth*, 54.
11. Lincoln, *Collected Works*, 3:29.
12. Oates, *With Malice toward None*, 32.
13. Diggins, *On Hallowed Ground*, 47, 99.
14. Hamilton, *Writings*, 70.
15. Hamilton, 70, 71, 72, 76–77.
16. Rossiter, *Federalist Papers*, 121, 122–23. Emphasis in the original.
17. Hamilton, *Papers on Public Credit*, 190.
18. Hamilton, 204–5, 234, 220, 211.
19. Hamilton, 239–40.

20. Rossiter, *Federalist Papers*, 331, 395, 392.
21. Rossiter, 400.
22. Rossiter, 402.
23. Walling, *Republican Empire*, 141.
24. Hyneman and Carey, *Second Federalist*, 174.
25. McDonald, *Presidency of George Washington*, 90–95.
26. McDonald, *Alexander Hamilton*, 199.
27. Hoadley, *Origins of American Political Parties*, 106, 51.
28. Walling, *Republican Empire*, 124. Walling also recognizes this distinction.
29. Walling, 146. Article I, Section 1, of the Constitution limits Congress to "all powers herein granted." Those powers are largely granted in Article I, Section 8. The executive grant of power in Article II, Section 1, simply says, "The executive Power shall be vested in a President of the United States." So the executive power is less defined than the legislative power, giving the executive more freedom to act.
30. Hamilton, *Writings*, 805.
31. Walling, *Republican Empire*, 126. See Locke's *Second Treatise*, chapter 12, especially paragraphs 145–47.
32. Hamilton, *Writings*, 808.
33. Walling, *Republican Empire*, 152.
34. Quoted in Howe, *Political Culture of the American Whigs*, 11.
35. Howe, 16.
36. Holt, *Rise and Fall of the American Whig Party*, 7.
37. Watson, *Andrew Jackson vs. Henry Clay*, 215.
38. For an example of Jacksonian opposition to government action, see Jackson's veto of the Maysville Road internal improvement bill. Watson, 175–81. One also has to note that by the Jacksonian age, and certainly by the presidency of James K. Polk, Democratic opposition to government power in the realm of economics was to a large extent driven by the fear of any argument that might suggest government power over slavery. See Howe, *What Hath God Wrought*, 356–65.
39. Holt, *Rise and Fall of the American Whig Party*, 86.
40. Howe, *Political Culture of the American Whigs*, 13.
41. Holt, *Rise and Fall of the American Whig Party*, 3.
42. Holt, 2.
43. Guelzo, *Abraham Lincoln*, 57.
44. Remini, *Henry Clay*, 226, 229–30.
45. Watson, *Andrew Jackson vs. Henry Clay*, 150.
46. Remini, *Henry Clay*, 39–40.
47. Holt, *Rise and Fall of the American Whig Party*, 68–70. In later years, Republican partisans Charles Francis Adams and William Seward would argue that the Republicans gained their support from the hard-working and industrious middle class, while Democrats got their support from

Notes to Pages 88–92

the very rich and poor, the "aristocracy and the ignorance" (Foner, *Free Soil*, 34–35).

48. Holt, *Rise and Fall of the American Whig Party*, 951–52.
49. Watson, *Andrew Jackson v. Henry Clay*, 187, 196.
50. Howe, *What Hath God Wrought*, 6.
51. Diggins, *On Hallowed Ground*, 47.
52. Neely, *Last Best Hope*, 10. Note Lincoln's faint, and somewhat amusing, praise of farmers in his address to the Wisconsin State Agricultural Society:

> I presume I am not expected to employ the time assigned me in the mere flattery of the farmers as a class. My opinion of them is that, in proportion to numbers, they are neither better nor worse than other people. In the nature of things they are more numerous than any other class; and I believe there really are more attempts at flattering them than any other, the reason of which I cannot perceive, unless it be that they can cast more votes than any other. (Lincoln, *Collected Works*, 3:472–73)

53. Lincoln, *Collected Works*, 1:5.
54. Lincoln, 1:32–33, 39, 42.
55. Lincoln, 1:49–50.
56. Lincoln, 1:159–79.
57. Lincoln, 1:165.
58. Lincoln, 1:480–90. While waiting out the lengthy time between his election and actual service in Congress, Lincoln served as a delegate to the Chicago Rivers and Harbors Convention. This industrial convention came out in favor of a broad construction of the Constitution, a Pacific railroad, and free labor.
59. Lincoln, 1:483.
60. Lincoln, 1:487.
61. Nevins, *Emergence of Lincoln*, 1:355–56.
62. Lincoln, *Collected Works*, 4:430.
63. Lincoln, 5:240–43.
64. Lincoln, 4:492.
65. See Lincoln's speech in 1848 in opposition to the Mexican-American War and his mocking of the "manifest destiny"–preaching Young America movement in his "Second Lecture on Discoveries and Inventions." Lincoln, *Collected Works*, 1:431–42 and 3:356–63.
66. Danoff, "Lincoln and Tocqueville," 711.
67. Lincoln, *Collected Works*, 5:537.
68. Lincoln, 7:282.
69. The South would still have had a major voice in the government through its control of the Senate and Supreme Court, as Alexander Stephens noted to his fellow Georgians as the state pondered secession. By seceding they gave total control to their enemies. This suggests that the South

226

read the writing on the wall and realized its future in the Union spelled disaster for a rural agrarianism built upon the foundation of slavery.

70. Curry, *Blueprint for Modern America.*
71. Pestritto, *Woodrow Wilson,* 58.
72. Theodore Roosevelt, "What Is a Progressive?," in Pestritto and Atto, *American Progressivism,* 40–41.
73. Croly, *Promise of American Life,* 87–88.
74. Pestritto and Atto, *American Progressivism,* 273.
75. Cuomo, *Why Lincoln Matters.* Indeed, the book even has a mock "State of the Union" speech for Lincoln to address twenty-first-century problems.
76. Cuomo, 6, 8.
77. McGovern, *Abraham Lincoln,* 152.
78. Holzer and Garfinkle, *Just and Generous Nation,* 259–60.
79. Barack Obama, "Illinois Senator Barack Obama's Announcement Speech," *Washington Post,* February 10, 2007, http://www.washingtonpost.com/wp -dyn/content/article/2007/02/10/AR2007021000879.html.
80. A similar project has been taken on by Jason Jividen in his fine work *Claiming Lincoln.* I can recommend the work, although those who read it will see that I am less concerned than Jividen with the notion of equal opportunity, while my own review of Jividen's book in the journal *American Political Thought* (Spring 2013) suggests that Jividen does not adequately appreciate the change in the American economy caused by industrialization. As will be seen, I think this change is meaningful if we are to aptly apply Lincoln's economic theory to current circumstances.
81. This is not the place for a comprehensive overview of the American founding. For a good summary of the differences between the founding political science and that of Progressives, see Sidney Pearson's introduction to the Transaction edition of Croly's *Progressive Democracy,* xi–li.
82. Roosevelt, "New Nationalism."
83. Roosevelt, "Commonwealth Club Address."
84. Roosevelt, "Commonwealth Club Address."
85. Roosevelt, "Commonwealth Club Address."
86. Roosevelt, "First Inaugural Address."
87. W. Wilson, *Congressional Government,* 53–54.
88. W. Wilson. "Study of Administration."
89. Quoted in Ronald J. Pestritto, "Woodrow Wilson, the Organic State, and American Republicanism," in Frost and Sikkenga, *History of American Political Thought,* 558.
90. Croly, *Promise of American Life,* 115, 382.
91. See, for example, Pika, Maltese, and Rudalevige, *Politics of the Presidency,* 13–14.
92. Quoted in Pestritto and Atto, *American Progressivism,* 185.
93. W. Wilson, *Constitutional Government,* 68.
94. Quoted in Pestritto, "Woodrow Wilson," 556.

95. W. Wilson, *Constitutional Government*, 60.
96. Ellis, *Development of the American Presidency*, 16.
97. W. Wilson, *Congressional Government*, 4.
98. Wilson, 54–55. Wilson means the English Whig Party, not the American Whigs, who obviously did not exist at the time of the American founding.
99. Wilson, 56–57.
100. Pestritto, *Woodrow Wilson*, 6, 57.
101. Croly, *Progressive Democracy*, 51, 232, 44–45, 47.
102. Croly, 284, 280.
103. Roosevelt, "Campaign Address at Oglethorpe University."
104. Lincoln, *Collected Works*, 4:531–32.
105. Lincoln, 6:404.
106. Lincoln, 8:253–54.
107. Lincoln, 5:433–34.
108. Lincoln, 6:29.
109. Lincoln, 6:30.
110. Lincoln, 4:168–69.
111. Quoted in Marshall, "Strange Stillbirth of the Whig Party," 446.
112. Lincoln, *Collected Works*, 2:1–5.
113. Lincoln, 1:501–16.
114. Lincoln, 4:262.
115. Lincoln, 7:398.
116. Allen Guelzo, "Abraham Lincoln or the Progressives: Who Was the *Real* Father of Big Government?," The Heritage Foundation, February 10, 2012, http://www.heritage.org/research/reports/2012/02/abraham-lincoln-was-not-the-father-of-big-government. In the 2017 fiscal year, the federal government spent about $4.147 trillion, or approximately 142 times the 1865 inflation-adjusted budget. This accounted for 21.5 percent of GDP. See "2017 United States Federal Budget," Wikipedia, https://en.wikipedia.org/wiki/2017_United_States_federal_budget (last modified May 18, 2018).
117. Guelzo, "Abraham Lincoln or the Progressives." Again, by comparison, in 2015 the Federal Register of regulations ran over 80,000 pages. Clyde Wayne Crews, "Bureaucracy Unbound: 2015 Is Another Record Year for the Federal Register," Competitive Enterprise Institute, December 13, 2015, https://cei.org/blog/bureaucracy-unbound-2015-another-record-year-federal-register.
118. "Annual Report to Congress on White House Office Personnel, as of June 30, 2017," https://www.whitehouse.gov/sites/whitehouse.gov/files/docs/disclosures/07012017-report-final.pdf (accessed May 14, 2018).
119. Lincoln, *Collected Works*, 2:220-221
120. Holzer and Garfinkle make just this claim in relation to the passage quoted (see *Just and Generous Nation*, 75–76). The immediate claim here

is not that Lincoln would not support such a Progressive state, although I think that is true, but that this particular passage does not support Holzer and Garfinkle's interpretation.

121. This is the basic error of Holzer and Garfinkle. They conflate the Whig belief that "government should do more" with "there should be no limits on government," and when discussing contemporary views they set up a false distinction between supporting either the Progressive state or an anarchist social Darwinism. The accusation of social Darwinism is simply a straw man, in that virtually no one actually advocates such a minimalist state, and sets up a false dichotomy, as if the Progressive state and anarchy are the only two alternatives.

122. Fornieri, *Abraham Lincoln*, 19.

123. Howe, *Political Culture of the American Whigs*, 20.

124. McPherson, *Abraham Lincoln*; Beard and Beard, *Rise of American Civilization*, 2:54.

125. See, for example, DiLorenzo, *Real Lincoln*; and Hummel, *Emancipating Slaves*.

126 Rossiter, *Federalist Papers*, 311, 305.

127. For Lincoln's commentary on *Dred Scott* and the Supreme Court, see *Collected Works*, 2:398–410, and his first inaugural speech, 4:268.

128. For an argument regarding Progressives as both a break from the founding and as part of the modern political tradition, see Deneen, *Why Liberalism Failed*.

129. Edward McPhail, "Distributism and 'Modern Economics,'" in Lanz, *Beyond Capitalism and Socialism*, 98.

130. Levin, *Fractured Republic*, 204.

131. Belloc, *Servile State*, 16.

132. Belloc, 37, 16.

133. Leo XIII, *Rerum Novarum*, 3, 28, 61.

134. Pius XI, *Quadragesimo Anno*, 54. Even John Paul II, normally considered more friendly to free markets than earlier pontiffs, writes of capital and labor in the nineteenth century in *Centesimus Annus*: "A new form of *property* had appeared—capital; and a *new form of labour*—labour for wages, characterized by high rates of production which lacked due regard for sex, age or family situation, and were determined solely by efficiency, with a view to increasing profits" (4). As the title of the encyclical suggests, it was written on the centenary of *Rerum Novarum*.

135. Belloc, *Servile State*, 52, 54.

136. Médaille, *Toward a Truly Free Market*, 196, 53.

137. Thomas Storck, "Capitalism and Distributism: Two Systems at War," in Lanz, *Beyond Capitalism and Socialism*, 69.

138. Médaille, *Toward a Truly Free Market*, 164–65, 137.

139. Belloc, *Servile State*, 6.

140. S. Sagar, "Distributism," in Sharpe, *Distributist Perspectives, Volume II*, 93.

141. Arthur J. Penty, "Distributism: A Manifesto," in Sharpe and O'Huallachain, *Distributist Perspectives, Volume I*, 87.

142. Chesterton, *Three Works on Distributism*, 48.

143. Belloc, *Servile State*, 64.

144. Médaille, *Toward a Truly Free Market*, 164–65.

145. Belloc, *Servile State*, 70–71, 69.

146. Thomas H. Naylor, "Averting Self-Destruction: A Twenty-First Century Appraisal of Distributism," in Sharpe and O'Huallachain, *Distributist Perspectives, Volume I*, 17.

147. Sale, "Forward," xi.

148. Storck, "Capitalism and Distributism," 78.

149. Médaille, *Toward a Truly Free Market*, 136.

150. Chesterton, *Three Works on Distributism*, 46.

151. Belloc, *Servile State*, 13.

152. McPhail, "Distributism and 'Modern Economics,'" 105.

153. Harold Robbins, "The Buttress of Freedom," in Sharpe and O'Huallachain, *Distributist Perspectives, Volume I*, 65.

154. McPhail, "Distributism and 'Modern Economics,'" 111.

155. Leo XIII, *Rerum Novarum*, 46.

156. Pius XI, *Quadragesimo Anno*, 63.

157. Pius XI, 65.

158. Lanz, "Editor's Preface," in *Beyond Capitalism and Socialism*, vi.

159. Quoted in Zieba, *Papal Economics*, 10.

160. Leo XIII, *Rerum Novarum*, 12, 13, 45.

161. Leo XIII, 57.

162. Esolen, *Reclaiming Catholic Social Teaching*, 153.

163. Pius XI, *Quadragesimo Anno*, 33.

164. Pius XI, 34.

165. Leo XIII, *Rerum Novarum*, 45.

166. Distributists might point to the good number of employee-owned corporations in the United States, particularly in the supermarket industry, as examples of distributism in action, as well as the rise in farmers' markets. The Spanish corporation Mondragon also runs on distributist principles. Still, no major national economy has adopted distributist principles in any large measure.

167. Guelzo, *Abraham Lincoln*, 106.

168. Winger, *Lincoln, Religion, and Romantic Cultural Politics*, 127.

169. See Donald, *Lincoln*, 110 and 234; and Boritt, *Lincoln and the Economics of the American Dream*, 114, 122, and 124.

170. Donald, *Lincoln*, 234.

171. Boritt, *Lincoln and the Economics of the American Dream*, 128. Emphasis in original.

172. Boritt, 169.

173. Lincoln, *Collected Works*, 1:412.

174. Lincoln, 3:459.
175. Lincoln, 3:311–12.
176. Lincoln, 3:459.
177. Lincoln, 4:24.
178. Lincoln, 4:24.
179. Lincoln, 5:51.
180. Lincoln, 3:477.
181. Lincoln, 3:477.
182. Lincoln, 3:478.
183. Lincoln, 5:52.
184. Lincoln, 5:52.
185. Lincoln, 5:52.
186. Foner, *Free Soil*, xxvi.
187. Lincoln, *Collected Works*, 3:462–63.
188. Lincoln, 3:478–79.
189. Lincoln, 3:479.
190. Guelzo, *Abraham Lincoln*, 122.
191. Howe, *What Hath God Wrought*, 542.
192. Lincoln, *Collected Works*, 3:481.
193. Friedman, *Capitalism and Freedom*, 12.
194. Lincoln, *Collected Works*, 1:8.
195. Lincoln, 1:8.
196. Lincoln, 3:479–80.
197. Lincoln, 4:24.
198. Lincoln, 2:220.
199. Rupert Ederer, "Heinrich Pesch and the Idea of a Catholic Economics," in Lanz, *Beyond Capitalism and Socialism*, 91.
200. Lanz, "Editor's Preface," viii.
201. Baumgarth and Regan, *Aquinas on Law*, 191.
202. Winger, *Lincoln, Religion, and Romantic Cultural Politics*, 7.
203. John Sharpe, introduction to Lanz, *Beyond Capitalism and Socialism*, xxiii.
204. Peter Chojnowski, "Father Vincent McNabb's 'Call to Contemplatives,'" in Lanz, *Beyond Capitalism and Socialism*, 51.
205. Anthony Cooney, "I Fear No Peevish Master: The Romance of Distributism," in Lanz, *Beyond Capitalism and Socialism*, 13.
206. Howe, *Political Culture of the American Whigs*, 103, 105.
207. Quoted in Foner, *Free Soil*, 22.
208. Quoted in Howe, *Political Culture of the American Whigs*, 117.
209. Winger, *Lincoln, Religion, and Romantic Cultural Politics*, 132.
210. Howe, *What Hath God Wrought*, 540–41.
211. Howe, *Political Culture of the American Whigs*, 115.
212. Howe, 115–16, 118.
213. Foner, *Free Soil*, 37.
214. Howe, *Political Culture of the American Whigs*, 119.

215. Howe, 121–22.
216. Howe, 297.
217. Howe, 297.
218. Foner, *Free Soil*, xxxvi.

4. Lincoln and the Second American Revolution

1. Paludan, *Presidency of Abraham Lincoln*, xiii.
2. For example, the massive biographies of Lincoln by David Herbert Donald and Michael Burlingame respectively say virtually nothing about any public policy in the Lincoln presidency except that pertaining to the Civil War. If one reads Doris Kearns Goodwin's highly successful *Team of Rivals*, ostensibly about Lincoln's management of his cabinet, one will learn more about the social scene of Civil War–era Washington than about nonwar public policy, as she has nothing to say about the latter.
3. The argument of Leonard Curry is considered in detail below. See also Frank J. Williams and William D. Pederson, "Lincoln as an Advocate of Positive Government," in Deutsch and Fornieri, *Lincoln's American Dream*, 393–97.
4. Beard and Beard, *Rise of American Civilization*, 2:53–54.
5. Randall, *Lincoln: The Liberal Statesman*, 177–78.
6. See, for example, T. Harry Williams, "Lincoln and the Radicals," in McWhiney, *Grant, Lee, Lincoln and the Radicals*, 114; and Norman A. Graebner, "Abraham Lincoln: Conservative Statesman," in Graebner, *Enduring Lincoln*, 68.
7. McPherson, *Abraham Lincoln*, 39–40.
8. McPherson, 40.
9. Curry, *Blueprint for Modern America*; Moore, *Social Origins*; Boritt, *Lincoln and the Economics of the American Dream*.
10. McPherson, *Abraham Lincoln*, 42.
11. McPherson, 12.
12. One assumes McPherson is counting Woodrow Wilson as a New Jerseyan, where Wilson was governor and resided immediately before ascending the presidency, rather than a Virginian, where Wilson was born.
13. McPherson, *Abraham Lincoln*, 12–13.
14. McPherson, 25, 25–29, 29–37, 37, 37–38, 39, 40.
15. Beard and Beard, 2:22–23.
16. Beard and Beard, 2:7, 53.
17. Beard and Beard, 2:39–40, 54. The Beards seem to assume that abolition was the only serious antislavery position of the 1850s.
18. Beard and Beard, 2:56–57.
19. Beard and Beard, 2:99.
20. Moore, *Social Origins*, 112, 121, 123–24.
21. Boritt, *Lincoln and the Economics of the American Dream*, 155, 191–92.
22. Boritt does argue that Lincoln's antislavery position was part of a broader economic vision. Boritt, 192.

23. Curry, *Blueprint for Modern America*, 14, 15–16.
24. Beard and Beard, *Rise of American Civilization*, 2:108, 109.
25. Moore, *Social Origins*, 126, 143, 136–37.
26. Boritt, *Lincoln and the Economics of the American Dream*, 99, 149–50.
27. Boritt, 197.
28. Curry, *Blueprint for Modern America*, 101.
29. Curry, 135–36.
30. Curry, 179.
31. Beard and Beard, *Rise of American Civilization*, 2:56.
32. Boritt, *Lincoln and the Economics of the American Dream*, 148, 195, 228, 198.
33. Boritt, 208, 209, 217, 227.
34. Curry, *Blueprint for Modern America*, 207, 9.
35. Ellis, *Development of the American Presidency*, 15–16.
36. Greenstein, 45.
37. Greenstein, 45–46, 49.
38. Neustadt, *Presidential Power*, i, 1, 6.
39. Neustadt, 6. As Neustadt writes, "[f one wants effective policy in the American system, danger does not lie in our dependence upon a man; it lies in our capacity to make ourselves dependent upon a man who is inexpert" (181). Unlike the founders, Neustadt's only worry about concentrating virtually all power in one branch of government is the possibility that the head of that branch might be "inexpert."
40. Neustadt, 80.
41. Neustadt, 54, 158–59, 132.
42. Edwards, *At the Margins*, 1.
43. Bond and Fleisher, *President in the Legislative Arena*, 7.
44. Quoted in Leuchtenburg, *FDR Years*, 17.
45. Posner and Vermeule, *Executive Unbound*, 185.
46. Suri, *Impossible Presidency*, 177.
47. Nichols, *Myth of the Modern Presidency*, 10, 62.
48. Jeffrey Tulis, "The Constitutional Presidency in American Political Development," in Fausold and Shank, *Constitution and the Modern Presidency*, 139. Emphasis in the original.
49. Tulis, 139.
50. Tulis, 139–40, 140.
51. Kernell, *Going Public*, 19–20, 78–81.
52. Kernell, 85, 89–90.
53. Frendreis, Tatalovich, and Schaff, "Predicting Legislative Output."
54. W. Wilson, *Congressional Government*, 57, 47–48, 253–54, 255.
55. Lowi, "American Business," 677–715. See also Birkland, *Introduction to the Policy Process*, 132–41.
56. Lowi, "American Business," 689–90.
57. Lowi, 690, 693.

58. Ripley and Franklin, *Congress*, 102.
59. Ripley and Franklin, 102.
60. Lowi, "American Business," 691.
61. Lowi, 697.
62. Lowi, 705.
63. Ripley and Franklin, *Congress*, 121, 123.
64. Lowi, "American Business," 689.
65. Lowi, *Personal President*, 56–57.
66. Redistributive policy did not develop in full force until the New Deal. But it will be argued below that among the most significant acts of the Civil War Congresses was the passage of legislation providing for the regulation banks and the money supply.
67. It should be noted that there is a distinction between a "critical election" and a "realignment." As stated before, realignments occur over a period of years, often crystallizing, though, in one critical election. Properly speaking, the late 1850s made up a realigning era punctuated by the critical election of 1860. While being somewhat distinct phenomena, they both can be explained by the same theories as a critical election, which is in fact a kind of subset of a realignment.
68. Key, "Theory of Critical Elections," 3.
69. Key, 11.
70. Campbell, Converse, Miller, and Stokes, *Elections and the Political Order*, 126.
71. Campbell, Converse, Miller, and Stokes, 74–76.
72. Campbell, Converse, Miller, and Stokes, 76.
73. Burnham, writing in 1970, speculated that 1968 may signal a realignment toward Republicanism. This proved to be false. Most political scientists argue, rather, that since the late 1960s/early 1970s we have seen a "dealignment," meaning a breakdown of party loyalty within the electorate. My own view is that the rise of primary elections and changes in campaign finance law have neutered the two political parties and have given rise to the interest group as the instrument of change in American politics. Political parties have ceased to be the central organizing principle of American elections and thus partisan realignment as traditionally understood is almost impossible.
74. Burnham, *Critical Elections*, 181, 6–10.
75. MacDonald and Rabinowitz, "Dynamics of Structural Realignment," 778.
76. MacDonald and Rabinowitz, 778–79.
77. MacDonald and Rabinowitz, 779.
78. Skowronek, *Politics Presidents Make*, 3, 4, 20–21.
79. Skowronek, 30.
80. Skowronek, 30.
81. Skowronek, 37, 38.
82. Skowronek, 50, 51.

83. Skowronek, 199, 201.
84. Skowronek, 202–3, 203, 205–6, 210–11.
85. Skowronek, 212, 212–13.
86. This should not be confused with the Union Party created in 1860 by conservative Northern and Border State Democrats who supported the Union but had strong Southern sympathies.
87. Skowronek, *Politics Presidents Make*, 213.

5. Whigs and Lincoln: A Realignment Reconsidered

1. Sundquist, *Dynamics of the Party System*, 50.
2. Mayfield, *Rehearsal for Republicanism*, 4.
3. Chase, *Salmon P. Chase Papers*, 1:86.
4. Mayfield, *Rehearsal for Republicanism*, 101–2.
5. Mayfield, 68–69.
6. Mayfield, 189–90.
7. Porter and Johnson, *National Party Platforms*, 13.
8. Porter and Johnson, 14.
9. Porter and Johnson, 14–15.
10. Holt, *Political Crisis*, 237, 242.
11. Sundquist, *Dynamics of the Party System*, 69.
12. Porter and Johnson, *National Party Platforms*, 20–21.
13. Sherman, *Sherman's Recollections*, 96.
14. Sherman, 113.
15. McKay, *Henry Wilson*, 86–87.
16. Fessenden, *William Pitt Fessenden*, 62.
17. Donald, *Lincoln*, 138–41.
18. Fessenden, *William Pitt Fessenden*, 42.
19. Holt, *Political Crisis*, 238–39.
20. Holt, 244–45.
21. Holt points out that there was a bit of coincidence to the seeming local nature of the political restructuring that suggests this was not a thought-out party-building strategy. It just so happened that the 1854–55 local elections were the first post–Kansas-Nebraska elections where the Republicans and Know-Nothings even existed. Neither party was willing to wait until 1856 and the presidential election to make its move. A contemporary third-party movement of any significance would almost certainly wait for a presidential election to make its move.
22. Holt, *Political Crisis*, 251–56.
23. Crandall, *Early History of the Republican Party*, 9.
24. Mayfield, *Rehearsal for Republicanism*, 108.
25. Chase, *Salmon P. Chase Papers*, 1:119–20.
26. Holt, *Political Crisis*, 247.
27. Stevens, *Selected Papers*, 108.
28. Sherman, *Sherman's Recollections*, 92–93.

29. Fessenden, *William Pitt Fessenden*, 46–47.
30. McKay, *Henry Wilson*, 113.
31. The slave state of Missouri would be the one exception to the line.
32. Obviously Douglas guessed wrong. The controversy over his bill made him politically unviable in 1856.
33. Greeley, *Recollections*, 294.
34. Cross, *Justin Smith Morrill*, 29; Crandall, *Early History of the Republican Party*, 107.
35. Trefousse, *Thaddeus Stevens*, 88.
36. Sherman, *Sherman's Recollections*, 97–98.
37. Chase, *Salmon P. Chase Papers*, 1:384.
38. In fact, James Sundquist shows that Republican votes correlate better with past Free-Soil votes than with Whig votes (*Dynamics of the Party System*, 86).
39. Ilisevich, *Galusha A. Grow*, 86, 108–14.
40. Hunt, *Hannibal Hamlin*, 88–90.
41. Hunt, 82.
42. Hunt, 80.
43. Taylor, *William Henry Seward*, 92.
44. Ilisevich, *Galusha A. Grow*, 100.
45. Sherman, *Sherman's Recollections*, 101–3.
46. Smith, *Schuyler Colfax*, 49.
47. Cook, *Baptism of Fire*, 60.
48. Sherman, *Sherman's Recollections*, 110–11.
49. Gienapp, *Origins of the Republican Party*, 66; Holt, *Political Crisis*, 291–92; Crandall, *Early History of the Republican Party*, 14–15.
50. Stevens, *Selected Papers*, 152; Smith, *Schuyler Colfax*, 51–53; Gienapp, *Origins of the Republican Party*, 48–60.
51. Trefousse, *Thaddeus Stevens*, 91.
52. Mayfield, *Rehearsal for Republicanism*, 114–15.
53. Porter and Johnson, *National Party Platforms*, 10.
54. Foner, *Free Soil*, 170; Sundquist, *Dynamics of the Party System*, 79.
55. Foner, *Free Soil*, 113.
56. Crandall, *Early History of the Republican Party*, 97–98.
57. Fessenden, *William Pitt Fessenden*, 64–65.
58. Ilisevich, *Galusha A. Grow*, 105.
59. Crandall, *Early History of the Republican Party*, 198.
60. Crandall, 283–84.
61. Nevins, *Emergence of Lincoln*, 2:303.
62. Stevens, *Selected Papers*, 156.
63. Ilisevich, *Galusha A. Grow*, 80, 83.
64. Ilisevich, 184–86.
65. Smith, *Schuyler Colfax*, 131–32.
66. Bensel, *Yankee Leviathan*, 76. "Pro-Buchanan" Democrats were opposed on many issues by Democrats like Stephen Douglas, who ultimately

parted ways with the administration over the organization of the Kansas state. Of the bills mentioned, these anti-administration Democrats opposed only the rivers and harbors bill and the railroad bill but also did not support the other measures in the uniformity that Republicans did.

67. Porter and Johnson, *National Party Platforms*, 32–33.
68. Porter and Johnson, 33.
69. Foner, *Free Soil*, 174.
70. Chase, *Salmon P. Chase Papers*, 1:415.
71. Chase, 2:25–27.
72. Gienapp, *Origins of the Republican Party*, 70–71.
73. Foner, *Free Soil*, 73–74.
74. Chase, *Salmon P. Chase Papers*, 2:30.
75. Fessenden, *William Pitt Fessenden*, 49.
76. Fessenden, 51.
77. Gienapp, *Origins of the Republican Party*, 203–8.
78. Gienapp, 190.
79. Ilisevich, *Galusha A. Grow*, 93.
80. Stevens, *Selected Papers*, 148–49.
81. Gienapp, *Origins of the Republican Party*, 192–203; Sherman, *Sherman's Recollections*, 106.
82. Cook, *Baptism of Fire*, 58–59.
83. Crandall, *Early History of the Republican Party*, 15.
84. Chase, *Salmon P. Chase Papers*, 2:10.
85. Crandall, *Early History of the Republican Party*, 108.
86. Crandall, 68.
87. Gienapp, *Origins of the Republican Party*, 179.
88. Gienapp, 264–68; Crandall, *Early History of the Republican Party*, 67.
89. Crandall, *Early History of the Republican Party*, 163.
90. Chase is particularly suspect as at one time or another in his political life he was associated with the Whig Party, the Liberty Party, the Free-Soil Party, the Democratic Party, the Know-Nothing Party, and the Republican Party. A man of almost blinding ambition, he seemed to take whatever course suited that ambition.
91. Donald, *Lincoln*, 126–29.
92. Donald, 126–27.
93. Lincoln, *Collected Works*, 2:158–59.
94. Lincoln, 2:135–57.
95. Lincoln, 2:288.
96. Donald, *Lincoln*, 177.
97. Lincoln, *Collected Works*, 2:247, 254–56, 273.
98. Donald, *Lincoln*, 169–71.
99. Lincoln, *Collected Works*, 2:316–17.
100. Lincoln, 2:340–41; Donald, *Lincoln*, 190–91.
101. Lincoln, *Collected Works*, 2:361–66.

102. Lincoln, 2:358, 374–75.
103. Lincoln, 3:396, 400–462, 463–82, 495–507.
104. Lincoln, 3:522–54, 4:1–30.
105. Foner, *Free Soil*, 213–14.
106. Beard and Beard, 2:56–57.
107. Lincoln, *Collected Works*, 2:385.

6. The Domestic Lincoln and Congressional Government

1. Boritt, *Lincoln and the Economics of the American Dream*, 195.
2. Donald, *Lincoln Reconsidered*, 59.
3. Hendrick, *Lincoln's War Cabinet*, 4.
4. Donald, *Lincoln Reconsidered*, 110–11.
5. Bogue, *Congressman's Civil War*, 121.
6. Bogue, 140–41.
7. Cross, *Justin Smith Morrill*, 209.
8. Trefousse, *Thaddeus Stevens*, 303.
9. Nicolay and Hay, *Abraham Lincoln*, 6:247.
10. Boritt, *Lincoln and the Economics of the American Dream*, 197.
11. Hendrick, *Lincoln's War Cabinet*, 332.
12. Fessenden, *William Pitt Fessenden*, 193–95.
13. McPherson, *Abraham Lincoln*, 40.
14. Lincoln, *Collected Works*, 4:202.
15. Curry, *Blueprint for Modern America*, 101.
16. Porter and Johnson, *National Party Platforms*, 33.
17. *Cong. Globe*, 37th Cong., 2nd Sess., 136 (1861).
18. *Cong. Globe*, 136.
19. *Cong. Globe*, 910.
20. *Cong. Globe*, 1938.
21. *Cong. Globe*, 1951, 1035.
22. *Cong. Globe*, 2147–48.
23. Cross, *Justin Smith Morrill*, 84.
24. Curry, *Blueprint for Modern America*, 111–12; *Cong. Globe*, 37th Cong., 2nd Sess., 2275–77.
25. *Cong. Globe*, 2769–70.
26. *Cong. Globe*, 2634, 2770.
27. Porter and Johnson, *National Party Platforms*, 33.
28. Porter and Johnson, 31.
29. *Cong. Globe*, 37th Cong., 2nd Sess., 1578–79.
30. *Cong. Globe*, 1578.
31. *Cong. Globe*, 1596. Emphasis in original.
32. *Cong. Globe*, 1590; Lincoln, *Collected Works*, 5:156–57.
33. *Cong. Globe*, 37th Cong., 2nd Sess., 599.
34. *Cong. Globe*, 1708.
35. *Cong. Globe*, 1698–1711.

36. *Cong. Globe*, 2654–55.
37. *Cong. Globe*, 2655.
38. Curry, *Blueprint for Modern America*, 131; *Cong. Globe*, 37th Cong., 2nd Sess., 2906.
39. *Cong. Globe*, 37th Cong., 2nd Sess., 2840, 2906.
40. Burlingame and Ettlinger, *Inside Lincoln's White House*, 133–34.
41. Ellis, *Development of the American Presidency*, 172–73.
42. Chase, *Salmon P. Chase Papers*, 1:423.
43. *Cong. Globe*, 37th Cong., 2nd Sess., 458.
44. *Cong. Globe*, 523–24.
45. *Cong. Globe*, 524.
46. *Cong. Globe*, appendix, 25.
47. *Cong. Globe*, appendix, 25.
48. *Cong. Globe*, appendix, 26.
49. *Cong. Globe*, 525. Emphasis in original.
50. *Cong. Globe*, 525–26. Emphasis in original.
51. *Cong. Globe*, 525.
52. *Cong. Globe*, 639.
53. *Cong. Globe*, 640.
54. *Cong. Globe*, 664–65. Emphasis in the original.
55. *Cong. Globe*, 657.
56. Sherman, *Sherman's Recollections*, 271.
57. *Cong. Globe*, 37th Cong., 2nd Sess., 772.
58. *Cong. Globe*, 772.
59. *Cong. Globe*, 774.
60. *Cong. Globe*, 774–75.
61. *Cong. Globe*, 802.
62. *Cong. Globe*, 789.
63. Chase, *Salmon P. Chase Papers*, 3:322–23.
64. *Cong. Globe*, 37th Cong., 2nd Sess., 804, 939.
65. Lincoln, *Collected Works*, 5:522–23.
66. Lincoln, 6:60–61.
67. Lincoln, 5:522–23.
68. *Cong. Globe*, 37th Cong., 2nd Sess., 1114.
69. *Cong. Globe*, 1117.
70. *Cong. Globe*, 840–41.
71. *Cong. Globe*, 821.
72. *Cong. Globe*, 842.
73. *Cong. Globe*, 874.
74. *Cong. Globe*, 874.
75. Chase, *Salmon P. Chase Papers*, 3:425–26.
76. Sherman, *Sherman's Recollections*, 298–99.
77. Boritt, *Lincoln and the Economics of the American Dream*, 200–201.
78. *Cong. Globe*, 37th Cong., 3rd Sess., 897, 1148 (1863).

79. *Cong. Globe*, 37th Cong., 1st Sess., 315 (1861).

80. *Cong. Globe*, 37th Cong., 2nd Sess., 221.

81. Curry, *Blueprint for Modern America*, 160.

82. *Cong. Globe*, 37th Cong., 2nd Sess., 1217.

83. *Cong. Globe*, 1217–18, 1412, 2446.

84. Davis, Hughes, and McDougall, *American Economic History*, 172.

85. Greenleaf, *American Economic Development*, 41.

86. Foote, *Civil War*, 1:801.

87. White, *Eloquent President*, 108. In contrast, Barack Obama in his first term gave 1,852 "speeches, remarks and comments," 699 of which were formal enough to require a teleprompter. Mark Knoller, "Obama's First Term by the Numbers," CBS News, January 13, 2013, http://www.cbsnews .com/news/obamas-first-term-by-the-numbers/.

88. Ellis, *Development of the American Presidency*, 361–62.

89. McPherson, *Abraham Lincoln*, 42.

90. Surely Lincoln and Chase did not have the personal attachment Washington and Hamilton had. It is well known that Chase was highly critical of Lincoln's pursuit of war aims and on these matters sought to undermine Lincoln with Congress. The volatility between the two men reached such a fever pitch that, under pressure from Lincoln, Chase resigned as secretary of the Treasury in 1864.

91. Suri, *Impossible Presidency*, 162.

92. Posner and Vermeule argue that the complexity of modern economies and government necessitate a presidency-centered government (*Executive Unbound*, 31–32).

93. Lowi, *Personal President*, 20.

94. Lowi, 51.

95. Nichols, *Myth of the Modern Presidency*, 10.

96. Suri, *Impossible Presidency*, xv–xvi.

97. Rossiter, *Federalist Papers*, 29.

98. See, for example, Judis, *Populist Explosion*; Müller, *What Is Populism?*; and Mounk, *People vs. Democracy*.

99. Ceaser, *Presidential Selection*, 11–14.

100. Mansfield, *Taming the Prince*, 266.

101. It is worth noting, for example, that in the decade before becoming a Republican president, Trump had donated financially to campaigns of leading Democrats such as Charles Schumer, Nancy Pelosi, and Harry Reid. His 2016 opponent Hillary Clinton was an attendee at Trump's 2005 wedding.

102. Bernie Sanders nearly captured the Democratic nomination the same year despite literally not being a Democrat. Sanders, a socialist-leaning Independent, had to change his party registration to run for the Democratic nomination.

103. One of the biggest complaints of members of Congress is that they spend an inordinate amount of time on constituency service, tied to reelection, and not enough time actually educating themselves about legislation. See Davidson, Oleszek, and Lee, *Congress and Its Members*, 120.
104. This phenomenon is not limited to the presidency. In my state of South Dakota, candidates for an open U.S. House seat announced nearly a year and a half before the November 2018 election.
105. Doherty, *Rise of the President's Permanent Campaign*, 150–52, 163.
106. See Rod Dreher, "How Bobby Jindal Wrecked Louisiana," *American Conservative*, February 6, 2015, http://www.theamericanconservative .com/dreher/how-bobby-jindal-wrecked-louisiana/.
107. See Kiewe, *Modern Presidency*.
108. Lowi, *Personal President*, 170.
109. Mansfield, *Taming the Prince*, 14, 251.
110. Mansfield, 257; Rossiter, *Federalist Papers*, 421–23.
111. Rossiter, *Federalist Papers*, 306.
112. Rossiter, 379.

Conclusion

1. See, for example, Vance, *Hillbilly Elegy*; and Hochschild, *Strangers in Their Own Land*.
2. For the "mantle of anger" quote see Ryan Teague Beckwith, "Read the Full Transcript of the Sixth Republican Debate in Charleston," *Time*, January 15, 2016, http://time.com/4182096/republican-debate-charleston -transcript-full-text/.
3. Lincoln, *Collected Works*, 5:345.
4. Randall, *Lincoln: The Liberal Statesman*, 177.
5. Randall, 184–86.
6. Fornieri, *Abraham Lincoln*, 25.
7. Brookhiser, *Founders' Son*, 6.
8. Randall, *Lincoln: The Liberal Statesman*, 179.
9. Lincoln, *Collected Works*, 3:315.
10. Lincoln, 1:111.

Bibliography

Aristotle. *Nicomachean Ethics*. Translated by Martin Ostwald. New York: Bobbs-Merrill, 1962.

———. *The Politics*. Translated by T. A. Sinclair. New York: Penguin, 1962.

Baumgarth, William P., and Richard J. Regan, eds. *Aquinas on Law, Morality and Politics*. Translated by Richard J. Regan. Indianapolis: Hackett, 2002.

Beard, Charles A., and Mary R. Beard. *The Rise of American Civilization*. 2 vols. New York: Macmillan, 1927.

Belloc, Hilaire. *The Servile State*. 1912. Reprint, San Bernardino, Calif.: Seven Treasures Press, 2008.

Bennett, Lerone. *Forced into Glory: Abraham Lincoln's White Dream*. Chicago: Johnson, 2000.

Bensel, Richard Franklin. *Yankee Leviathan: The Origins of Central State Authority in America, 1859–1877*. New York: Cambridge University Press, 1990.

Birkland, Thomas. *An Introduction to the Policy Process: Theories, Concepts, and Models of Public Policy Making*. Armonk, N.Y.: M. E. Sharpe, 2001.

Bogue, Allan. *The Congressman's Civil War*. New York: Cambridge University Press, 1989.

Bond, Jon, and Richard Fleisher. *The President in the Legislative Arena*. Chicago: University of Chicago Press, 1990.

Boritt, Gabor. *Lincoln and the Economics of the American Dream*. Urbana: University of Illinois Press, 1994.

Bibliography

Brookhiser, Richard. *Founders' Son: A Life of Abraham Lincoln*. New York: Basic Books, 2014.

Burke, Edmund. *Reflections on the Revolution in France*. New York: Penguin Classics, 1968.

Burlingame, Michael. *Abraham Lincoln: A Life*. 2 vols. Baltimore: Johns Hopkins University Press, 2008.

Burlingame, Michael, and John R. Turner Ettlinger, eds. *Inside Lincoln's White House: The Complete Civil War Diary of John Hay*. Carbondale: Southern Illinois University Press, 1999.

Burnham, Walter Dean. *Critical Elections and the Mainsprings of American Politics*. New York: W. W. Norton, 1970.

Campbell, Angus, Philip Converse, Warren Miller, and Donald Stokes. *Elections and the Political Order*. New York: John Wiley and Sons, 1966.

Cavanaugh, William. *The Myth of Religious Violence: Secular Ideology and the Roots of Modern Conflict*. New York: Oxford University Press, 2009.

Ceaser, James. *Presidential Selection: Theory and Development*. Princeton: Princeton University Press, 1979.

Chase, Salmon P. *The Salmon P. Chase Papers*. 4 vols. Kent, Ohio: Kent State University Press, 1993.

Chernow, Ron. *Alexander Hamilton*. New York: Penguin Press, 2004.

Chesterton, G. K. *The Everlasting Man*. Reprint, San Francisco: Ignatius Press, 1993.

———. *Three Works on Distributism*. Lexington, Ky.: Creative Space Independent Publishing Platform, 2009.

Clor, Harry M. *On Moderation: Defending an Ancient Virtue in a Modern World*. Waco, Tex.: Baylor University Press, 2008.

Cook, Robert. *Baptism of Fire: The Republican Party in Iowa, 1838–1878*. Ames: Iowa State University Press, 1994.

Crandall, Andrew. *The Early History of the Republican Party*. Boston: R. G. Badger, 1930.

Croly, Herbert. *Progressive Democracy*. New York: Macmillan, 1914. Reprint, New Brunswick, N.J.: Transaction, 1998.

———. *The Promise of American Life*. 1909. Reprint, Boston: Northeastern University Press, 1989.

Cross, Coy F. *Justin Smith Morrill: Father of the Land-Grant Colleges*. East Lansing: Michigan State University Press, 1999.

Cuomo, Mario. *Why Lincoln Matters: Today More Than Ever*. New York: Harcourt, 2004.

Curry, Leonard. *Blueprint for Modern America: Nonmilitary Legislation of the First Civil War Congress*. Nashville: Vanderbilt University Press, 1966.

Danoff, Brian. "Lincoln and Tocqueville on Democratic Leadership and Self-Interest Properly Understood." *Review of Politics* 67 (Fall 2005): 687–719.

Davidson, Roger H., Walter J. Oleszek, and Frances E. Lee. *Congress and Its Members*. 13th ed. Washington, D.C.: CQ Press, 2012.

Davis, Lance E., Jonathan R. T. Hughes, and Duncan M. McDougall. *American Economic History*. Homewood, Ill.: Richard Irwin, 1969.

Deneen, Patrick. *Why Liberalism Failed*. New Haven, Conn.: Yale University Press, 2018.

Deutsch, Kenneth L., and Joseph R. Fornieri, eds. *Lincoln's American Dream: Clashing Political Perspectives*. Washington, D.C.: Potomac Books, 1994.

Diggins, John Patrick. *On Hallowed Ground: Abraham Lincoln and the Foundations of American History*. New Haven: Yale University Press, 2000.

DiLorenzo, Thomas. *The Real Lincoln: A New Look at Abraham Lincoln, His Agenda, and an Unnecessary War*. Roseville, Calif.: Forum, 2003.

Doherty, Brendan J. *The Rise of the President's Permanent Campaign*. Lawrence: University Press of Kansas, 2012.

Donald, David Herbert. *Lincoln*. New York. Simon and Schuster, 1995.

———. *Lincoln Reconsidered: Essays on the Civil War Era*. New York: Vintage Books, 1961.

Edwards, George C., III. *At the Margins*. New Haven: Yale University Press, 1989.

Ellis, Richard J. *The Development of the American Presidency*. 2nd ed. New York: Routledge, 2012.

Emerson, Jason. *Lincoln the Inventor*. Carbondale: Southern Illinois University Press, 2009.

Engeman, Thomas S., ed. *Thomas Jefferson and the Politics of Nature*. Notre Dame, Ind.: University of Notre Dame Press, 2000.

Esolen, Anthony. *Reclaiming Catholic Social Teaching: A Defense of the Church's True Teachings on Marriage, Family, and the State*. Manchester, N.H.: Sophia Institute Press, 2014.

Fausold, Martin, and Alan Shank, eds. *The Constitution and the Modern Presidency*. Albany: State University of New York Press, 1991.

Fehrenbacher, Donald. *Slaveholding Republic: An Account of the United States Government's Relations to Slavery*. New York: Oxford University Press, 2002.

Ferguson, Andrew. *Land of Lincoln: Adventures in Abe's America*. New York: Atlantic Monthly Press, 2007.

Fessenden, Francis. *Life and Public Services of William Pitt Fessenden in Two Volumes*. New York: Houghton Mifflin, 1907.

Foner, Eric. *Free Soil, Free Labor, Free Men: The Ideology of the Republican Party before the Civil War*. New York: Oxford University Press, 1995.

Foote, Shelby. *The Civil War*. 3 vols. New York: Vintage, 1986.

Fornieri, Joseph R. *Abraham Lincoln: Philosopher Statesman*. Carbondale: Southern Illinois University Press, 2014.

Frendreis, John, Raymond Tatalovich, and Jon Schaff. "Predicting Legislative Output in the First One-Hundred Days, 1897–1995." *Political Research Quarterly* 54 (Winter 2001): 853–70.

Friedman, Milton. *Capitalism and Freedom*. Chicago: University of Chicago Press, 1982.

Frost, Bryan-Paul, and Jeffrey Sikkenga, eds. *History of American Political Thought*. New York: Lexington, 2003.

Gienapp, William E. *The Origins of the Republican Party*. New York: Oxford University Press, 1997.

Goodwin, Doris Kearns. *Team of Rivals*. New York: Simon and Schuster, 2006.

Graebner, Norman, ed. *The Enduring Lincoln*. Urbana: University of Illinois Press, 1959.

Greeley, Horace. *Recollections of a Busy Life*. Miami, Fla.: Mnemosyne, 1969.

Greenleaf, William. *American Economic Development Since 1860*. New York: Harper and Row, 1968.

Greenstein, Fred. "Change and Continuity in the Modern Presidency." In *The New American Political System*, edited by Anthony King, 45–85. Washington, D.C.: American Enterprise Institute, 1978.

Guelzo, Allen C. *Abraham Lincoln: Redeemer President*. Grand Rapids, Mich.: Wm. B. Eerdmans, 1999.

Haidt, Jonathan. *The Righteous Mind: Why Good People Are Divided by Religion and Politics*. New York: Vintage, 2013.

Hamilton, Alexander. *Papers on Public Credit, Commerce, and Finance*. New York: Liberal Arts Press, 1957.

———. *Writings*. New York: Library of America, 2001.

Healy, Gene. *Cult of the Presidency: America's Dangerous Devotion to Executive Power*. Washington, D.C.: Cato Institute, 2009.

Hendrick, Burton J. *Lincoln's War Cabinet*. Boston: Little, Brown, 1946.

Hoadley, John F. *Origins of American Political Parties, 1789–1803*. Lexington: University Press of Kentucky, 1986.

Hochschild, Arlie Russell. *Strangers in Their Own Land: Anger and Mourning on the American Right*. New York: New Press, 2016.

Hofstadter, Richard. *The American Political Tradition*. New York: Vintage, 1948.

Holt, Michael. *The Political Crisis of the 1850s*. New York: Norton, 1983.

———. *The Rise and Fall of the American Whig Party*. New York: Oxford University Press, 1999.

Holzer, Harold. *Lincoln at Cooper Union: The Speech That Made Lincoln President*. New York: Simon and Schuster, 2006.

Holzer, Harold, and Norton Garfinkle. *A Just and Generous Nation: Abraham Lincoln and the Fight for American Opportunity*. New York: Basic Books, 2015.

Howe, Daniel Walker. *The Political Culture of the American Whigs*. Chicago: University of Chicago Press, 1979.

———. *What Hath God Wrought: The Transformation of America, 1815–1848*. New York: Oxford University Press, 2007.

Hummel, Jeffrey Rogers. *Emancipating Slaves, Enslaving Free Men*. Peru, Ill.: Open Court, 1996.

Hunt, H. Draper. *Hannibal Hamlin of Maine: Lincoln's First Vice-President*. Syracuse, N.Y.: Syracuse University Press, 1969.

Hyneman, Charles, and George W. Carey. *Second Federalist: Congress Creates a Government*. New York: Appleton-Century-Crofts, 1967.

Ilisevich, Robert D. *Galusha A. Grow: The People's Candidate*. Pittsburgh: University of Pittsburgh Press, 1988.

Jaffa, Harry V. *Crisis of the House Divided: An Interpretation of the Issues in the Lincoln-Douglas Debates*. Chicago: University of Chicago Press, 1982.

Jividen, Jason. *Claiming Lincoln: Progressivism, Equality, and the Battle for Lincoln's Legacy in Presidential Rhetoric*. DeKalb: Northern Illinois University Press, 2011.

John Paul II. *Centesimus Annus* [papal encyclical on the hundredth anniversary of *Rerum Novarum*]. 1991. Accessed June 2015. http://w2 .vatican.va/content/john-paul-ii/en/encyclicals/documents/hf_jp-ii _enc_01051991_centesimus-annus.html.

Judis, John B. *The Populist Explosion: How the Great Recession Transformed American and European Politics*. New York: Columbia Global Reports, 2016.

Kalb, James. "Technocracy Now." *First Things* 225 (2015): 25–31.

Kernell, Samuel. *Going Public: New Strategies of Presidential Leadership*. Washington, D.C.: CQ Press, 1997.

Key, V. O. "A Theory of Critical Elections." *Journal of Politics* 17, no. 1 (February 1955): 3–18.

Kiewe, Amos, ed. *The Modern Presidency and Crisis Rhetoric*. Westport, Conn.: Praeger, 1994.

Knott, Stephen F. *Alexander Hamilton and the Persistence of Myth*. Lawrence: University Press of Kansas, 2002.

Kraynak, Robert. *Christian Faith and Modern Democracy: God and Politics in the Fallen World*. Notre Dame, Ind.: University of Notre Dame Press, 2001.

Lanz, Tobias J., ed. *Beyond Capitalism and Socialism: A New Statement of an Old Ideal*, Norfolk, Va.: Light in the Darkness Publications, 2008.

Leo XIII. *Rerum Novarum* [papal encyclical on rights and duties of capital and labor]. 1891. Accessed February 2015. http://w2.vatican.va/content /leo-xiii/en/encyclicals/documents/hf_l -xiii_enc_15051891_rerum -novarum.html.

Bibliography

Leuchtenburg, William. *The FDR Years: On Roosevelt and His Legacy.* New York: Columbia University Press, 1995.

Levin, Yuval. *The Fractured Republic: Renewing America's Social Contract in the Age of Individualism.* New York: Basic Books, 2016.

———. *The Great Debate: Edmund Burke, Thomas Paine, and the Birth of Right and Left.* New York: Basic Books, 2014.

Lincoln, Abraham. *The Collected Works of Abraham Lincoln.* Edited by Roy P. Basler. 9 vols. New Brunswick, N.J.: Rutgers University Press, 1953–55.

Lind, Michel. *What Lincoln Believed: The Values and Convictions of America's Greatest President.* New York: Doubleday, 2004.

Locke, John. *Second Treatise of Government.* Edited by C. B. Macpherson. Indianapolis: Hackett, 1980.

Lowi, Theodore J. "American Business, Public Policy, Case Studies and Political Theory." *World Politics* 16 (June 1964): 677–715.

———. *The Personal President: Power Invested, Promise Unfulfilled.* Ithaca: Cornell University Press, 1985.

MacDonald, Stuart Elaine, and George Rabinowitz. "The Dynamics of Structural Realignment." *American Political Science Review* 81, no. 3 (September 1987): 775–96.

MacIntyre, Alasdair. *After Virtue: A Study in Moral Theory.* 3rd ed. Notre Dame, Ind.: University of Notre Dame Press, 2007.

Mansfield, Harvey C., Jr. *Taming the Prince: The Ambivalence of Modern Executive Power.* Baltimore: Johns Hopkins University Press, 1993.

Marshall, Lynn L. "The Strange Stillbirth of the Whig Party." *American Historical Review* 72 (January 1967): 445–68.

Mayer, George H. *The Republican Party, 1854–1966.* New York: Oxford University Press, 1967.

Mayfield, John. *Rehearsal for Republicanism: Free Soil and the Politics of Antislavery.* Port Washington, N.Y.: Kennikat Press, 1993.

McDonald, Forest. *Alexander Hamilton: A Biography.* New York: W. W. Norton, 1982.

———. *The Presidency of George Washington.* Lawrence: University of Kansas Press, 1974.

McGovern, George. *Abraham Lincoln.* New York: Times Books, 2008.

McKay, Ernest. *Henry Wilson: Practical Radical.* Port Washington, N.Y.: Kennikat Press, 1971.

McPherson, James M. *Abraham Lincoln and the Second American Revolution.* New York: Oxford University Press, 1991.

———. *Battle Cry of Freedom: The Civil War Era.* New York: Oxford University Press, 1988.

McWhiney, Grady, ed. *Grant, Lee, Lincoln and the Radicals: Essays on Civil War Leadership.* Evanston, Ill.: Northwestern University Press, 1964.

Médaille, John C. *Toward a Truly Free Market: A Distributist Perspective on the Role of Government, Taxes, Health Care, Deficits, and More.* Wilmington, Del.: ISI Books, 2010.

Meier, Kenneth. "Drugs, Sex and Rock and Roll: A Theory of Morality Politics." *Policy Studies Journal* 27, no. 4 (1999): 681–95.

Miller, Eugene. "Democratic Statecraft and Technological Advance: Abraham Lincoln's Reflections on 'Discoveries and Inventions.'" *Review of Politics* 63 (Summer 2001): 485–515.

Miller, William Lee. *President Lincoln: The Duty of a Statesman.* New York: Vintage, 2008.

Moore, Barrington, Jr. *Social Origins of Dictatorship and Democracy: Lord and Peasant in the Making of the Modern World.* Boston: Beacon Press, 1966.

Morel, Lucas. *Lincoln's Sacred Effort: Defining Religion's Role in American Self-Government.* Lanham, Md.: Lexington Books, 2000.

Mounk, Yasha. *The People vs. Democracy: Why Our Freedom Is in Danger and How to Save It.* Cambridge, Mass.: Harvard University Press, 2016.

Müller, Jan-Werner. *What Is Populism?* Philadelphia: University of Pennsylvania Press, 2016.

Neely, Mark E., Jr. *The Fate of Liberty: Abraham Lincoln and Civil Liberties.* New York: Oxford University Press, 1992.

———. *The Last Best Hope of Earth: Abraham Lincoln and the Promise of America.* Cambridge, Mass.: Harvard University Press, 1995.

Neustadt, Richard. *Presidential Power: The Politics of Leadership.* New York: Wiley and Sons, 1960.

Nevins, Allen. *The Emergence of Lincoln.* 2 vols. New York: Charles Scribner's Sons, 1950.

Nichols, David. *The Myth of the Modern Presidency.* University Park: Pennsylvania State University Press, 1994.

Nicolay, John, and John Hay. *Abraham Lincoln: A History.* 10 vols. New York: Century, 1890.

Oates, Stephen B. *With Malice toward None: The Life of Abraham Lincoln.* New York: Harper and Row, 1977.

O'Connor, Flannery. *Collected Works.* New York: Library of America, 1988.

Paludan, Phillip Shaw. *The Presidency of Abraham Lincoln.* Lawrence: University of Kansas Press, 1994.

Pestritto, Ronald J. *Woodrow Wilson and the Roots of Modern Liberalism.* Lanham, Md.: Rowman and Littlefield, 2005.

Pestritto, Ronald J., and William J. Atto, eds. *American Progressivism: A Reader.* New York: Lexington Books, 2008.

Peterson, Merrill D. *Lincoln in American Memory.* New York: Oxford University Press, 1995.

Pika, Joseph A., John Anthony Maltese, and Andrew Rudalevige. *The Politics of the Presidency*. 9th ed. Washington, D.C.: CQ Press, 2017.

Pius XI. *Quadragesimo Anno* [papal encyclical on reconstruction of the social order]. 1931. Accessed June 2015. http://w2.vatican.va/content/pius -xi/en/encyclicals/documents/hf_p-xi_enc_19310515_quadragesimo -anno.html.

Porter, Kirk H., and Donald Bruce Johnson. *National Party Platforms, 1840–1956*. Urbana: University of Illinois Press, 1956.

Posner, Eric A., and Adrian Vermeule. *The Executive Unbound: After the Madisonian Republic*. New York: Oxford University Press, 2010.

Postman, Neil. *Amusing Ourselves to Death: Public Discourse in the Age of Show Business*. 20th Anniversary Edition. New York: Penguin Books, 2005.

———. *Technopoly: The Surrender of Culture to Technology*. New York: Vintage, 1993.

Randall, J. G. *Lincoln: The Liberal Statesman*. New York: Dodd, Mead, 1947.

———. *Lincoln: The President*. Vol. 1, *Springfield to Gettysburg*. 1945. Reprint, Gloucester, Mass.: Peter Smith, 1976.

Remini, Robert. *Henry Clay: Statesman for the Union*. New York: W. W. Norton, 1991.

Ripley, Randall B., and Grace A. Franklin. *Congress, the Bureaucracy, and Public Policy*. Belmont, Calif.: Wadsworth, 1991.

Roosevelt, Franklin D. "Campaign Address at Oglethorpe University." May 22, 1932. George Info: An Online Georgia Almanac. https://georgiainfo .galileo.usg.edu/topics/history/related_article/progressive-era-world -war-ii-1901-1945/franklin-d.-roosevelts-twenty-third-visit-to -georgia/fdr-oglethorpe-university-commencement-address -may-22-1932.

———. "Commonwealth Club Address." September 23, 1932. TeachingAmericanHistory.org. http://teachingamericanhistory.org/library/index .asp?document=447.

———. "First Inaugural Address." March 4, 1933. TeachingAmericanHistory .org. http://teachingamericanhistory.org/library/index.asp ?document=89.

———. "The New Nationalism." August 10, 1910. TeachingAmericanHistory .org. http://teachingamericanhistory.org/library/index.asp ?document=501.

Rossiter, Clinton, ed. *The Federalist Papers*. With an introduction by Charles Kesler. New York: Mentor, 1999.

Sasse, Ben. *Them: Why We Hate Each Other—and How to Heal*. New York: St. Martin's Press, 2018.

Sharpe, J. Forrest, ed. *Distributist Perspectives, Volume II*. Norfolk, Va.: IHS Press, 2008.

Bibliography

Sharpe, J. Forrest, and D. Liam O'Huallachain, eds. *Distributist Perspectives, Volume I*. Norfolk, Va.: IHS Press, 2004.

Sherman, John. *John Sherman's Recollections of Forty Years in the House, Senate and Cabinet*. Chicago: Werner, 1895.

Skowronek, Steven. *The Politics Presidents Make*. Cambridge, Mass.: Harvard University Press, 1997.

Smith, Willard H. *Schuyler Colfax: The Changing Fortunes of a Political Idol*. Indianapolis: Indiana Historical Bureau, 1952.

Stevens, Thaddeus. *The Selected Papers of Thaddeus Stevens*. Edited by Beverly Palmer. Pittsburgh: University of Pittsburgh Press, 1997.

Storing, Herbert. *What the Anti-Federalists Were For*. Chicago: University of Chicago Press, 1981.

Striner, Richard. *Father Abraham: Lincoln's Relentless Struggle to End Slavery*. New York: Oxford University Press, 2007.

Sundquist, James. *The Dynamics of the Party System: Alignment and Realignment of Political Parties in the United States*. Washington, D.C.: Brookings Institute, 1983.

Suri, Jeremi. *The Impossible Presidency: The Rise and Fall of America's Highest Office*. New York: Basic Books, 2017.

Taylor, John M. *William Henry Seward: Lincoln's Right Hand*. Washington, D.C.: Brassley's, 1991.

Thurow, Glen E. *Abraham Lincoln and American Political Religion*. Albany: State University of New York Press, 1976.

Tocqueville, Alexis de. *Democracy in America*. Translated by Harvey Mansfield and Delba Winthrop. Chicago: University of Chicago Press, 2002.

Trefousse, Hans Louis. *Benjamin Franklin Wade: Radical Republican from Ohio*. New York: Twayne, 1963.

———. *Thaddeus Stevens: Nineteenth-Century Egalitarian*. Chapel Hill: University of North Carolina Press, 1997.

Tulis, Jeffrey. *The Rhetorical Presidency*. Princeton: Princeton University Press, 1987.

Vance, J. D. *Hillbilly Elegy: A Memoir of a Family and Culture in Crisis*. New York: Harper, 2016.

Vodolazkin, Eugene. "The New Middle Ages." *First Things* 256 (2016): 31–36.

Walling, Karl-Friedrich. *Republican Empire: Alexander Hamilton on War and Free Government*. Lawrence: University of Kansas Press, 1999.

Watson, Harry L. *Andrew Jackson vs. Henry Clay: Democracy and Development in Antebellum America*. New York: Bedford/St. Martin's, 1998.

White, Ronald C. *The Eloquent President: A Portrait of Lincoln through His Words*. New York: Random House, 2005.

Williams, Frank J., William D. Pederson, and Vincent J. Marsala, eds. *Abraham Lincoln: Sources of Style and Leadership*. Westport, Conn.: Greenwood Press, 1994.

Wills, Garry. *Lincoln at Gettysburg: The Words that Remade America.* New York: Touchstone Books, 1992.

Wilson, Douglas L. *Lincoln's Sword: The Presidency and the Power of Words.* New York: Vintage Books, 2006.

Wilson, Woodrow. *Congressional Government.* Boston: Houghton Mifflin, 1885.

——. *Constitutional Government in the United States.* New York: Columbia University Press, 1908. Reprint, New Brunswick, N.J.: Transaction Publishers, 2002.

——. "Study of Administration." November 1, 1886. TeachingAmericanHistory .org. http://teachingamericanhistory.org/library/index.asp ?document=465.

Winger, Stewart. *Lincoln, Religion, and Romantic Cultural Politics.* DeKalb: Northern Illinois University Press, 2003.

Zieba, Maciej. *Papal Economics: The Catholic Church on Democratic Capitalism, from "Rerum Novarum" to "Caritas in Veritate."* Wilmington, Del.: ISI Books, 2013.

Index

abolitionism, 22, 33, 51, 162; 1837 resolution denouncing, 26–27; immoderate and imprudent stances, 36–37

abstract justice, 5, 22, 31, 42, 45, 76

abstract rights, 57, 73–78

Adams, Charles Francis, 184, 197

Adams, Henry, 85

Adams, John Quincy, 86, 87, 92

agrarianism, 81–82, 109, 125–27, 177–78

Alley, John, 186

American Revolution of 1776, 135

American System of economics, 80, 85–88, 161, 196; internal improvements, 89–90, 170

Ames, Fisher, 84

Appeal of the Independent Democrats (Chase, Giddings, and Sumner), 173–74

Aquinas, Thomas, 125

aristocracies, 59, 71–72, 88

Aristotle, 11–12, 13–17, 25, 36, 38, 76

Articles of Confederation, 81, 107

authority, executive, 44, 59, 75–76, 85, 91, 100, 142, 167, 186–87, 192

Bank of the United States, 86, 144

banking and currency, 88, 142, 171, 186–95; Treasury notes, 185. *See also* Legal Tender Act of 1862; National Bank Act of 1863

Banks, Nathaniel, 169, 175

Barger, Harold, 147–48

Bates, Edward, 173, 187

Beard, Charles A., 135, 137–40, 142, 144, 177

Beard, Mary R., 135, 137–40, 142, 144, 177

Belloc, Hilaire, 109–12, 113–14

Benjamin, Julian, 165

Bennett, Lerone, 18, 21, 28, 34, 36–37

Bingham, John, 188

Blair, Frank, 174

Boritt, Gabor S., 118, 136, 137, 139–44, 180, 193
Brookhiser, Richard, 65, 210
Brown, John, 211
Bryan, William Jennings, 153
Buchanan, James, 51, 165, 170–74, 176, 177, 182, 183, 201, 236n66
Burke, Edmund, 73–74, 77
Burnham, Walter Dean, 155
Bush, George W., 200, 203

campaign, permanent, 201–3
Campbell, Angus, 154–55
Campbell, James, 184
candidate-centered elections, 201–2
capitalism, 108–10, 136–39, 153, 229n134
Carey, Henry C., 117, 127–28
Cass, Lewis, 52, 163
Catholic social thought, 108–15, 125
Cavanaugh, William, 38
Ceaser, James, 200–202
centralization, 87, 94–99, 105, 112, 146
Chase, Salmon P., 18, 51, 34, 36–37, 237n90, 240n90; banking legislation and, 186–97; as organizer of Republican Party, 162, 166, 169, 172–76, 179; as Treasury secretary, 143, 181, 193–94, 196–97
Chernow, Ron, 79
Chesterton, G. K., 1–2, 109, 111, 113
Chicago Tribune, 174
citizenry, acculturating, 4, 14, 21–22, 25, 28–29, 40, 199
Civil War: currency as wartime measure, 188–89; Emancipation Proclamation as war measure, 34–35, 102; legislation during, 7, 92, 104, 124, 134–39, 143–44, 161; Lincoln acts without permission

of Congress, 91, 197, 204; as "second American Revolution," 7, 107, 133–35, 144, 194, 208
Clay, Henry, 18, 46, 64, 163, 165, 185, 217n6; "American System" of economics, 80–81, 85–88, 143, 161, 196; "corrupt bargain," 86; Declaration of Independence, view of, 58; Douglas's use of, 52, 55; Liberty Party and, 26–27; state of nature views, 58–59
Clinton, Hillary, 208, 240n101
Clor, Harry, 15, 36–37
Colfax, Schuyler, 169
Collamer, Jacob, 191–92
Commentaries (Story), 187
commercial society, 82–83, 87
Compromise of 1850, 49, 52, 163–64, 167
Confederate States of America, 36–37
Congress, 6–7; First, 84, 196; Thirty-Third, 163; Thirty-Fourth, 169; Thirty-Sixth, 171; Thirty-Seventh, 92, 134, 144, 159, 181, 198; Thirty-Eighth, 134, 144, 159; abolition of international slave trade, 56; in Articles of Confederation, 81; committee system, 150–51; dominance, 144, 146–47; Douglas's view, 54–56; factions, 141–42; Lincoln acts without permission of, 91–92, 197, 204; power to ban slavery, 48, 56–57, 64; presidential deference to, 7, 144–45, 147, 180, 194, 197; Republican, 180–81; in touch with people, 103
Congressional Government (Wilson), 97
Conkling, F. A., 188
Conkling, Roscoe, 188

consent of the governed, 30–31, 36–38, 47

conservatism, 135–37, 209–10

Constitution: abolition of international slave trade, 56; Article I, Section 1, 148, 225n29; Article I, Section 8, 89–90, 187; Article II, 85, 148; congressional factions and, 141–42; exploitation of ambiguities in, 91, 98, 188–89; living constitution, 99–100, 107; as monarchy, 100; nullification crisis of 1832, 52; protections for slavery, 31, 37, 38; respect for, 21; strict constructionism, 107

Constitutional Convention, 148

constitutionalism, 5, 95, 148, 211

Converse, Philip, 154

Cooney, Anthony, 125

corporations, 96–98, 108, 110, 126–27

Crandall, Andrew, 166, 168, 174

crisis, routinized, 106, 199, 203–5, 208

Croly, Herbert, 93, 95, 97, 100–101

Cross, Coy, 169

Cuomo, Mario, 93–94

Curry, Leonard P., 136–37, 139, 141, 144

Danoff, Brian, 92

Davis, Lance E., 194

Declaration of Independence, 1, 21, 77, 79, 102–3, 222n42; all people included, 64; Douglas accused of undermining, 44–45; natural rights in, 43–47, 60, 100, 211; as "standard maxim for free society," 46–47; as standard of progress, 105–6; undermines slavery, 34, 44; Wilson's view, 100, 103

demagoguery, 4, 15–17, 38–39, 21–22, 199–200, 207–08

democracy: as dangerous to legitimate authority, 75–76; direct, 101; liberalism associated with, 2, 209–10; natural rights as democratic poetry, 72–78; popular sovereignty undermines, 59, 73, 211; preference for as prejudice, 25; saving Union as tantamount to, 34; shaping of democratic soul, 6, 32, 73

Democratic Party, 45, 51, 56, 67, 236–37n66; anti-Nebraska, 164, 169, 174, 176; Appeal of the Independent Democrats, 173–74; as inheritor of Lincoln, 94; Jacksonian, 138–39, 153, 158, 161, 225n38; limited government, view of, 170; pro-Douglas and anti-Douglas factions, 177; states' rights faction, 85; Whigs and, 164–65

despotism, 59, 63, 86, 199–200, 221n3

Diggins, John Patrick, 80

dignity, 59, 75, 78, 109

DiLorenzo, Thomas, 18

discoveries and inventions, 65–72; "Negroes" as, 70–71; speech and writing as, 69–70

distributism, 7, 108–17, 120, 230n166; areas of agreement with Lincoln, 123–30; critiques, 116–17; decentralization, 113; explained, 110–17; solidarity, 114–15, 124; subsidiarity, 114–16, 124

distributive policy, 150–52

District of Columbia, 33, 47–48, 164

domestic policy, 2, 91, 133–34; distributive, regulatory, and redistributive, 150–52; electoral

domestic policy (*continued*)
theory, 137, 154–55; elite introduction of issues, 155–58; legislative role of president, 146–50; modern presidency literature, 137, 145; party realignment theory, 152–59, 234n73; political science perspectives, 146–59; public policy and presidential power, 149–52; public policy literature, 137, 145–46, 150. *See also* legislation
Donald, David Herbert, 117–18, 180
"don't care" policy/indifference, 30, 48, 54, 59–62, 210
Douglas, Stephen, 6; 1858 senatorial race, 29–30; accused of undermining Declaration, 44–45; "Black Republican" rhetoric, 29–30, 50; as chair of Senate Committee on Territories, 49, 67; "don't care" policy, 30, 48, 54, 60–62; as immoderate statesman, 30; Kansas-Nebraska Act and, 167–68; Know-Nothing comments about, 12–13; Lincoln's natural rights rebuttal to, 47–65; moderation, presentation of, 51–55; natural rights and, 43; popular sovereignty approach, 29–31, 43, 51, 59, 73, 176, 210–11; racism, appeals to, 50–51; Young America movement and, 67–69
Douglass, Frederick, 50, 51
Dred Scott decision, 54, 64, 107
due process, 2, 25, 37–38

Ederer, Rupert, 124
education, 70–72, 122–23, 144
Edwards, George, 147
Eisenhower, Dwight, 147
electoral system, 201–2, 241n103

electoral theory, 137, 154–55
Ellis, Richard J., 99, 146, 186, 194
Emancipation Proclamation, 34–35, 102
Engeman, Thomas S., 80
equality, 36, 46, 53; as central idea of republic, 29, 32; natural, 26, 34, 37, 46, 59, 71–72
Esolen, Anthony, 115
Evans, George Henry, 127
Everett, Edward, 127
The Everlasting Man (Chesterton), 1–2

Father Abraham: Lincoln's Relentless Struggle to End Slavery (Striner), 18
Federalist Papers: No. 1, 199; No. 23, 82, 89, 188; No. 44, 42; No. 48, 204; No. 49, 107; No. 51, 42, 62–63, 105; No. 55, 221n3; No. 62, 204; No. 70, 83, 148, 204; No. 71, 83
Federalists, 72–73, 80, 86–87, 142
federative power, 91
Fenton, Reuben, 191
Ferguson, Adam, 128
Ferguson, Andrew, 3
Fessenden, Samuel, 184
Fessenden, William Pitt, 164, 167, 170, 173, 181, 184, 189–90, 193
Fillmore, Millard, 168, 175, 201
First Bank of the United States, 88
flattery, 59, 83, 199–200, 226n52
Foner, Eric, 120, 126, 173, 176
Foote, Shelby, 17
Fornieri, Joseph, 13, 17, 56, 66, 106, 209, 222n36
founders/founding fathers, 21–22, 44, 79–80; change and continuity, 209–10; creation of half slave,

half free nation, 53, 55; Lincoln as departure from, 93–94; questioning of, 95–100; slavery, position on, 55–56
Franklin, Grace, 151–52
Free-Soil Party, 127, 143, 160–67, 170, 236n38, 237n90
free-soil position, 54
Frémont, John C., 34, 102, 170, 176
frontier thesis, 96

Garfinkle, Norton, 94, 229n121
Garrison, William Lloyd, 161–62
Gettysburg Address, 34, 56
Giddings, Joshua Reed, 51, 173, 174
Gilded Age, 128
goods: balancing, 34; competing, 26–27, 34, 37; consent and, 28–29; distributing, 150–51; exaggerating, 16–17; liberty, 110
government powers, 5, 6, 80–86; broad interpretation, 7, 89–93, 98, 106, 226n58; centralization, 87, 94–99, 105, 146; domestic policy and, 91; federal spending power, 83; maintenance of order as basic task, 104–5, 124; to regulate currency, 193–94; routinized crisis, 106. See also presidency
Great Depression, 149, 152, 153
Greeley, Horace, 34, 127, 168, 174, 175
Greenleaf, William, 194
Greenstein, Fred, 146, 147
Grow, Galusha, 168, 171, 181, 182
Guelzo, Allen, 48, 55, 59, 103–4, 121, 218n20

habit, 38, 76–77
Hamilton, Alexander, 6, 79–80, 88, 107; in First Congress, 196; presidency, views of, 80–85, 91–92, 148, 188; railroad legislation and, 185; *Report on Manufactures*, 80, 82–83, 89; as Treasury secretary, 84. See also *Federalist Papers*
Hamlin, Hannibal, 168
Hammond, James Henry, 119
Hay, John, 181, 186
Healy, Gene, 6
Hendrick, Burton, 180
Henry, Anthony, 192
Herndon, William, 47
Hoadley, John F., 84
Hofstadter, Richard, 80
Holt, Michael, 86–87, 165, 235n21
Holzer, Harold, 17–18, 94, 229n121
Homestead Act, 7, 92, 104, 124, 135, 139, 142, 171, 173; silence of administration, 182–83, 193, 196
homestead legislation, 127, 162–63, 171, 177–78
House Finance Committee (Illinois General Assembly), 89
Howe, Daniel Walker, 85, 121–22, 126, 128
Hughes, Jonathan R. T., 194
Hunter, David, 34

ideologue, 16–17, 24, 40, 211
ideology, 16–17, 78, 156
Illinois and Michigan Canal, 90
Illinois General Assembly, 174, 176
immigrants, white, 45–46, 54
Independent Treasury, 88
Industrial Revolution, 7, 118
industrialization, 95–99, 110, 118, 138, 142–43
interest groups, 201
internal improvements, 89–90, 143–44, 164, 170–71

Internal Revenue Act of 1862, 136, 192–93
"iron triangle," 151

Jackson, Andrew, 52, 86, 88–90, 98, 103, 107, 144, 153, 156–58, 161, 198, 219n28, 225n38
Jaffa, Harry, 13, 17, 22, 36, 80, 81
Jefferson, Thomas: agrarianism, 81, 82, 96, 126, 156; Lincoln's view of, 79–80; narrow interpretation of government power, 88–89, 100, Progressive view of, 93, 107, *See also* Declaration of Independence
Jindal, Bobby, 202
Jividen, Jason, 227n80
John XXIII, 117
Johnson, Lyndon, 138, 198
Julian, George, 182, 183
A Just and Generous Nation (Holzer and Garfinkle), 94
"Just Wage," 116
justice: abstract, 5, 22, 31, 42, 45; incomplete, 38; "not sole question," 28, 30, 42

Kansas, 167; "Bleeding Kansas," 30, 64
Kansas-Nebraska Act of 1854, 27, 42–43, 48, 57, 64, 139, 211; Northern opposition to, 174; passage of, 163; rise of Republican Party and, 139, 140–41, 166–68
Kennedy, John F., 149
Kernell, Samuel, 149
Key, V. O., 154
Knott, Stephen F., 81
Know-Nothings, 12–13, 141, 165, 168, 175, 218n2, 235n21
Kraynak, Robert, 75, 77

labor, 108–17; as both physical and mental, 113, 123; free, 108–17, 119; free, as source of value, 118, 123; Lincoln on, 117–23; "mud-sill" theory, 109, 119–20, 122–23; as political theory, 110; "right to rise," 88, 120–21, 161, 177; slavery contrasted with free, 118–19, 122; small producers, 117–18, 120–21; wage labor and free labor compared, 118–21
Land-Grant College Act, 7, 81, 104, 124, 135, 144, 171, 173, 181–82, 193, 196
Lanz, Tobias, 114–15, 125
Legal Tender Act of 1862, 7, 92, 135–36, 181, 186, 192–95
legislation, 7, 92, 104, 124, 134–39, 143–44, 161; land-related, 182–85; presidential leadership, 146–50, 182, 194–96. *See also* banking and currency; domestic policy; *individual legislation*
Leo XIII, 109, 110, 114–15, 125
Levin, Yuval, 73, 74, 109
liberalism, 209–10
Liberator (abolitionist newspaper), 161–62
Liberia solution to slavery, 27–28
libertarians, 107
Liberty Party, 26–27, 166
limitations, 5–8; angel analogy, 62–63; centralization of government, 96–97; on equality, 46; natural rights and, 42–44, 47–48, 55, 72–74, 78; obligations, 73–74; on presidency, 7, 81, 84, 104–5, 134, 146, 198–99, 209; president responsible for educating citizens, 22, 32, 40, 42, 68, 71, 81, 204–5; Progressives oppose, 7, 84,

99–101, 105–8, 137; self-imposed,
5; shaping of democratic soul, 6,
32, 73; tyranny as absence of, 42,
59, 65

Lincoln, Abraham: 1832 run for political office, 122; 1858 senatorial
race, 29; ability to stand inside
and outside democracy, 1–2; acts
without permission of Congress,
91–92, 197, 204; avoidance of
extremes, 12–13, 28, 178–79, 196,
205, 218n2; on banks, 89, 190;
biblical language, use of, 66–69;
"Black Republican" attack on,
29–30, 50; claimed by all parties
and politicians, 94–96; in Congress, 90, 174; as conservative,
135–36, 178–79; countermands
emancipation orders, 33–34, 102;
on Declaration of Independence,
43–47; deference to Congress, 7,
144–45, 147, 180, 194, 197; distri-
butionism, areas of agreement
with, 123–30; on free labor,
117–23; Hamiltonian views of,
88–92, 128–29; "house divided"
rhetoric, 30, 31, 49–50, 52–54, 64;
Illinois General Assembly, first
attempt, 89; influence with Congress, 181; on Know-Nothings,
12–13; on lawlessness, 19–21; as
liberal statesman, 209; National
Bank Act and, 191–93; non-extension view of slavery, 33, 46–47,
80, 175–76; policy pronouncements, restraint in, 194; political
economy of, 88–92; as precursor
to Progressive movement, 92–95,
137; as "premodern" president,
137, 198; Progressivism, contrast
with, 95, 101–8; prosecution of

Civil War, 91, 180; on prudence
and moderation, 12, 17–25;
on public opinion, 24–25, 32;
realignment theory of, 154–55;
Republican Party, role in forming, 173–79; on reverence for law,
21; as "revolutionary," 135, 137,
138–39, 159, 178–79, 194–95; slavery, approach to, 25–35; on slaves
as equals, 28; thoughtfulness,
25–26; as "Whig in the White
House," 180, 198; witnesses slave
sales, 47; *Speeches*: 1838, "On the
Perpetuation of Our Political
Institutions" (Springfield Young
Men's Lyceum), 18–22, 25, 31, 32,
63, 102; 1848, on abolitionists, 33;
1854, Peoria, on Kansas-Nebraska
Act, 27–28, 42, 62; 1856, Chicago,
29–30; 1858, Republican Convention, 30; 1859, "Address before
the Wisconsin State Agricultural
Society," 119; 1859, Agricultural
Fair, Milwaukee, 109; 1860,
Cooper Union, 17–18, 43–45,
56–57; 1861, annual message to
Congress, 109, 119; 1861, Independence Hall, Philadelphia,
43–47; 1862, annual address,
190; first inaugural address, 33,
103; Gettysburg Address, 34, 56;
"Lectures on Discoveries and
Inventions," 65–72, 123, 223n58;
second inaugural address, 35;
Washington Temperance Society,
18, 22–25, 31, 32; "Young America," 67–69; *Writings*: "Fragment,"
1854, 104–5; "Fragment on Free
Labor," 1859, 118

Lincoln-Douglas debates, 31, 44,
50–52, 118, 158, 176, 210–11

Locke, John, 85
Louisiana Purchase, 85
Lovejoy, Elijah, 20–21
Lovejoy, Owen, 51, 176
Lowell, Massachusetts, 128
Lowi, Theodore J., 137, 150–52, 198–99, 203
Lyceum speech, 1838 (Lincoln), 18–22, 25, 31, 32, 63, 102

MacDonald, Stuart Elaine, 155–56, 158
MacIntyre, Alasdair, 76–77
Madison, James, 42, 62–63, 79, 107
majority rule, 5, 28–29, 34, 41–42, 47, 53
"manifest destiny," 68, 226n65
Mansfield, Harvey, 203–4
McDougall, Duncan M., 194
McDougall, James, 189–90
McGovern, George, 94, 95
McIntosh (lynching victim), 19–21
McKinley, William, 153, 154
McNabb, Vincent, 125
McPhail, Edward, 114
McPherson, James M., 135–39, 181; historians on Lincoln's leadership, 144–46; "second American Revolution," 7, 107, 133–35, 144, 194–95; sources, 139–44
Médaille, John, 110, 111, 113, 124
Medill, John, 174
Meier, Kenneth, 20
Mexican-American War, 26, 33, 88, 175
Miller, Eugene, 71
Miller, Warren, 154
Miller, William Lee, 37
Missouri Compromise of 1820, 43, 48–49, 53, 117, 139, 167–68
mob justice, 19–21, 32, 63, 218–19n28

"moderates," 11, 26
moderation, 3, 5–6, 39, 207; Aristotelian definitions, 11–12, 13–17; Douglas's approach, 51–55; as relative, 14–15; slavery, approach to, 25–35
modern presidency, 137, 145–47, 180, 196–99
Moore, Barrington, Jr., 136, 137, 139–44
moral excellence, 76–77
Morel, Lucas, 23–24, 38
Morrill, Justin, 182, 184, 188
Morrill, Lot, 168

National Bank, 84, 86
National Bank Act of 1863, 7, 92, 135–36, 142, 181, 186, 191–95
National Republicans, 85–86, 161. See also Whig Party
nationalism, economic, 86–87, 140, 143, 161, 191, 195–98
Native American Party ("Know-Nothings"). See Know-Nothings
nativist movement, 169–70, 176, 209
natural equality, 26, 34, 37, 46, 59, 71–72
natural rights, 3, 5, 41–78, 207, 210; as authority, 59, 75; critiques of, 73–75; in Declaration of Independence, 43–47, 60; as democratic poetry, 72–78; dignity, 59, 75, 78; Douglas's role in, 43; of family, 115; limitations inherent in, 42–44, 47–48, 55, 72–74, 78; obligations and, 73–76; political economy and, 129; Progressive rejection of, 99, 101; rebuttal to Douglas, 47–65; as self-evident truths, 44–45; slavery as wrong, 43, 61–62, 118; "state of nature"

philosophy, 46, 55, 57–59; taste vs. moral considerations, 61–62; technology and, 65–72

Nebraska Territory, 49, 167

"necessary and proper" clause, 89–90, 187

Neely, Mark, 89

Neustadt, Richard, 147, 203, 233n39

Nevins, Allen, 90, 172

New Deal, 138, 154, 234n66

New Mexico Territory, 49, 67

New York Tribune, 173, 174

Newtonian theory, 99

Nichols, David K., 148–49, 199

Nicolay, John, 181

Nicomachean Ethics (Aristotle), 13–15

non-extension view of slavery, 33, 46–48, 80, 175–76; Free-Soil Party and, 162–63

Northwest Ordinance, 53

Oates, Stephen, 80

Obama, Barack, 94–95, 200, 203, 240n87

O'Connor, Flannery, 37, 220n84

ownership, 67–69; distributist view, 110–13, 124; in production, 113–14

Pacific Railroad Act, 7, 92, 104, 124, 135, 171, 181, 183–85

Paludan, Phillip, 134

Panic of 1837, 86

party-centered system, 201–2, 234n73

Paul VI, 117

Pennsylvania, 170–71

Penty, Arthur, 112

perfection, pursuit of, 17

Pericles, 14

Pierce, Franklin, 164, 165, 168, 174, 201

Pike, Frederick, 188–89

Pius XI, 109, 110, 114–16, 229n134

plebiscitary system, 201–3

pluralism, institutionalized, 149

poetry, democratic, 72–78

political economy, 5–6, 79–130; "American System" of economics, 80; Clay, Whigs, and an American System, 85–88; commercial society, 82–83, 87; distributism, 108–17; economic dynamism, 5–6, 161; economic nationalism, 86–87, 140, 143, 161, 191, 195–98; free labor concepts, 108–17, 119; Hamiltonian views of Lincoln, 88–92; Hamilton's views, 80–85; Lincoln as precursor to Progressive movement, 92–95; Lincoln's, 88–92; majority rule and material wealth, 129–30

political religion, 38, 79, 102

political science perspectives, 146–59; legislative role of president, 146–50; party realignment theory, 152–59, 234n73; public policy and presidential power, 149–52

Politics (Aristotle), 15–16

Polk, James, 26, 33, 88, 90

popular sovereignty, 29–33, 37–38, 48, 176; democracy undermined by, 59, 73, 211; Douglas and, 29–31, 43, 51, 59, 73, 176, 210–11

positive liberal state, 106

Posner, Eric A., 148

presidency, 5–6; as check on public opinion, 83–84; commander-in-chief power, 34–35; "constitutional," 98; contemporary expectations of, 134, 198–200, 203; cult of, 6; "going public," 149, 197, 202–3; Hamilton's view,

presidency (*continued*)
80–85, 91–92, 148, 188; influence, restraint in, 191–92; legislative leadership, 146–50, 182, 194–96; as limited office, 7, 81, 84, 104–5, 134, 146, 198–99, 209; modern, 137, 145–47, 190, 196–97, 199; modest, 195–205; order affirming/creating/shattering, 156–58; permanent campaign, 201–3; "premodern," 137, 148–49, 197–98, 200; prerogative power, 84–85, 99, 148, 181; public attention to, 146; as public relations office, 202; reconstructive, 157; reelection concerns, 201–2, 241n103; responsibility for educating citizens, 22, 32, 40, 42, 68, 71, 81, 204–5; strong executive, 83, 103, 133–34, 146–49, 156; transformative characteristic of, 156–58; Union preservation as responsibility, 91; veto, 144; Whig suspicion of, 90–91, 103; White House staff, 104, 146, 197; Wilson on, 98–99. *See also* government powers
presidency-centered government, 3, 6–7, 133, 198
Progressive Party platform of 1912, 93
Progressivism, 6–7, 84, 92–95; historicism of, 95, 101; Lincoln, contrast with, 95, 101–8; Lincoln as precursor to, 92–95, 137; natural rights, rejection of, 99, 101; principles of political thought, 95–101; unlimited government, tendency toward, 7, 84, 99–101, 105–8, 137
The Promise of American Life (Croly), 93

protectionism, 83, 87–88, 117, 128, 172
prudence, 3, 6, 207; Aristotelian definitions, 11–17; going from theory to practice, 22–23
public opinion, 15, 24–25, 41, 149, 210; abolitionism as beyond, 37; executive as check on, 83–84; natural rights arguments, 49–50; persuasion and, 42, 147; statesman must address, 31; tyranny as threat, 32
public policy literature, 137, 145–46, 150–51, 180

Quadragesimo Anno (Pius XI), 109, 110, 114–16, 229n134

Rabinowitz, George, 155–56, 158
Radical Republicans, 29–30, 35, 52, 168
railroads, 48–49, 90, 135, 143, 171–72, 183–85
Randall, James G., 49, 80, 135, 209
Reagan Ronald, 156, 198
realignment theory, 152–59, 161, 177, 195, 234n67; elite introduction of issues, 155–57; "top-down" vs. "bottom-up," 153–54, 158, 195
reconstructing, politics of, 157–58
redistributive policy, 150–52, 234n66
regulatory policy, 150–52
Remini, Robert, 88
Report on Manufactures (Hamilton), 80, 82–83, 89
Republican Party, 7, 12, 51, 92–94; 1860 campaign, 7, 66, 92, 103, 135, 137, 139–40, 153, 171–72; agrarian policy and, 127; ascendancy of, 139–42, 152–53; birth of, 166–72; domestic agenda, 160–61;

economic issues and birth of,
169–72, 177–78, 195; as inheritor
of Lincoln, 94; as instrument
of capitalist class, 138–39, 153;
lack of strength, 201–2; leadership and realignment, 173–79;
legislation, Civil War era, 7, 92,
104, 124, 135–36, 138–39; Lincoln's
role in forming, 173–79; national
committee, 174; nomination of
Lincoln, 172; Radical Republicans, 29–30, 35, 52, 168; wealth
redistribution and, 135–36
Rerum Novarum (Leo XIII), 109,
110, 114–15
"right to rise," 88, 120–21, 161, 177
Ripley, Randall, 151–52
Robbins, Harold, 114
Roosevelt, Franklin Delano,
96–97, 101, 138, 153, 154, 156; as
benchmark, 146–47; elite-to-elite
bargaining, 149; "First Hundred
Days," 136, 146, 149
Roosevelt, Theodore, 93, 95, 97, 98
rule of law, 5, 6, 15, 21–22, 63; due
process, 37–38; political religion
concept, 38, 102; undermined by
tyrants, 32

Sale, Kirkpatrick, 113
Sargent, Aaron, 184–85
Scott, Winfield, 164, 175
secession, 34, 92, 138, 142, 158,
226–27n69
"second American Revolution," 7,
107, 133–35, 144, 194–95
self-government, 31, 62, 71, 75, 92,
126
self-interest, 42, 55, 60, 64–65, 71;
distributist approach and, 125;
Federalist approach, 72–73

Senate Committee on Commerce,
168
Senate Committee on Territories,
49, 67
separation of powers, 42, 63, 98–99,
107
The Servile State (Belloc), 110
Seward, William, 168, 169–70, 173,
175, 218n2
Sharpe, John, 125
Sheffield, William, 188
Sherman, John, 164, 166–67, 168,
172, 189–92
Skowronek, Steven, 156–58
slavery: attrition approach, 26–27;
colonization option, 27–28;
Compromise of 1850, 49, 52, 53,
163, 167; congressional power to
ban, 48; free labor contrasted
with, 118–19, 122; as instrument of
division, 30; as invention, 70–71;
natural rights critique of, 43,
60–62, 118; no incentive to eliminate, 64; non-extension view,
33, 46–48, 80, 162–63, 175–76;
prudent and moderate approach
to, 25–35; self-government arguments against, 31, 62; self-interest
arguments, 42, 55, 60, 64–65;
snake analogy, 31–32, 56–57; as
violation of moral relationships,
48–50
Smith, Al, 154
social Darwinism, 99–100, 229n121
social science, 97, 101
socialism, 110–11, 124
solidarity, 114–15, 124
Sorenson, Ted, 149
South: Jacksonian political
stranglehold, 138; literacy, 72;
secession, 34, 92, 138, 142, 158,

Index

South (*continued*)
226–27n69. *See also* Democratic
Party
Spaulding, Elbridge, 186–87, 190–91
Speed, Joshua, 47
Stanton, Edwin, 184
"state of nature" philosophy, 46, 55,
57–59
statesman, 217n6; criteria for judging, 36; fundamental qualities,
11–12; gardener metaphor, 210; as
political educator, 4, 14, 21–22, 25,
28–29, 40, 42–43, 72
statesmanship: balancing of political goods, 15–17, 34; contemporary complaints, 11; liturgy of,
36–40; time metaphor, 4–5
Stevens, Thaddeus, 142, 166, 168, 171,
173, 180–81, 193
stewardship theory, 98
Stokes, Donald, 154
Stone, Dan, 26, 47
Storck, Thomas, 110, 113, 123
Storing, Herbert, 72–73
Story, Joseph, 187
Striner, Richard, 18
subsidiarity, 114–16, 124
Sumner, Charles, 18, 36, 145, 169,
173, 174, 175, 191
Sundquist, James, 161–62
Supreme Court, 54, 64, 138
Suri, Jeremi, 148, 198, 199

Taft, William Howard, 98
tariffs, 83, 87–88, 117, 128, 135, 142,
170–71, 181
taxes, 136, 144–45
Taylor, Zachary, 47, 103, 164, 166
technology, 65–72
temperance, 22–24
Temperance Society speech, 1842
(Lincoln), 18, 22–25, 31, 32

territories: Free-Soil Party opposition to slavery in, 162; lack of
sovereignty, 167; Missouri Compromise of 1820, 43, 48–49, 53,
167; police regulation, 54; "state of
nature" philosophy, 46, 55, 57–58
Texas, 26, 67, 88, 162
"A Theory of Critical Elections"
(Key), 154
third-party movements, 165
Thurow, Glenn, 4
Tocqueville, Alexis de, 2, 59, 75,
219n36
Toombs, Robert, 165
transportation, 87, 89, 139, 142; military concerns, 184–85; railroads,
48–49, 90, 143, 171–72
Trefousse, Hans, 168
Trent Affair, 37
Trumbull, Lyman, 33, 51, 184
Trump, Donald, 39, 41, 200–203,
208, 240n101
Tulis, Jeffrey, 148–49, 179, 194
Turner, Frederick Jackson, 96
twentieth-century liberalism, 106
Twenty-Second Amendment, 148
tyranny, 5, 21–22, 32, 42; limits and,
42, 59, 65

Union Party, 158, 188, 235n86
Utah Territory, 49

Van Buren, Martin, 86, 162–63
Vermeule, Adrian, 148
veto, 103, 144, 204
virtue, 38, 42; as mean between excess and deficiency, 14–15; modern political thought as danger
to, 76–77. *See also* moderation;
prudence
virtue ethics, 76–77
Vodolazkin, Eugene, 5

264

Index

Wade, Benjamin, 168, 173, 192

Walling, Karl-Friedrich, 85

Washburn, Israel, 126–27

Washington, George, 79, 84, 88, 146, 196

Wayland, Francis, 117

Weber, Max, 101

Webster, Daniel, 86, 103, 143

Weigel, George, 115

welfare-state liberalism, 117

Welles, Gideon, 184

Western states, 92, 170–72, 181–83

Whig Party, 6, 7, 51–52, 55; "American System" and, 85–88; Conscience Whigs, 163; Cotton Whigs, 164; deference to president, 144; demise of, 160–66; Free-Soil Party and, 127, 143, 160–66; industrialization, support of, 126–28, 129, 138–39; Kansas-Nebraska Act and, 166–68; National Democrats

and, 161; Northern Whigs, 139, 163–67; origins of, 85–86; positive liberal state vs. twentieth-century liberalism, 106; "right to rise," 88, 120–21, 161, 177; Southern Whigs, 164; suspicion of presidency, 90–91, 103

"Who Is a Progressive?" (Roosevelt), 93

Wills, Garry, 80

Wilmot, David, 173

Wilmot Proviso, 33, 173, 174

Wilson, Douglas, 13, 65

Wilson, Henry, 164, 167, 169

Wilson, Woodrow, 84, 93, 97–99, 101, 133, 232n12; *Congressional Government*, 97; living constitution, 99–100

Winger, Stewart, 67, 71, 125, 127

workingmen's unions, 115, 123–24

Young America movement, 67–69

★ ★ ★ ★ ★

Jon D. Schaff is a professor of political science at Northern State University in Aberdeen, South Dakota, where he teaches courses on American political institutions and political thought. He has authored various pieces on Abraham Lincoln and Alexis de Tocqueville and is a coauthor of a forthcoming book on the depiction of our anxious age in popular culture.